BE YOUR OWN HOUSE DETECTIVE

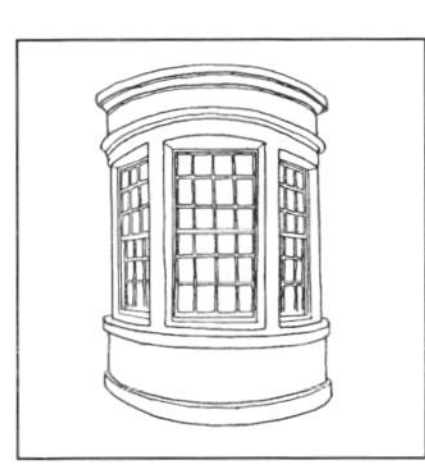

BE YOUR OWN HOUSE DETECTIVE

DAVID AUSTIN,
MAC DOWDY AND
JUDITH MILLER

BBC BOOKS

This book is published to accompany the television series entitled *The House Detectives* which was first broadcast in 1997. The series was produced by BBC Music and Arts.
Executive Producer: Roly Keating
Series Producer: Sally Angel

Published by BBC Books,
an imprint of BBC Worldwide Publishing,
BBC Worldwide Limited, Woodlands,
80 Wood Lane, London W12 0TT

First published 1997

ISBN 0 563 38314 3

Designed by Harry Green
Illustrations by Mac Dowdy
Map on p.65 by David Austin

Set in Berkeley & Copperplate
Printed in Great Britain by Cambus Litho Limited, East Kilbride
Bound in Great Britain by Hunter and Foulis Limited, Edinburgh
Colour separations by Radstock Reproductions Limited, Midsomer Norton
Jacket printed by Lawrence Allen Limited, Weston-super-Mare

PREVIOUS PAGES This thatched cottage at Higher Uppacot in Dartmoor, Devonshire, certainly dates from the early seventeenth century, yet the mullioned window with the rainhood could be sixteenth century. The detectives would look for further sixteenth-century clues on the inside.

OPPOSITE An early photograph of Dunsby Fen Farm that confirmed the existence of a drive where today there is a field.

PICTURE CREDITS
With thanks to Paul Bricknell for special photography.
Paul Bricknell / © BBC pages 3, 134, 138, 162, 170–1, 172, 173, 174, 175, 178, 179, 181, 182, 183, 184, 185, 186, 190, 191, 194, 195, 196, 197, 198, 199, 201, 202, 203, 206, 207, 209.

Arcaid/Chris Blane 118; © BBC 6–7; Richard Bryant 87, 142; David Churchill 31; G.P. & J. Baker 158 above right; Derry Brabbs 38–9, 66–7, 78, 81, 121; Colin Burt 167; Cole & Son 156, 158; Cheshire Record Office 46, 53; Alison and Norman Corbett /Courtesy of Great Little Places of Wales 215; The Design Archives 158 above left; Mac Dowdy 7, 14–14, 18, 27, 84, 94, 99, 102–3, 111; Dulux Paints 154 above; Edifice/Pippa Lewis 22–3, 26, 34, 107, 126–7; Gillian Darley 34–5, 71; ERA Technology 166; Farrow and Ball Ltd 155; Fired Earth 154 below; The Master and Governors of Sutton's Hospital, Charterhouse (London Metropolitan Archive), Crown Copyright Reserved 56, 57, 58–59; Courtesy Dr William Harcus 195 above left; House and Interiors/David Copsey 10–11, David Markson 125; Images Colour Library 80–1, 82–3, 114–5; A.F. Kersting 2–3, 122; Allyson McDermott 163; Manningtree Museum and Local History Group 184; National Trust/Andreas von Einsiedel 74–5, 130; Public Record Office 51; Julie Phipps 98; Sanderson 159; Courtesy Veronica Watts 186; Welsh Folk Museum 90–1, 95; Zuber 158–9.

CONTENTS

ACKNOWLEDGEMENTS

David Austin, Mac Dowdy and Judith Miller would like to thank the following people:

Tim Dunn, first and foremost, for his invaluable contribution and commitment to the book and for his unfailing enthusiasm; Sally Angel, the Series Producer, for her constant support and keenness in getting the series off the ground and seeing it through; Jo Hatley for keeping us all in order and paying the expenses; Roly Keating, the Executive Producer; the directors Emma Worster, Samira Osman, Flavia Rittner, Nicky Pattison, Sarah Aspinall; the researchers Maggi Gibson and Alison Priestley; Harry Green, the designer of this book; Khadija Manjlai, the editor; Allyson McDermott; Neil Loader; John White; Norman Corbett, Dr William Harcus, Philip Kitchen and Veronica Watts; ERA Technology; Carole Knight; all the records offices who supplied material, including The Public Record Office, Cheshire Record Office and Charterhouse (London Metropolitan Archives); and Manningtree Museum and Local History Group.

We would also like to thank all the families who took part in the television series for welcoming us into their homes and allowing us to uncover the secrets of the real stars, the houses themselves.

INTRODUCTION

Be *Your Own House Detective* will help you learn the skills used by the three detectives, David Austin, Mac Dowdy and Judith Miller, in the popular BBC television series. The book offers a systematic, step-by-step guide to finding out for yourself the history of your home. This involves careful detective work investigating documentary evidence, building materials, the layout of your house and its architectural and stylistic features.

If your investigation goes to plan, you should be able to discover the age of your house, how it has been altered over the

HOUSE DETECTIVE

NAME: Judith Miller

TITLE: Author on interiors and antiques

SPECIAL SKILLS: Recognizing style features, interior design, social history

INTERESTS: Terraced housing and cornices

BIRTHPLACE: Late Victorian tenement flat in Galashiels, Scotland

FAVOURITE PERIOD OF ARCHITECTURE: Victorian

TYPE OF HOUSE LIVES IN: Suburban Edwardian end-of-terrace house

HOUSE DETECTIVE

NAME: David Austin

TITLE: Professor of Archeology, University of Wales, Lampeter

SPECIAL SKILLS: Archeology, reading, medieval documents, interpreting maps and understanding the house in the landscape

INTERESTS: Rural settlements, landscapes and castles

BIRTHPLACE: Brocket Hall (war hospital), Hatfield, Hertfordshire

FAVOURITE PERIOD OF ARCHITECTURE: Romanesque

TYPE OF HOUSE LIVES IN: Semi-detached Edwardian town house

HOUSE DETECTIVE

NAME: Mac Dowdy

TITLE: Architectural Historian and Fellow of Wolfson College, Cambridge

SPECIAL SKILLS: Recognizing and dating architectural features; preparing house surveys

INTERESTS: Dowsing and climbing about in roofs

BIRTHPLACE: A Victorian terraced house in Peterborough

FAVOURITE PERIOD OF ARCHITECTURE: From the eleventh to the late twentieth century

TYPE OF HOUSE LIVES IN: Small nineteenth-century village house.

years and, perhaps most interestingly, who lived there in the past. Being your own house detective can be hard work, but it is also great fun and very rewarding. Once your work is complete you will be amazed at how the way you view your house has changed. It will increase your understanding of your home and you will love it more than ever.

There are many well-worn clichés about homes: 'Home is where the heart is'; 'An Englishman's home is his castle'; 'Home sweet home' and, yes, 'There's no place like home'. They bear repeating simply because they prove the point that where you live is important: it matters to us.

Of course there's a certain cachet about having the 'right' postcode, but your relationship with your home goes deeper than that. Your home witnesses the momentous events of your life: marriages, births, baptisms and other celebrations. And, yes, deaths. In old houses, these events become manifold.

Be Your Own House Detective covers houses from medieval times through to the early twentieth century. It focuses on vernacular architecture or ordinary buildings in local regional style, rather than polite architecture, which covers the significant buildings from the past plus the more special, architect-designed houses of later years.

Vernacular architecture is generally the work of local craftsmen and builders, speculators, paternalistic employers and even social visionaries. It provides homes for the vast majority of people and, consequently, a wide array of social groups.

Vernacular buildings include terraces, cottages, farmhouses and townhouses. Often they will imitate the tastes and fashions of the finest houses. But much also depends on the geographical location of the house and any number of local, often idiosyncratic, influences. This makes detective work all the more fascinating, not least because in a small way you may be breaking new ground.

This book will arm you with the necessary approach and guidelines to be a successful house detective. It will enable you to recognize different architectural styles and periods, as well as teaching you how to date style details.

Because there are so many nuances – and indeed, so many contradictions – in house-detective work, it may be necessary to refer to more specialist books, which are listed in the bibliography on page 219. This book also tells you where to track down archive material and what to look for when you find it.

How deep into the case you go depends on how much time you've got to spare, but don't be surprised if you become completely enthralled. The most important thing is to enjoy searching for clues and piecing together the history of your home. Uncovering key evidence and then building up a wider picture is very exciting. Of course, there will be setbacks, red herrings, dead ends and evidence that just does not add up, but that's all part of being a detective!

Your research can also be sociable, bringing you into contact with former owners of your house, as well as local people who pass down the oral history – an important source of evidence. You will undoubtedly hear many myths and legends about your house and town or village. There may well be tales of hidden treasure, scandal, intrigue, romance, broken promises, fortunes won and lost, and even dodgy dealings on the fringes of society.

Like any good detective, you should embark on your work with a healthy scepticism, but be prepared for the unexpected. In the six houses investigated in the television series, the detectives heard, among other stories, that the notorious Witchfinder General had lodged in one; that James I planted a mulberry tree in the garden of another and that a third was the scene of a battle between Roundheads and Cavaliers during the English Civil War. There was also the story of a reluctant heiress who was rumoured to have sealed her most valued possessions in the cellar, and of non-conformists plotting to assassinate King Charles II!

One of the most interesting parts of being your own detective is that you step back into another world and find out how former owners of your house lived, worked and played. In many respects, it is similar to tracing your family tree. Your home has a lineage and during its history it has been home to any number of families. You may own your house, but perhaps it would be more accurate to view yourself as having a time share in history.

More than two-thirds of British homes are now owner-occupied. Older houses are highly sought after and about 45 per cent of the country's houses are more than 50 years old. These have invariably undergone many changes. As the way people lived altered and fashions changed, new wings or lean-tos were added on, façades modernized and interiors gutted and redesigned. This can make the work of the detective complicated and makes it all the more important to be well organized and systematic about what you do. Follow up all the leads you have, even the more implausible ones, but make sure you prioritize and record your findings clearly.

Your detective work can also have very practical benefits, especially if you're planning to restore your house. Many people want to restore their houses to the way they used to be. This often proves to be impossible. Because houses develop organically, sometimes over several centuries, there is no way of pinpointing any one date in the past to aim for. For example, to restore a medieval timber-framed building to its original state may well mean ripping away a Jacobean façade, destroying an Elizabethan chimney stack or pulling down fine Georgian cornices to expose beams.

By finding out how your house developed you will be more sensitive to how, and if, it can be 'restored'. If your house is of any architectural interest, the chances are that it is listed or part of a conservation area, in which case any changes need to be approved by the relevant authority.

As any estate agent will tell you, the provenance of a house is a good selling point, in the same way that knowing the origins of an antique can push up its value. To be able to refer to the house's history in the particulars for sale – 'A fine period house built by a Victorian urban squire'; 'This property was modernized by a wealthy merchant in the sixteenth century and it served as a manor house for several centuries' – will fire the imagination of the potential purchaser. Your research on the house will almost certainly be of interest to future owners and

FOR SALE

If you are considering buying a house, take a closer look at some of the features when you are being shown around by the owner. Try to work out how much of the house has been modernized and note any features, interior and exterior, that might give clues to help you date the house. You might also want to ask whether there is existing archive material in the owner's possession. If you are thinking of selling your house, point out any interesting features to prospective buyers and tell them about the history you have uncovered so far.

can be passed down, like the deeds, over generations to come.

Being a house detective is an inexact science, but one of the joys of studying ordinary buildings is that there are an infinite number of possibilities and a great, often undiscovered wealth of detail and influence. Much work remains to be done on the age of ordinary British houses and there are many hidden secrets. Over the last 20 years or so, academic studies in Devon and King's Lynn, Norfolk, have uncovered many medieval buildings that had been concealed and were therefore unrecorded.

You can contribute to this ongoing historical study of British buildings personally, but be warned: if you do own a house going back several centuries it will not be a straightforward, open-and shut case. Rare is the house that gives away its history without a struggle. That said, statistically, you are much more likely to own a house that was built in the last 200 years or so, which should make your task less onerous but still a challenge.

There is no right or wrong way to go about being a house detective, but if you take a systematic approach your investigation will go more smoothly. Each house is different and there are various routes to the truth, so do not be afraid to think laterally. Houses hold so many wonderful secrets: the best detectives uncover these with a blend of organization, determination and imagination.

ON THE TRAIL

The key to solving the mystery of your house lies in carrying out a systematic investigation aimed at building up a body of evidence. To find out the age of the building and names of former occupants requires work on a number of fronts. In this chapter you will find out how to amass evidence about the layout, fabric and stylistic details of your house, as well as getting a general feel for its location.

You may decide to do your practical investigation around the house concurrently with the archive research (see Chapter 2) for the sake of variety. This is certainly feasible, as long as your approach is logical and well organized.

Before you start looking for clues, it is worth creating a file to collate your findings. By the time you have finished, you should have built up an impressive catalogue of notes, photographs (old and new), video footage, sketches, plans, maps, surveys and photocopies of key archive material, concluding hopefully with a summary of the history of your own home.

Having opened your casebook, you will also need to assemble some basic items of kit (see panel, p.25) – plus a trusty sidekick can come in useful!

ASSESSING THE EXTERIOR

Your first task is to take a close look at the exterior of your house, starting with the front.

It is a good idea to photograph or sketch what you see. Photographs will be particularly useful when you are trying to compare individual features with illustrations or photographs in reference books. Some detectives prefer the clearer outlines of black-and-white photos, but it is really just a matter of taste.

You may even find it instructive to follow through your own survey with a camcorder if you have one, doing your own commentary as you go.

SEEING THROUGH A FAÇADE

It is useful at this stage to compare the façade of your house with the nine examples of typical vernacular houses from different periods illustrated in this chapter. These are merely a sample: they are in no way totally representative and are only intended to give you a feel for architectural styles. It is unlikely that your house will be similar in every respect to any one of these houses because of the huge number of regional and style variations that were fashionable at any given period.

While getting a rough idea of the

period of your home is a valuable starting point, your first impression is liable to change. Of the six houses investigated in the television series, only two – significantly, the most recent houses – could be dated accurately from the façade alone. You may well find that your house has features from one or more of the examples shown here, which can mean, among other things, that it was built and added on to in stages.

It may also be down to the whim of the builder. Neo-Classical, Gothic, Baroque, Rococo, Regency and other polite or upmarket styles of architecture have been revived, adapted and mixed in to ordinary houses over several centuries. However, this has not been a linear progression and does not fit neatly into any one century or the reign of any one monarch or royal dynasty.

Developments in printing techniques and publishing in the eighteenth century meant that the designs of leading architects like Inigo Jones, James Gibbs and the Italian Palladio began to appear in pattern books which became widely available and copied. Speculative builders from the late seventeenth century onwards began to borrow ideas from polite architecture and were able to dress up the shabbiest of structures with the latest decorative features.

With improvements in communications in the last century, Victorian builders experimented with a wide range of styles and materials, influenced, for example, by the prevailing nostalgia for the Middle Ages in the cases of Gothick architecture and the Arts and Crafts movement, which promoted a return to traditional building skills.

What all this tells us is that, however well you grasp the history of polite and vernacular architecture, you will always face the problem that no single piece of evidence or the appearance of the façade is enough to date your house. It is quite possible that one piece of conflicting evidence will undermine your whole case and point you in the direction of new avenues of research.

A DETACHED POINT OF VIEW?

The first fact you need to note is whether your house is detached (stands on its

Dateline of Main Architectural Periods

Use this simplified history of the principal architectural periods and styles for general background only; it is not intended to provide definitive answers to dating your house.

Date	Period	Style
to c.1480	Middle Ages	Medieval – vernacular Gothic
to c.1550	Early Tudors	Tudor – early Renaissance
to c.1620	Later Tudors	Elizabethan – later Renaissance
to c.1680	Stuarts and Commonwealth	Jacobean – Baroque
to c.1750	William and Mary to George I	Early Georgian – Neo-Classical
to c.1810	The Later Hanoverians	Later Georgian – Neo-Classical
to c.1840	Regency and William IV	Regency – Neo-Classical
to c.1860	Early Victoria	Early Victorian – eclectic, including Neo-Gothic
to c.1900	Later Victoria	Later Victorian – eclectic, including Neo-Gothic, Neo-Classical and Arts and Crafts
to c.1920	Edward VII	Edwardian – eclectic, hints of many styles, including Art Nouveau, Arts and Crafts, early Modernist

TIMBER-FRAMED HALL HOUSE
The Little Hall at Lavenham, Suffolk still displays all the hallmarks of its fifteenth-century origins. This exterior view shows the large window of what was the open hall and two jettied crosswings. The hall was given a second storey around the late sixteenth century. The silvery studwork is the result of a coating of protective lime-wash.

own), semi-detached (joined to another on one side by a common wall) or terraced (in a row of identical houses sharing common dividing walls). Terraced housing dates from the Middle Ages when rows of linked cottages and almshouses were built, but only became widespread in towns from the late seventeenth century. About this same time, semi-detached houses began emerging in rural areas but they did not have their heyday until the development of suburbia in the nineteenth century.

USEFUL MATERIALS

Early in your investigation you need to establish the material your house is built of. This could be brick, timber, stone, concrete or even mud.

If it is brick, look at the way in which the bricks are laid and compare the coursing with the examples on p.72. Look closely at the size, shape and colour of the bricks, because this can be a clue to their age and their geographical origin.

You can do the same for stone houses, but try also to assess the quality of the stone: there is a key distinction between finely cut rectangular blocks of dressed ashlar stone used on some façades and the wide variety of shapes and sizes you find with roughly cut rubble stone. Also, before the transport revolution in the late eighteenth and nineteenth centuries, ordinary houses were built of whatever stone was available locally, which means that there are many regional differences (see Chapter 3, pp.76–77).

It may be impossible to tell what your house is built of from the front because the walls are rendered or cladded, but this in itself can provide good evidence.

If it's not obvious, don't worry: you may have more luck in finding out what material your house is built of when you inspect the back, the side or the interior.

Altered images

When you look at your house it is essential to keep your eyes peeled for signs of modernization, alterations and extensions. Houses that have not been developed are definitely in a minority. The sort of clues to look out for are changes in the colour, shape, size and bonding of bricks. If your house is stone-built, check for a narrow course of stone above the ground-floor window lintels – it could mean that the upper floors were added later. Another clue to watch for is when a decorative pattern such as a row of different coloured bricks is cut off abruptly for no apparent reason.

Identifying main features

It is worth trying to assess the main features of your house in the most general sense, paying particular attention to styles that do not ostensibly fit together.

The sort of clues that will help you here include the position, shape and size of the doors and windows, and the pitch and shape of the roof, as well as the roofing material. For example, you may notice that the doors and windows are symmetrical on one side but totally out of proportion on the other. Anomalies like this often give away that a house has been modernized.

Windows of opportunity

If some of the windows seem to be oddly positioned it could mean that the front of the house has been built in different stages. This was a clue that helped us understand the house we investigated in Bidston, Merseyside.

Blind windows are also of interest, because they may have been filled in following the introduction of a window tax in 1696. Equally, there could have been other practical reasons for filling in windows: for example, in the house we looked at in Manningtree, Essex, there was a blind mullioned window in an attic room that was no longer being used. This was evidence that the old living quarters had at one time extended into the roof space and, more importantly, proved that the neighbouring property was a later abutment.

It is worth making a note of the type of windows you see: determine whether they are horizontal landscape windows or vertical portrait windows and assess if they are of the mullioned, casement, sash or dormer type (see Chapter 5, pp.129–133).

You should also make yourself aware of key dates: in 1851, for example, the window tax was repealed which led to the building of more projecting bay windows, previously heavily taxed.

However, like so many other features, the windows you see now may not be original to the house and, if you are not careful, could start you on a false trail. One side of the house in Manningtree had Victorian bay windows, but on closer inspection the building itself turned out to be seventeenth century.

Telltale doors

Look at the front door or doors in a similarly analytical manner and make a note of the door itself, its surround and whether there is a porch or a verandah.

Doors can be very revealing and are a subject of study in themselves.

In general, you should be analyzing the door itself and the shape of the doorway: is it arched or rectangular? The style of the surround provides its own clues: for example, moulded columns or *pilasters* (a decorated half-column projecting from a wall), together with a low-pitched gable or *pediment* at the top, were popular in the late eighteenth century. Ornamental cast-iron porches, which were fashionable from the early nineteenth century, are also good evidence, as are glass fanlights in their different forms.

Other clues worth noting are the door furniture, the hinges, door knockers, letterplates and the remnants of earlier bell pulls. The whole subject of doors is covered in more detail in Chapter 6.

Other giveaways

Be aware of other features, including the shape of the roof and gable end (if there is one) and decorative bargeboards on the edge of a roof and chimney stacks, which can also provide very helpful information. In the Manningtree investigation, an imposing brick stack with six shafts was immediately identifiable as late sixteenth century.

Parapets are also worth noting because these were a popular innovation during the Georgian period, when they were a fashionable feature and used to conceal dormer windows in the roof. In fact, you should analyze anything that sticks out, because it could provide you with useful evidence – for example, a course of bricks protruding from the wall above a window could be a rainhood dating from the Elizabethan period.

Exterior Checklist for the Front

1. Overall style of the façade
2. Features that contradict the general impression
3. Material your house is built of: timber, stone, brick or cob
4. Roof shape, style and materials
5. Window size, shape and style (mullion, casement, sash or dormer)
6. Window panes: plate-glass or quarries, stained glass or plain
7. Front door: type and position (that is, recessed in archway or under a porch)
8. Style of door surround and fanlight (if there is one)
9. Size of chimney stack and number of pots
10. Other features: rainhood, keystone with mask, mouldings, quoins or corner stones, decorative ironwork, guttering, bargeboarding, datestones, etc

It's possible to quote examples ad infinitum, but the best advice is to be thorough; do not leave anything out and make sure you highlight features that contradict a neat general picture. Remember: all leads need to be followed up.

A word of warning

A note of caution needs to be rung here: beware of datestones. Just because there is a datestone above a door, on the chimney, on an external wall or on a rainwater head, it should not be taken as proof of the age of the house. It is a common mistake to assume that such dates mark the year the house was first built. In fact, the datestone could signify the date the house was modernized or may be designed to commemorate a marriage or another event.

You would not assume that the Tower

of London was built in 1843 because that is the date on its rainwater heads, so do not be tempted to do so with your own house. It is possible that a datestone originates from another house and is of no relevance at all. A datestone becomes a more useful source when it includes the name or initials of a former owner, because this will be a good lead when you come to investigate documentary records.

Fire insurance plaques can also be helpful and it is worth trying to track down the records of the insurance company that put up the plaque. This in itself involves detective work because the company may have been taken over by another concern many years ago. It is worth persevering since the records should provide you with names of former owners and possibly a plan of the house

STONE-BUILT HOUSE
This house at Barnack, near Stamford, has been built in the locally quarried stone with stone slates from nearby Collyweston. Its features reveal a number of periods: the oldest (in the upper window in the gable), is late fifteenth century; the window below it is sixteenth century; the gable-stop – that is, the raised edge of the end wall which is topped with a finial – is early seventeenth century... and so it goes on. Whenever the owners have had the money, they have modernized their home a bit!

as it was in the past. Again, you should be careful: old insurance plaques are sold as antiques which could mean you have a fake on your hands.

Back and sides

Once you have combed the front of the house for clues, you should analyze the back and sides if they are accessible. This will enable you to do an initial sketch of the overall shape of the house. You will also have a growing list of features that you can compare with the illustrations and photographs in later chapters.

In many cases, the back and sides will give you a more reliable indication of how your house has changed: do not be surprised if your findings contradict your impression of the front. The façade is the most likely part of the exterior to be altered to keep up with the latest architectural fashion, while the back and sides are more probably the scene of an extension or later addition.

Form an impression of what has been tacked on and build up a picture of the original layout of the property. As a general rule, the original building, whether it be a medieval long-house, a Georgian country house or a Victorian terrace, will have conformed to a logical, if not entirely regular plan. Examples of the classic plans for the main periods are included in Chapter 4 (see p.96).

If the current layout is more like 'the house that Jack built' with a warren of small rooms and corridors, you are probably looking at any number of alterations. Houseowners typically build into any space available at the back or sides to create more rooms. In the case of a classic single-fronted Victorian terraced house two rooms deep, you will often find a kitchen extension at the back with an additional bedroom built on top of that and even a conservatory.

It is worth doing a quick sketch of how you think the plan of your house would have looked when it was first built. Try to work out the reasons behind future developments, for example, larger families, the introduction of inside toilets and bathrooms, or the gentrification of your area. The changing fortunes of a neighbourhood are very revealing in themselves and may well have affected the layout of your house.

Exterior Checklist for the Back and Sides

1. Gable ends: shape and type of building material; Flemish style or crowfeet?
2. Changes in building material and in shape/size of bricks or stone
3. Signs of alterations, extensions, lean-tos: style and materials used
4. Any changes to the roof line?
5. Spacing of windows: compare with those at front
6. Evidence of filled-in windows or doors
7. Back door: location, style, shape, evidence it has been moved
8. Back alley or path leading to back of house
9. Porch or balcony: is there evidence that one may have existed?
10. Steps or other evidence that back has been raised or lowered

ANALYZING THE INTERIOR

Once you are confident you have completed your work on the outside and have ticked off the checklists (see panels, p.17 and above) you can go inside and do the same. It is important to follow a logical progression, starting at the front and going round, floor by floor, making sure that you do not forget the cellar or attic, if they exist in your house and are accessible.

You should attempt to analyze the interior in two distinct ways: first, through its overall plan and structure, and second, in terms of the style of practical and decorative features. Again the best tip is to be suspicious and accept nothing at face value: change is the norm and imported or reproduction features are widespread. The reason is simple: if an owner had money, he or she was unlikely to have retained out-of-date styles.

As far as interiors are concerned, a period of destruction is invariably followed by a period of reproduction, restoration and imitation. It is not always easy to distinguish between the authentic and the fake. For example, if there are timber beams in any of your rooms you need to check if they serve any structural purpose or have just been stuck on to a wall or a ceiling to imitate an 'olde worlde' effect.

Studying the layout

The first thing you need to do is get a feel for the current layout and proportions of the house, as this will provide clues to what has been added and will help you to build up a picture of the shape of the original house. By drawing a plan and section (see 'How to do your own house plans', p.25), you will have a template that can be compared with the illustrations in Chapter 4.

The way people live in houses has changed over the centuries, so although the plan can help you date your home it is unlikely to give you a clear-cut answer. When assessing the way people lived in the past, it is easy to forget the fundamental changes and improvements in sanitation that have taken place during this century. Nowadays we take for granted bathrooms, indoor toilets and kitchens with all mod cons and few people would live in a house without these facilities. However, a matter of three generations ago, people washed in metal tubs in front of the fire in the kitchen or living room and the toilet was a draughty shed at the end of the garden.

Has it been modernized?

When you are surveying the interior you should always be looking for evidence of alterations. In some cases, the clues will be obvious: lumps or hollows in plasterwork, or *cornices* (mouldings) that end abruptly at a wall and then continue on the other side in a neighbouring room. The latter is invariably a telltale clue in first-floor rooms at the front of Victorian and Georgian houses. These were traditionally the smartest and most spacious rooms in houses: the drawing room on the *piano nobile*, the main reception rooms through which guests would circulate. In this century, however, they have often been converted into bedrooms. You may find a house's most elaborate fireplace here or evidence of a walled-up hearth.

Tapping into your walls

When there is no immediate evidence of change, you should go around tapping the walls with your knuckles. This will enable you to distinguish between partition walls and load-bearing structural ones. The partition walls will give a hollow wooden ring, while structural walls emit a lower, more solid sound. As a rule of thumb, the main supporting walls are less likely to have been rearranged than the more temporary partition walls.

It is also a good idea to measure the thickness of the walls, because a particularly thick wall in the middle of a house may mean that it was once an exterior wall. When houses are extended, some of the outside walls take on a new role as interior walls.

If you suspect that alterations have taken place, look for signs that there were once windows or another door in the wall. There may still be evidence of a lintel, but most clues will be concealed: windows or doors may have been filled in and plastered over or adapted to form part of a new feature, perhaps a service hatch or even a cupboard. Again, knocking on the wall with your knuckles can reveal changes in material and thickness. Keep knocking and listening until you have built up an outline of a shape which should reveal whether you are dealing with a window or a door.

Do the proportions look right?

You should look critically at the proportions of each room and examine the spatial relationship between the skirting board, *dado* (panelling or rail on the lower part of a wall) and cornice, if they exist. If it looks wrong, something has been changed. The position of windows and lintels inside a room can also reveal alterations. It is worth checking whether the windows appear to be unusually close to the floor or the ceiling, because this could indicate that the house has been restructured.

Changes in floor levels should raise questions in your mind: they could mean that the house has been extended onto a higher, or lower, piece of ground. If you suspect you are living in a late-medieval farmhouse, a change in levels could be significant. In traditional rural longhouses of the highland regions, the animals were kept under the same roof in a byre at one end. This byre was generally at a lower level than the rest of the house to prevent animal slurry from flowing back into the living quarters.

Getting to the top and bottom of it

You will find, to your frustration, that previous owners have done their best to conceal old features: they will have boxed in beams, concealed them beneath dropped ceilings, boarded over fireplaces, imprisoned panelling behind hardboard walls and, in the worst-case scenario, just ripped out historic features.

However, there is certainly one place, and possibly two, where clues are not hidden away: attics and cellars. If they have not been filled in or converted into living areas, these can be a real Aladdin's cave for house detectives. Attics and cellars are areas that were not intended to be seen and where the truth is not hidden artfully from the world.

Armed with a powerful torch and taking care where you walk, you should go up into the attic and analyze the rafters, *purlins* (the main horizontal timber supporting the common rafters), beams and other timbers. If there is a complex skeleton of heavy-looking solid

1614

MELLOWING BRICK
A comparatively small building, this lodge at Thurlow in west Suffolk dates back to 1614 – which could be a modernization date. The quality of the bricks and a coursing that appears part-random, part-English bond, suggests a date some 50 or more years earlier. The doorway with carvings in the spandrels (the areas between the curve of the arch and the square of the opening) is sixteenth century. The windows and their surrounds are heavily restored but remain sympathetic to the house.

timbers, you should start investigating the possibility that this is a timber-framed building. Look for evidence of wooden pegs, peg holes, roughly hewn timbers and decorative moulding or chamfering on principal beams, all of which would suggest that at one time they would have been exposed.

If the roof has been replaced or raised, the old cut-off rafters may still be present and there may be noticeable differences in the brick or stonework at the level of the *eaves* (the overhang of the roof slope). It is crucial to take a close look at the brick- or stonework in the attic because this may be your first real opportunity to see what the house is really built of, especially if the exterior has been rendered over, cladded or hidden in some other way. You may discover filled-in windows or doorways or solid floorboards and well-worn stairs which could mean that the attic was once a bedroom, possibly used for servants.

You should look at the cellar with a similar analytical eye and make a note of any clues as to how it would have been used and when it might have been built. In many cases, cellars will have been sealed up or filled in because they had become more of a problem than they were worth.

Hidden cellars are intriguing places and conjure up a certain romance. You may have a hunch where the cellar entrance was but, before you dig it up, it is worth remembering that all you are likely to find is a mass of rubble infill or a dark, damp hole full of unpleasant gases and infested with rodents. There was undoubtedly a good reason for closing it up in the first place!

Burning Evidence

Fireplaces are interesting because for centuries they were literally the heart of a household. They have undergone a major revival in popularity in recent years and are once again considered to be the focus of a room.

If you are lucky, fires can be the source of clues going right back to the earliest vernacular houses. When you are in the attic look for blackened timbers, because this could be evidence that your house was once a one-storey medieval hall with an open fire in the middle of the floor.

However, perhaps more than any interior feature, you need to be careful when dating fireplaces. For example, it is all too easy to jump to the conclusion that an inglenook fireplace is an early feature, when in fact it may be the product of a twentieth-century mock-Tudor fad. Neither should you assume that a perfectly proportioned and totally stylish fire surround with pilasters is necessarily Georgian: it may be just a convincing modern reproduction.

There is also a large market in antique fireplaces and a growing number of fireplace thefts, both of which make life more difficult for house detectives. One useful tip is to look at changes in the surrounding skirting boards for evidence that a new fireplace has been introduced.

Interior Checklist

1. Staircase: style, material, details – newel post, banisters and balusters
2. Doors and door surrounds: style, position and size
3. Evidence of old beams on ceiling or floor
4. Floorboards or other floor covering
5. Walls: differences in sound when you tap?
6. Cornices, dado rails, ceiling roses, skirting boards and other mouldings
7. Fireplace: style and period
8. Roof construction in attic
9. Other clues in attic or cellar: change in brick or stone type, timber framing, filled-in windows?
10. Remnants of old, disused fixtures and fittings
11. Wall coverings: paint, paper, timber, anaglypta, lincrusta, panels
12. Any changes in floor level between rooms?

Peeling Back the Years

Other useful techniques include pulling back carpets to find old floors; checking the height and material of the skirting boards; analyzing decorative mouldings like cornices, dados and ceiling roses, and seeking remnants of early wall coverings. You may be able to date the floor coverings, whether they're tiles, linoleum or stone. A heavily worn floor would suggest frequent usage and is a clue as to the way the house was lived in. It may even point the way to the entrance to a sealed-up cellar.

You may find old wallpaper behind existing paper or inside cupboards, or perhaps mere fragments behind a skirting board or other feature. The latter may require forensic assistance (see Chapter 6, pp.163–164); with the help of specialist books you should be able to identify decorative plasterwork which was very popular in both Georgian and Victorian homes.

Keeping a Record

The other main task, and possibly the most enjoyable one, is to analyze and create a record of the style features of your home. This is vital if you are planning to restore part or all of your house, but can also provide you with some very important clues as to the age of your house and key periods of development.

However, this is an area fraught with dangers and you must question your every assumption. Interior details and decorations are most at the mercy of the whims of fashion, and you must ask yourself if the features are original and fit in with the overall structure of the house. There may be examples where the answer is obvious: a fireplace that is clearly out of proportion with the rest of the room or a traditional-looking six-panel door with a hollow ring to it.

However, there will be cases where any innovation is subtle and intensive detective work is required to get to the truth. In old houses, staircases are likely to have been modernized as building techniques improved and tastes changed. As well as noting the characteristics of the modern staircase, look for evidence of an earlier one next to a chimney stack or in a cellar or attic. During the television series, we looked at one house where a brand new staircase had been put in during a period of gentrification earlier this century, and in another, we discovered the remaining few steps of an Elizabethan spiral staircase in the attic.

HOW TO DO YOUR OWN HOUSE PLANS

Before embarking on your own survey it is worth finding out if your solicitor or building society already has floor plans with the deeds. Having said that, even if the work has been carried out by someone else it is still worth taking your own measurements because it is a useful discipline that focuses the mind. By doing your own systematic survey any alterations to the house and any anomalies should become clear.

Before getting started you will need the following equipment

- Hardbacked notepad or clipboard
- Squared paper and tracing paper
- 30-m steel or linen tape measure (plus assistant!)
- 2-m folding rule or retractable metal rule
- Plumbline (a weight attached to a length of string)
- Spirit level
- Pencil, eraser and drawing pen
- Set square, protractor, compasses and spring bows
- Ruler
- Bright torch and binoculars

MEASURING UP INSIDE

Before you get down to the detailed measuring, it is a good idea to do a rough sketch of the floorplan of the house, marking in windows, doors, the approximate thickness of walls, fireplaces and stairs or steps. At this stage the plan does not have to be perfect, but it is sensible to make it large enough to give you space to write in the measurements.

The key to successful measuring is to take a systematic and comprehensive approach. You start by choosing the room you want to do first and measure the horizontal distance between the walls,

THE YEOMAN'S HOUSE The yeomen of England are symbols of noble strength, and this house at Appledore, near Tenterden in Kent, exudes those timeless qualities. It is brick built to 2½ storeys – note the downer which gives it the half, in the manner of the developed long-house of, say, the 1640s. This means it could be older, and only a detailed search would reveal the likely date. The door will open on to the side of the chimney breast, the baffle position.

moving around in a clockwise direction. Once you have completed these so-called 'running measurements', you need to cross-check them by measuring the diagonal distance across the room. The next task is to go back round the room in the same direction measuring the following: the length across the base of each door and window; the width of the fireplace and any other features, including baths, sinks, radiators and built-in cupboards; the width of the walls (which can be done at a door or window opening); the width of the staircase and dimensions of each tread. This can be a time-consuming process, but it is worth doing well because you will be surprised by the amount of evidence that it can uncover.

Once you are satisfied with your measurements for the floor plans, you should retread the same ground all over again measuring the vertical dimensions instead of the horizontal ones. It is best to start in each room with the straightforward distance between the floor and the ceiling, followed by the height of doors, windows, fireplaces, etc. from the bottom to the top of the frames or surrounds. Make sure you do not forget any changes in floor level.

The thickness of floors can be measured in stairwells, but this should also

EIGHTEENTH-CENTURY TOWN HOUSE
Wisbech in Cambridgeshire has many fine eighteenth-century houses, and this one in Museum Square is among them. It was built in the 1790s by Joseph Medworth, who lived there for a time. Apart from the central white door, which replaced a window, the windows and the quietly elegant porch are typical of the period. A curious note is that in this and other of Medworth's houses the ground floor features are not exactly in vertical alignment with the upper storeys.

be double-checked by doing a measurement of the height of the whole house, excluding the roof space and cellar. The most practical place to do this is in the stairwell using a plumbline. By subtracting the height of individual rooms on each floor from the total height, you have the combined thickness of the floors and ceilings. This can sometimes be a useful clue: if the figure is surprisingly high, it may mean that there is a suspended ceiling designed to conceal old beams or reduce the height of the rooms.

It is also worthwhile continuing your measurements in the attic or roof space: this can be of particular value if you have a timber-framed house. The dimensions of individual beams, rafters, purlins, joists, posts and other timbers should all be measured individually, as well as the width of any floorboards.

You should also work out the pitch of the roof. The simplest way to do this is to measure the distance between the attic floor and the inside ridge of the roof, and the horizontal distance between the base of the rafters. This can be cross-checked by using a protractor to measure the angle of the rafters.

Measuring up outside

To complete your survey, you will need to do the external measurements of your house. This can be very challenging, especially if you live in a tall house, but there are a few useful tips to help you avoid hanging off ladders.

As with the floor plans, it is a good idea to do a rough sketch of what you are looking at: one good way of doing this is to trace a photo of the house and enlarge it. You will then be able to write your measurements down next to the relevant part on the picture.

Again, you should start with the length of the walls, using a spirit level to make sure you are measuring a horizontal plane, and go around the whole house doing the vertical and horizontal dimensions of windows, doors, chimney stacks, the level of the eaves and the height of the gable end. The height of upstairs windows can be measured using the plumbline.

On the same page, you should also be making a note of the building materials, the style of the doors, windows and roof. If you find that parts of the elevation are

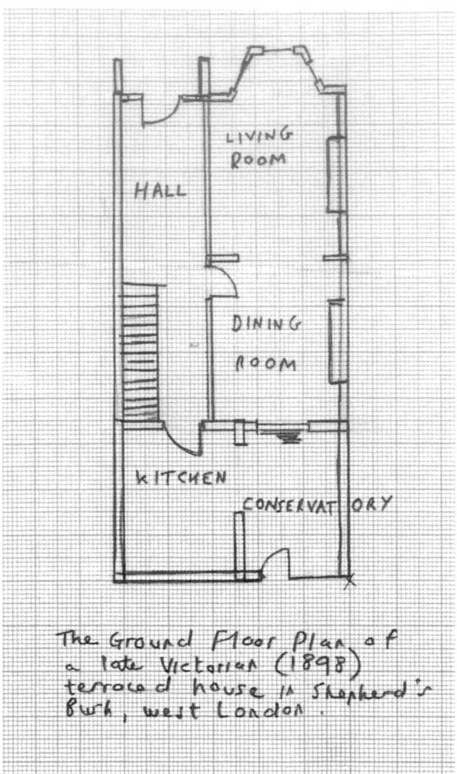

OUTLINE HOUSE PLAN Plans of your house are essential to your visual survey. They need to be simple but clear, showing an outline of the position of the rooms, doorways and windows and drawn as close to scale as you can make them (working on graph paper helps you with the scale). You need to do outline drawings of all floors and even one for the roof if you can. Then photocopy each drawing so that you have a number of copies of each plan to make your notes on.

inaccessible, you may be able to measure the height of the building by counting the number of brick courses and multiplying it by the height of each course. Of course, for this to be accurate, the bricks need to be of a regular size.

Drawing up the plans

Once you have collected all the measurements, it's time for the fun part: drawing up the plans. It is good advice to do this on tracing paper initially because your plan for one floor can be used as a template for others, which should be roughly the same.

First of all, you need to choose a scale: 1:100 is normally used for architectural plans, sections and elevations. You start by drawing a scale line of the width of the room and then, using compasses, mark the length of the side walls and the diagonal dimensions. Do not forget to indicate the thickness of the walls by using parallel lines.

Once you have marked on all the relative measurements, join them up freehand using a pencil – this looks more authentic than if you use a ruler. Once you are satisfied with your pencil versions of the plan, section and elevation, trace over them in pen, finishing the whole project off with the north point and details of the name and location of the house and the date of the survey.

Doing your own plans is a lot of hard work, but it is worth it. The plans may reveal a false ceiling or a secret room or blocked-up hideaway that you would otherwise have missed. They can also be passed on with the deeds of your house and a local history or vernacular buildings society may be interested to see your findings.

CHECKING OUT YOUR ENVIRONS

For the time being you have done all you can inside your house. You will almost certainly need to return to the attic or cellar or take another look at certain features in the light of what you discover later. The next stage of the inquiry is to get a feel for your local area, whether it be a town or city, a village, a suburb or the back of beyond. This will set you up for two very important aspects of house detection still to come: analyzing maps and finding out about local history.

Gardening tips

A quick look around your garden may throw up any number of clues. You should look at boundary walls and make a note of the materials and building technique used: a dry-stone wall is likely to be earlier than one with stone laid in lime mortar. If it is a brick wall, you should be able to date it.

Humps in the lawn or inexplicable changes in the level of the garden may be evidence of a former structure, like an old well or wall. If there is evidence of old walls, it could mean that the boundary has been moved and the plot enlarged. Compare the size of your plot with others nearby. If you are on the corner of a terrace, it could mean that yours is a prime plot that would have been reserved for the builder or a favoured client.

When you are gardening, look for signs of old building materials such as cobbles, old bricks and large pieces of stone that could have been part of a former building. Some people use metal detectors and search for archeological evidence, which can be revealing but will need specialist interpretation.

Trees and hedgerows, which are known as 'soft architecture', are also worth examining. Look at the pattern in which trees have been planted in relation to the house. During the television series, David Austin found the remains of an old orchard near a farmhouse we were investigating. By drawing a diagram and examining the orientation of the trees, he was able to work out that an earlier house would have been in a slightly different position to the new one.

Know your outhouses

It is important to take a close look at outhouses and ask yourself if they could ever have been living quarters or used as an outside kitchen or toilet – old sinks or other fittings and attachments on the wall are obvious clues.

In some cases, the earliest house on a site was relegated to a shed or junk store when a new building was built on the site. In a house we looked at in Gloucestershire, a building in the garden turned out to be a former school, which had closed in 1841. The upper floor was plastered and there were still drawings that had survived of a lady with a dog and a hot-air balloon: the work of a child more than 150 years ago.

Visit the neighbours

Your voyage of discovery should extend beyond your own boundaries into the surrounding area. The most valuable tip is: do not be afraid to be nosy. You will not be asked to produce a warrant – providing you are polite, friendly, reassuring and explain what you want and do not trespass or loiter suspiciously on other people's property.

One excellent first port of call is a neighbouring house. It can be extremely edifying to have a look around the inside of a neighbour's house and compare its layout with yours. Many terraces of Georgian, Victorian and Edwardian vintage are built with a great degree of uniformity, conforming to the pressure on builders to make money and the demands of building authorities. Many of these houses have been gutted on the inside and remodelled to suit late-twentieth-century tastes and needs. In so doing, any real sense of the original layout and ambience of the house is lost.

In some areas, the so-called gentrification of terraced housing is almost complete, and in others, former family houses have been converted into a warren of bedsits. However, there are cases where a house has gone a century or more almost untouched. If you can find such an example in a terrace near you, it will give you a real insight into how your house was designed to be lived in.

Local people can be a valuable source of information: ask around and you are sure to uncover a wealth of stories and legends that provide at best worthwhile leads, and are at worst plain entertaining. Your neighbours may also be able to fill you in with the names of former occupants and, if they have been living in the area a long time, can give you a very good potted history that will really get you started on your investigation.

Shop around

When you are walking around your area or shopping locally it is a good idea to look up from the shop fronts and take in the style of the buildings above street level. Do a rough tally of how many seem to be of the same period as your house and how many are different. You may be able to recognize a number of periods from the façades which is a useful clue as to when your area developed.

However, as with your own home, do not take other buildings at face value. It is also worth noting the most common building materials: it may be a useful clue if your house is built of stone in a predominantly brick area, or if your street is built of different materials than another local street. A difference in brick colour may be explained, for example, by the coming of the railways (see 'On the right tracks', p.32).

Talk to the experts

Estate agents, shopkeepers and especially publicans will invariably give you a rundown of the local mythology. However, the people you really need to get in touch with early in your investigation are local historians because they often have an inexhaustible knowledge of the local area and are generally keen to share it.

While it would be wrong to expect historians and other experts to provide you with all or any of the answers to your own particular house, they can certainly point you in the right direction as far as research and background reading is concerned. They will also provide you with a snapshot of your town or village in the past and let you know which famous, or indeed infamous, historical characters frequented your area. During the television series, we encountered many local experts, some of whom played an invaluable role in helping us close our cases. Most local historians are delighted to help out because your efforts will contribute to their own wider historical research.

Local historians will be able to tell you about the main historic sites in your area, some of which you may know about and may have visited. The sites of churches, ancient and modern, as well as other religious buildings like priories and abbeys, are important because before the Reformation in the sixteenth century the Church was a major landowner.

For the same reason you should find out about local manor houses, stately homes and castles because they may be a clue that your house once belonged to an estate. Nearby industries and mining activities should also be investigated, as there may be some link with your house.

NINETEENTH-CENTURY TOWN HOUSE

A very fine-looking semi-detached house in Surbiton, Greater London. Although simple in design and lacking elaborately decorative features it has a classiness about it and looks well proportioned, strong and reliable. Houses do have personalities! The angled bay is a striking feature. The stonework contrasts with the brick, and it is interesting that the first floor has horizontal rustication between the windows while the half-basement has a plain surface. The glazing in the windows at all levels appears to be modern yet does not spoil the appearance.

During the Industrial Revolution, some employers built homes for their workers. Disused malthouses, slagheaps, decaying textile mills, converted warehouses, old mines, closed-down steel mills or a disused railway line are all part of the nation's industrial heritage and can help to explain why your house was built in the first place.

ON THE RIGHT TRACKS

Transport links also provide valuable pointers. If there is a navigable river or canal flowing through your town, there is a strong chance that it would have brought waterborne trade and prosperity to local merchants. It is also useful to know if there is a railway station or if there ever was one, and to make a note of the main roads, where they come from and where they go to.

The position of your house in relation to key transport links may reveal when it was built and for what purpose. For example, housing developments in suburbs hinged on access to the town centre by public transport, so the building of a railway station may have been the motivating force behind the construction of your house.

At the beginning of your investigation it is worth obtaining an early edition 6-in or 25-in Ordnance Survey map made in the nineteenth century. Later in your investigation this will prove an invaluable source of evidence used in tandem with your new-found fascination with your area (see Chapter 2, pp.43–44).

Neighbourhood Watch Checklist

1. Trees in your garden or street or in neighbouring gardens or fields
2. Remains of outbuildings in garden, old cobbles or paths and walls or fences
3. Humps in lawn?
4. Size and position of your plot and its boundaries
5. Topographical features: streams, woods, orchards, parkland, field shapes, public gardens, etc.
6. Transport links: train stations, main roads, canals, waterways, tracks, lanes, drains
7. Historic sites in the area: stately homes, churches, castles, monuments, old factories or significant commercial buildings
8. Most commonly used building materials in area
9. Main local industry or craft
10. Local myths

GEOGRAPHICAL DIVERSITY

There are major regional differences in the way houses were built and the materials used. Architectural styles emerged in different places at different times. As a general rule, the further away you are from London and the south-east, the later new fashions and styles took hold. It is also important to distinguish between urban and rural architecture and to be aware of when your home city, town or village developed.

In the days before materials could be transported cheaply around the country, vernacular houses tended to be built from local stone, local timber, locally produced bricks or whatever other material was to hand. This has produced an often complex geographical diversity, both between regions and within limited local areas. It is not within the scope of this book to provide a comprehensive guide to localities, but Chapter 3 on building materials goes into this in greater detail and the map on p.65 gives some general guidelines. If you want to find out more about building materials in your area, you might find reference books on local geology helpful.

Know your history

A good house detective also needs to have an idea of the historical context of his or her region, without which it is difficult to interpret the truth about your home.

Most towns have been through at least one period of major rebuilding financed by growing prosperity over the centuries. In Kent and Sussex, a boom in trade in the fifteenth century led to the building of many timber-framed, open-hall houses of a style called *Wealden*. The Welsh counties of Glamorgan and Gwent were rebuilt from about 1560, while in Welsh and English highland areas, major building began in about 1670. In the cases of Northumberland, Durham and south and east Scotland there was large-scale reconstruction between 1720 and 1815.

In some cases, towns have had to be rebuilt because they were destroyed by fire or wartime bombing (for example, Coventry). The best-known example is London after the fire of 1666, but Warwick faced a similar conflagration in 1694 and Blandford Forum in Dorset had to be rebuilt for much the same reason in 1731.

Time-capsule towns

Around the country there are many towns which enjoyed their heydays centuries ago. Some, like Bath (now a World Heritage Site) and Cheltenham, have remained fashionable and are still closely associated with the grandeur of their Georgian and Regency buildings.

However, there are other towns whose rich architectural heritage is almost forgotten; a secret well kept from all but those who live there. Whitehaven on the Cumbrian coast is a prime example. In the eighteenth century it was one of the country's busiest ports and wealthy merchants built themselves imposing and elegant Georgian townhouses in long avenues running up from the harbour. When the bottom fell out of the trade and local industries went into decline, Whitehaven stood still, with the result that many of the town's fine buildings remain unchanged. Other port cities like Liverpool and Bristol possess equally fine eighteenth-century houses in areas like Toxteth and St Paul's, areas which are possibly better known today for inner-city deprivation.

For the historian of vernacular architecture, towns and areas like these are very enlightening. For example, the town of Montgomery in Wales was a regional capital in the Middle Ages, flourishing as a fortress town and an administrative and trading centre by dint of its location on the volatile border with Wales. However, by the end of the fifteenth century Wales had been absorbed into the English state and Montgomery's *raison d'être* as a colonial town had disappeared. It failed to evolve and today remains a frozen example of the Medieval period.

Lavenham in Suffolk is another excellent example of a town that has retained its original character, here because of a sudden and dramatic decline in the textiles trade. With no more money there could be no modernization, and today Lavenham is overflowing with medieval timber-framed houses.

EDWARDIAN TOWN HOUSE
A marvellous range of early-twentieth-century houses in which all the decorative details from the shaped barge-boarding on the gable to the brackets supporting the ground-floor window-sills have been cared for. The repeated pattern of the glazing bars in all the windows appears to be derived from perpendicular gothic. This range in Friern Barnet in Greater London dates back to 1904.

Unique designs

There are some towns and villages whose architecture is purely idiosyncratic, more down to a flight of fancy of a local landowner than any prevailing trend.

The village of Ripley in North Yorkshire is an excellent example of this. During a visit to northern France, the owner of Ripley Castle was so enamoured with the local architecture that on his return he rebuilt the whole of his village in that style. The houses, village school and hall all have a continental look about them that is quite at odds with other rural dwellings in the region.

European influences spread as local aristocrats returned from their Grand Tours of Europe and tried to imitate the style they had seen on their own estates. The sixth duke of Devonshire rebuilt the village of Edensor on his estate in Derbyshire in about 1840 in a veritable rash of styles, including Castellated, Gothic, Norman, Classical and Swiss Chalet. The Earl of Dorchester had the whole of the Dorset village of Milton Abbas rebuilt between 1771 and 1790 as 40 semi-detached cottages along a tree-lined avenue. The trend continued as ordinary people began to travel internationally in the last century, bringing more continental influences into British buildings.

BACK-TO-BACK HOUSING The early nineteenth century had rows upon rows of cramped dwellings in the industrial regions. Houses were built literally back-to-back until the middle of the century, but after that the Public Health Act of 1848 encouraged more space and improved sanitation facilities in backyards. These workers' houses in Saltaire, West Yorkshire, may well be called front-to-front housing.

Mass housing

With the coming of the Industrial Revolution, purpose-built housing was put up for factory workers. At one end of the scale were the cramped, back-to-back terraces, the majority of which have been demolished for health reasons. At the other were the many examples of practical and solid houses built by industrialists for their workers, many of which have survived. One such was Sir Richard Arkwright, who pioneered the water-powered industrial cotton mill and built decent terraced accommodation for his workers in Cromford, Derbyshire. This was repeated in many industrial towns across the country and is worth investigating, as are the visionary attempts by social reformers to create pleasant and healthy housing estates such as Hampstead Garden Suburb or the Old Oak estate in East Acton, London.

CHANGING USES

Be careful not to make assumptions about your house. Do not take it for granted, for example, that your house has always been a purely residential

dwelling. It is common for vernacular buildings to fulfil numerous roles in their history and to be reinvented on more than one occasion. Many people live in buildings that used to be schools, shops, farms, mills, churches, almshouses, inns or taverns, barns or pre-industrial centres of production.

Life on the farm

You may live in a town but don't discount the possibility that your house could have been a farm at one time. The Agricultural Revolution led to farmhouses being built in newly enclosed fields outside towns and villages. Existing farmhouses and associated buildings were in many cases converted into smaller living units for farmworkers because this was the cheapest way of providing them with accommodation. Better-off farmers tended to build labourers' cottages as part of the model farms, a good example of which can be seen at Dunsby Fen Farm in Lincolnshire (see Chapter 7, p.186).

Living above the shop

It is also worth bearing in mind that a pre-seventeenth century house built in the centre of a town would almost certainly have had a commercial role to play as well as a residential one. The front of the house at street level would have been a shop or a workshop, possibly a butchers or a blacksmiths. The name of your house may provide an initial clue which can be followed up by analyzing early street maps.

By the late seventeenth century, townhouses were being built purely for residential use and the occupants worked elsewhere. However, many of these houses were themselves converted into shops as the town expanded, which meant that the ground floor would have been extensively altered. Traditionally, the owner lived over the shop, but in more recent years because of insurance and other reasons, much living space above High Street shops has been left unoccupied.

Crafty clues

Before the Industrial Revolution, textiles and other durable products were produced by individual craftspeople in their own homes. This influenced the design of their houses and can be very useful evidence for identifying a house.

Excellent examples of this are spinners' and weavers' cottages in Lancashire, the Lake District and West Yorkshire, which can be instantly recognized by the long rows of windows on the upper floor. These were designed to let in as much light as possible. You would also expect to find surprisingly large rooms on this upper floor.

Watermills are another good example: they can go back as far as the Middle Ages but most of those that have survived are from the eighteenth and nineteenth centuries. Generally there was a mill house attached to the mill itself and in many cases the mill has been incorporated into the house and the machinery removed. If you think your house was an old mill because of its name or some other clue, you should look for the remains of fixtures and fittings in the walls and try to locate the millpond and stream. A mill would almost certainly feature on early Ordnance Survey maps and it is worth checking manorial records as mills were often owned by the local lord of the manor.

Houses with specific functions

The transport revolution in the second half of the eighteenth century gave birth to a range of clearly identifiable houses. A fine example of this is the toll house, built by the Turnpike Trusts to collect tolls from travellers on the new roads. The houses can be many-sided and invariably have large windows to give them good visibility along the road. Often situated right on the verge, these houses have in many cases fallen victim to road widening schemes.

Canalworkers' and lockkeepers' cottages are also very distinctive and were generally built in a uniform style by the canal companies. In recent years these have enjoyed something of a renaissance, thanks to the surge of interest in holidaying on Britain's inland waterways.

Railways, too, have had a considerable influence on the building of houses. In a general sense, the coming of the railways in the nineteenth century heralded a boom period in many towns at the same time as precipitating the decline of others ignored by the main lines. Signalmen's cottages were put up alongside often remote stretches of track, and the railway companies built terraced housing for their workers near the station, often using a mixture of different-coloured bricks arranged in patterns. There are examples of this in main railway junctions like Reading, Swindon and Crewe. Documents about the origins of these houses are generally kept by the companies involved or by their modern-day successors.

Old school ties

With improving transport links and changing education policy, many small rural schools have been forced to close and have since been converted into homes. There is an excellent example of this in Halsham, near Hull in East Yorkshire. This fine and rather rambling Elizabethan house is now a family home but for most of its long history, between 1584 and 1949, it was a boys' grammar school. There are many clues to this in the layout and size of the rooms and corridors and the surprisingly large number of windows, indicating former classrooms. The pupils themselves have left their own mark, too: an ancient wooden door on the first floor of the house still bears graffiti with names and dates from the early eighteenth century carved by naughty children. Halsham Grammar School was run by the Church and in such cases there are extensive documentary records to help with your investigation.

The Inn Look

It is not uncommon for former inns or taverns to be reborn as ordinary homes. Indeed, we came across an example during the television series: the house in Manningtree, Essex, had been a tavern in the eighteenth century. It was one of 29 in the town at that time, which seems remarkable by modern standards.

However, inns, taverns and alehouses were more numerous in the past and their functions were much more varied than they are today. Inns were generally of a higher status and would provide a bed for the night and refreshments for travellers, while taverns and alehouses were drinking venues, as well as being important meeting places where business deals were struck.

During the Middle Ages, the Church was a leading producer of ales, which were invariably sold in a Church House near the churchyard. The Church House also developed as an important social centre and typically had a large open room on the first floor with a series of smaller rooms and stores at ground level.

The Church's involvement in the alcohol trade was effectively ended by the Reformation, and Church Houses were often converted into private houses. There are numerous good examples in the west of England, at Braunton and Manaton in Devon, as well as Sherborne in Dorset. Prior to the Reformation, religious orders traditionally provided accommodation for travellers and built hostels or inns on busy routes. Following the Dissolution of the Monasteries, this function passed almost exclusively into secular hands.

Inns were generally built around courtyards, which were entered via an archway at the front. If you think you live in a former inn, look for evidence of an old archway that has been filled in or a former courtyard that has been covered to create more rooms. The coming of the railways sounded the death knell for many inns, and a considerable number became private houses. If you suspect from the name of your house that it was an inn, tavern or alehouse, there are numerous documentary sources available, including alehouses' recognizances and other licences. Modern-day breweries may also keep records.

INDUSTRIAL STYLE
Not all housing in the industrial areas presented plain functional façades. These terraced houses in Saltaire, west Yorkshire, have got quite a bit of style about them. The ground-floor windows and doorways have arched heads, the upper windows have emphasized lintels and sills and the symmetry of the range is underlined by taller, projecting houses.

THE PLOT THICKENS

The investigation now moves into the realm of documentary evidence, which comes from either primary or secondary sources. Primary sources are the original records, such as maps, deeds, census returns and parish registers, which are the bread-and-butter of historical research; secondary sources are history books and other studies, which can help you build up a picture of what was happening locally and nationally during the lifetime of your house. Oral history, which we have already mentioned in Chapter 1, is a third source. However, while it can provide excellent leads and some entertaining stories it is wise not to rely solely on this kind of evidence because it can become rather embroidered in the handing down.

HISTORY BOOKS AND SECONDARY SOURCES

Before you immerse yourself in old archive documents it is worth getting a basic grounding from local history and architectural books. These publications fall into two categories: weighty near-definitive tomes – sometimes part of a national series – and small booklets and collections of old photographs produced locally by enthusiasts. Your local library or bookshop should be able to help you track down both types of book without too much difficulty, but there are a number of general publications that you should refer to as a matter of course.

THE *VICTORIA COUNTY HISTORY*

The first must is the *Victoria County History* (*VCH*), a mammoth county-by-county encyclopaedia of English local history which has yet to be completed. Work began on it almost a century ago in 1899 and so far a massive 211 volumes have been published. You should first check to see if work on your county has been completed or is still in progress. So far, 14 counties have been finished and work is continuing on another 14. Some information is available on most of the remainder, but those volumes are effectively dormant.

Your local library should keep the *VCH* and will be able to get you the relevant volume if it does not stock it. It is a useful tip to start with the *Victoria County History General Introduction* (1970) and its 1990 supplement and refer to the contents of volumes published. The *VCH* should be able to tell you if your house is built on land once owned by a manor or a religious order, which would give you a head start when it comes to the primary sources. Books like the *VCH* have an enormous quantity of background material so you may find it easier to go to them in search of specific subject areas, for example maritime trade in the seventeenth century, rather than trawl through thousands of pages.

Buildings of England series

The *VCH*'s architectural equivalent is the *Buildings of England* series by Nikolaus Pevsner. In 1945, Pevsner, a German immigrant, undertook to produce a series of architectural history guidebooks, county by county. The first, on Cornwall, was published in 1951. Initially, Pevsner visited the buildings in the guidebooks himself during university vacations, but he later sought the help of other architectural historians. The work on England was completed in 1974 when Staffordshire became volume number 46. By this time plans for a separate series on Scotland, Wales and Ireland were afoot and, although Pevsner himself has now died, work is continuing on these volumes.

The *Buildings of England* series is revised at intervals and the later editions are the most useful ones for house detectives because they reflect the growing interest in vernacular architecture. If you want to find out the architectural history of a county, start with Pevsner as it is full of excellent background material. However, if your house happens to be featured it does not mean your work has already been done for you. Pevsner himself acknowledged that he did not have the time to get everything absolutely right and he was not always able to go inside the buildings, which is where some of the best clues to a house's origins are to be found.

Royal Commission on Historical Monuments

The other major source of background material is the inventories of the Royal Commission on Historical Monuments, a major survey launched early this century. It is worth contacting the National Monuments Record, which is the RCHM's public archive (see p.221), to see if your house has been surveyed. The collection, which is housed in Swindon, has three million buildings' records and photographs and has aerial photographs of the whole of England. Similar offices for Wales and Scotland are to be found in Aberystwyth and Edinburgh. The house we investigated in Manningtree High Street, Essex had been recorded in 1921, and while the information was not completely accurate it provided us with one or two useful clues and an archive photograph.

If you live in London, you should look into the Survey of London, which is now the responsibility of the RCHM. The survey was launched in 1894 as a volunteer project to record the historic fabric of the capital. Each volume in the main series examines a particular area, discusses its topographical and architectural history, gives a detailed description of buildings and includes archive photographs, maps and plans.

The Department of the Environment, the Welsh office (Cadw) and the Scottish and Northern Ireland offices also list buildings of historic importance and you will almost certainly be aware if your home is listed. If it is, contact your local authority planning department who should be able to offer you advice and help you gather material.

Further reading

There are a great many other societies and organizations who can be called on to help you in your quest for background information. They will be able to tell you about publications focusing on your area and may also be able to put you in touch with local groups. Among those you should consider contacting is the Vernacular Architecture Group as well as the various organizations specializing in specific architectural periods, such as the Victorian Society, the Georgian Group and the Twentieth Century Society. If you strike lucky, someone may have already gathered together most of the background material you want in one neat little volume.

One final tip: think laterally about your background reading. If there are local legends about well-known or notorious historical figures such as the Witchfinder General, Judge Jeffreys or Dick Turpin, you should read up on them. You never know, your town or village may get a mention; there is often an element of truth, however small, in myths. More importantly, they will give you a flavour of the past and enable you to develop a picture of life in former centuries.

PRIMARY SOURCES: WHERE TO GO AND WHO TO TALK TO

The real detective work begins when you get into the archives: this could involve analyzing old maps, poring over ancient tomes and sifting through long lists of names on microfiche which, in some cases, can be like looking for a needle in a haystack. It's important to take a systematic and logical approach, otherwise you could end up juggling a whole collection of random clues.

If at first the evidence seems disparate and confusing, do persevere. You will almost certainly be dealing with incomplete records, which will mean leapfrogging from one source to another and from one period to another, but most efforts pay off in the end.

The best approach is to start looking for the most recent information and progress backwards, making a note of any relevant names or clues and following them all up wherever possible. You will probably find that you can go back 150 years without too much difficulty and will be able to draw a fairly comprehensive 'family tree' for your house. Further back than that the records become more patchy; they may not have survived or they were quite simply never done.

Records Office

Your investigation will take you to a number of different places, both locally and in London or other centres. A good piece of advice is to find a sympathetic archivist or librarian to help you and point you in the right direction. If you know what you are looking for, and your enthusiasm is infectious, you should have little trouble in obtaining useful guidance. There is usually more than one person you can approach, so do not be deterred if the first one you ask is less than helpful.

Once you have gained all the information you can from your local library, your next port of call will be the County Records Office, which is normally in the county town and will hold a considerable number of wide-ranging documents. On your first visit you should come armed with a list of clues and other leads, as these will provide a starting point for going through the index.

As far as the earlier records are concerned, it is worth looking into all documents listed in the index of place names for your local area. This can be a painstaking process, but as long as you are focused about the area you are looking at, the task should be manageable.

You will often find that copies of records held elsewhere in the country, e.g. census returns, are available at your County Records Office, so it is worth checking before you make a wasted journey to London. For most people, the other main source of material will be the Public Record Office in Chancery Lane, London, and Kew, in Surrey. If you are in Wales, then the National Library of Wales is another important source.

In addition, there are numerous other places to look which we will come to later in this chapter, including the British Library, the Church Commission's Record Office, diocesan records' offices, the Guildhall Library, the General Register Office (London and Edinburgh) and Somerset House, London.

There are numerous rules and ways of doing things at records offices. For example, you will generally need a reader's ticket to view all original documents at a County Records Office, a procedure that requires you to fill out a slip and wait for about half an hour for the document to be produced. You will probably find that only three documents can be applied for at once. Remember to take a pencil with you to make notes because pens are not allowed, and if you are permitted to handle original documents you will be expected to don surgical-looking white gloves. Maps, directories and secondary sources tend to be kept on open shelves, which makes life easier.

When you go to the Public Record Office for the first time, you should take a formal document – a driving licence or a credit card bearing your name and signature – so that you can be issued with a reader's ticket free of charge. A £1 coin is also useful for a locker to put your possessions in as you are not allowed to take large bags in with you.

Maps

Maps are one of the single most fruitful areas of research for house detectives because the position of your house says a lot about its importance and its role in the past. You should start looking at maps fairly early on because they are one of the quickest ways of stripping away the history of a house. In the television series, the position of the house in the landscape – its *morphology* – provided crucial clues in no fewer than five out of the six cases.

Ordnance Survey maps

For house detectives, Ordnance Survey maps from the middle of the nineteenth century are essential, especially if they are used in conjunction with an aerial photograph of the area.

Ordnance Survey (OS) are the most detailed maps available, showing landscapes and communities before the major expansion of towns and cities in the second half of the last century. They come in different scales going right back to the beginning of the nineteenth century and are available for every area in the country. A local library or County Records Office should stock them.

The Ordnance Survey originally grew out of a decision to produce a military map of the Highlands of Scotland between 1747 and 1755; the project to produce maps of the whole country did not get underway until 1791. The first official map, of Kent, was published in 1801 at a scale of 1 inch to 1 mile. A second 1-inch map, this time of Essex, was published 10 years later. However, early production was sporadic because of financial stringency.

The old 1-inch maps are worth looking at, but to get the right amount of detail what you really need is a 6-inch Ordnance Survey map. These came in after the Ordnance Survey Act of 1841, which called for all public boundaries in the United Kingdom to be ascertained and recorded. In the second half of the nineteenth century, Ordnance Survey followed them up with a rapid succession of maps and engravings, including, in the 1870s, 25-inch maps.

A great deal of useful material can be discovered from 6-inch and 25-inch OS maps. They portray the ancient shape of the landscape and show clearly old boundaries and the original *burgage* plots, that is, pieces of land in the town granted by the lord of the manor. It is much more difficult to pick out key elements of a place's morphology in later maps: a good example is south-east Durham where maps that predate industrialization are essential because in later editions the development of Teeside has swallowed up original settlements shown on the map.

Making your own medieval map

The investigation we carried out in Manningtree, Essex, is a fine example of how OS maps can provide a major breakthrough. Armed with a photocopy of a 25-inch map mounted on cardboard, David Austin walked around the streets making a mental note of key locations and assessing how the town had changed. When you do this for yourself, look out for rivers or streams, churches, a marketplace, manor houses, mills, bridges, old pubs, the principal axial roads and sudden changes of direction in tracks and streets. Back home, try to work out an outline or skeleton of the medieval town.

The best way to do this is to attach tracing paper to the map and mark in all the key points in the town with different coloured pencils, starting with your own property. Analyze the size of the plot: compare it with others in the same street and see if it is any different to how it is now. In the Manningtree example this was a crucial clue. It was twice the width of neighbouring plots, which means that at some point two separate plots had been amalgamated.

These burgage plots were created in the Middle Ages and were generally rectangular in shape. In some cases, plots extended a long way to a back lane or alley, but it was the width of the frontage onto the street that was most important because this was the selling area in a town. Clearly, the original owner of the house in Manningtree had come into some money and doubled his frontage. It was this piece of evidence that enabled us to find the name of the owner from early-seventeenth-century documents.

Once you have drawn up and completed

your medieval skeleton, you should examine the position of your house in relation to other key locations. In Manningtree, the house is in a prime position right on the marketplace, which was the key selling area. It is also in the principal street running east/west and is literally a stone's throw from the harbour and the River Stour, which had been an important trading route. The morphological evidence suggested that whoever lived in the house was almost certainly involved in trade and was quite likely to be a prominent merchant.

The other clue worth following up was that, on the map, the house was right next door to a chapel. The chapel is no longer there but a plaque on the remains of the west wall explains that one was built in 1616 and was demolished in the mid-1960s. This again proved to be useful evidence (see 'Census Returns', p.50) and led us to investigate the history of the chapel in Manningtree and its links with the house.

Tithe maps

Ordnance Survey maps will be the focus of your investigation but there are other maps that you should inspect. Tithe maps were generally drawn up 20 or 30 years earlier than the detailed Ordnance Survey 6-inch maps and followed the Tithe Commutation Act of 1836.

Tithe was traditionally a payment in kind to the Church of one-tenth of the products of the land, but during the eighteenth century the system had fallen into disrepute and it was decided to replace it with a fixed rent.

The maps produced as part of this nationwide project vary greatly in scale, accuracy and size. Not all of them were the work of qualified land surveyors, because the cost of the survey had to be met by the landowners. Only about 1,900 tithe maps – one-sixth of the total – are accurate field-by-field, plot-by-plot, house-by-house descriptions. The rest, called unsealed or second-class maps, are a mixed bag, some of them little more than topographical sketches.

Strictly speaking, the tithe map and the tithe apportionment constitute a single document, but for practical reasons they are stored separately at the Public Record Office in Kew, near London. The tithe apportionments are a more uniform record than the maps and include the names of the owners or occupiers of land and the amount of rent they had to pay. They can provide you with some useful names for your investigation and also give you a clear idea of who the main landowners were.

Estate maps

If you have a hunch that your house is on land which was part of an estate, you should start immediately making enquiries about estate records, because these sometimes contain the most exquisite and revealing maps. The index in your local County Records Office should point you in the right direction. If not, the National Register of Archives should be able to help.

During the television series, we found two excellent examples of estate maps: one from the Charterhouse archives for Dunsby Fen Farm and one from the Kingston survey for Church Farm, Bidston (see pp.46 and 58–9). When you look at any of these maps, be aware of

any changes in the shapes and patterns of holdings, plots of land and the orientation of the buildings. Do not ignore anything, even the soft architecture like trees and hedgerows, because this will invariably be mapped with great accuracy. Straight lines of trees on a map, for example, can signify an early boundary, an old enclosure or the approach to a house. In the Bidston case, we were able to correlate a line of trees on a nineteenth-century OS map with an estate map from two

SEVENTEENTH-CENTURY ESTATE PLAN
This is a fragment of the large and colourful Kingston estate map of 1665. Initially it does not seem to bear any resemblance to a modern map of Bidston, but once you have identified a building that is still in existence, such as the church, the rest falls into place.

centuries earlier. Evidence of old roads or streams on early maps can also help you understand earlier settlements. At Mulberry Cottage in Swanage it emerged that a nineteenth-century extension to the house had been built on top of an old stream.

Transport records

If your house seems to have any connection with main transport routes, including roads, canals or railways, you should start investigating transport records. Railway companies and public authorities did detailed surveys and maps of land they were purchasing and these sometimes included adjoining land. The W. E. Hayward Collection at the Public Record Office may prove useful here: it includes Railway Clearing House maps, Johnston's maps of railway systems in Great Britain and junction diagrams between 1872 and 1967. Other railway, road and canal maps are held in the Transport Department section at Kew.

Very early maps

Enclosure awards, dating from about 1740, sometimes include maps and will be held at the Public Record Office or a County Records Office. Similarly, *terriers*, which mark the end of the open-field system, are inventories of estate land, including maps and details of individual properties.

City corporations, guilds, the Church and charities all produced maps of land they owned – indeed, printed maps have been available since Tudor times. Perhaps the best early maps were those by John Speed, whose *Theatre of the Empire of Great Britaine* (1612) contains 73 town plans, including Nottingham, Ipswich and Salisbury. There are also numerous eighteenth-century town plans that offer a valuable insight into urban morphology and can show, for example, changes in the names of streets.

THE DEEDS

Old deeds to your house can be invaluable. If you are lucky, you will find a whole bundle of different legal and other documents, including leases, conveyances, bonds, mortgages, plans, maps, wills and certificates of completion. Should these documents go all the way back to the origins of your house, they will give you an excellent head start: it is the equivalent of getting a confession at the scene of the crime.

Unfortunately, in most cases, such a comprehensive collection does not exist. Many householders nowadays have a modern piece of paper that merely marks the most recent transfer of the property. The Land Registration Act of 1925 enabled people to register their ownership of land, and in the ensuing years it became compulsory in different regions to do so, making the traditional system of deeds legally superfluous. This led to the destruction of many old documents, although some, which were considered to be of interest, were kept by the Land Registries or have been transferred to a local Records Office.

If you do not already have your deeds, they will be held by your solicitor or, if you have a mortgage, by the bank or building society. Your first call should be to your solicitor, because he or she will have seen all the relevant documents while acting on your behalf in the purchase of the house. Banks and building societies will normally demand a fee for providing copies of the deeds. If it emerges that you only have the modern transfer documents, it is worth calling your local Land Registry Office or making inquiries at the County Records Office to see if earlier deeds have been preserved. You may even find that the old deeds have been kept by former owners of the house or are to be found in the archives of a landed estate or religious organization.

Ancient deeds

It is worth having a brief look at the history of deeds as far back as the feudal period because an understanding of the processes and knowledge of the terms is useful. In medieval documents, the house and any land is referred to as a 'messuage' and was held in 'fee simple', which meant that the occupier had to perform services for the local lord. The transfer of property was carried out at a ceremony called a 'public livery of seisin', which traditionally involved the handing over of a symbolic stick, stone or piece of turf. There was no legal requirement to provide written proof of this transfer until the late seventeenth century, but from about the twelfth century early written deeds, known as 'charters of feoffment', were produced. These early charters were written in Latin and generally contained reference to some form of payment as well as annual services due to a lord.

Without a knowledge of Latin it is difficult to interpret these documents and, even if they are written in English, it will be an early form of the language written in old-fashioned handwriting. Deciphering these documents is a job in itself, but do not be put off. You may be on the verge of making an important breakthrough, so it is worth persevering.

Start off by copying out those parts of the documents that you can understand. Some people find it useful to trace over the words on a photocopy (not the original) of the document to get a feel for the handwriting. Often you can get this by simply identifying key words and names. Once you have got as far as you can, seek specialist advice from an archivist at your County Records Office or from the classics or medieval history department of a local college or university. The chances are that if you are investigating a medieval house they will be as interested as you to find out more.

Difficult deeds

If you have been unable to track down your deeds, it is worth investigating Quarter Sessions documents, which are generally held at County Records Offices. The Statute of Enrolments of 1536 stipulated that all 'bargains and sales', which were a type of conveyance, should be public documents. These enrolments of deeds of bargain and sale can be found among Quarter Sessions documents until the early eighteenth century. You should also be able to find the names and property details of Roman Catholics in the same place, because from 1715 so-called papists were required to register with the local Clerk of the Peace.

You may have given up on your deeds, only to find them in the most unusual of places. The case of the house in Manningtree High Street was a good example. The owners, David and Mandy Rose, had a modern transfer document that did not tell them anything they did not already know. The Land Registry was unable to trace the earlier deeds for the house and they were not in the Records Office. However, the deeds had not been entirely lost to posterity because, by an astonishing piece of luck, a local historian, Clarice Jacques, had seen them during the 1950s. Clarice borrowed the pile of old documents from the then owner of the house, a chemist called Charles Winter, and painstakingly copied them out in her own hand. Her efforts proved invaluable. From her notes we discovered that the house had been a bank throughout the last century and before that it had been a tavern, with cellars and vaults. The deeds also provided us with names, which we were able to follow up. This was just the type of evidence we had been looking for.

MORE RECENT HISTORY

If the deeds have yielded paltry information about former owners, your neighbours and other local people should be able to give you the names of the people who lived in your house over recent years. Once you have those, you will be able to trace the names through the General Register Office, which has records of births, deaths and marriages starting in 1837 in London and in 1855 in Scotland.

The registration certificates contain basic information, including names of parents, addresses, occupations, ages, dates and locations of the events. Any of these details could provide a lead and should be noted. Nowadays houses change hands regularly, but in the past the same family often lived in the same house for several generations. This has the advantage of allowing you to establish a distinct lineage. You can follow this up by seeking advice from the Society of Genealogists and researching published material on family trees. The Mormons, or the Church of Latter Day Saints, also keep comprehensive genealogical records, because it is an important tenet of their faith.

One of the single most fruitful sources for earlier this century are local authorities' rate books. The Domesday of the Rate of 1910, a nationwide survey carried out for tax purposes, is an excellent record of who was living where shortly before the First World War. You should also investigate the precursor of the rates, the Poor Law Returns, which were a form of local tax.

Both the General Register Office records and the rates books indicate the profession of the owner of a house. This is a valuable clue and can lead you directly to trade organizations or guilds, professional bodies and commercial directories. The latter first appeared around 1760 and really took off after 1820. A directory of this kind revealed a great deal about the man who built the house we investigated in Preston.

Trade guilds records can also prove fruitful. In London, the Guildhall Library is a dream come true for house detectives with its records of the city livery companies, including apprenticeship and enrolment books. The library's *pièce de résistance* is the list of the inhabitants of the City of London in 1695, which, sadly, is only useful if you live in a small area of the capital.

From the late eighteenth century until

the middle of this century, local directories were printed in many areas. They include details about the amenities, followed by lists of inhabitants. The directories vary in the way that the information is compiled and the amount of detail. Kelly's and other Post Office directories can be useful to house detectives, but be wary because these records are not complete: do not read anything into the absence of a person from these lists. In the late nineteenth century, the Board of Health responded to outbreaks of cholera by producing detailed lists of who lived where and what they did for a living. These were often accompanied by maps and can be revealing, if a little depressing.

As a general tip, it is helpful to write down everything you know about a family and think of the reasons why any aspect of their life may have been recorded. You can then go along to your Records Office and check in the index if such records exist.

ELECTORAL REGISTERS

Electoral registers are only of limited use because they are by definition incomplete records of who lived in a house. The universal right to vote is a relatively recent development: initially, it was limited to those owning larger properties, and it was only extended to women over 30 after the First World War and to women over 21 in 1928. You may also find patchy evidence in poll books, which listed qualified voters before 1872.

CENSUS RETURNS

Much more revealing than electoral registers, census returns provide excellent evidence of who lived in your house in the second half of the last century. The first census was carried out in 1841 and censuses have been taken every 10 years since; sadly for house detectives the details remain confidential for a century, which means the most recent census available to you is the one for 1891.

The records are kept on microfiche or microfilm in a number of places: in London at the Public Record Office and outside of the capital at County Records Offices and sometimes even local libraries. Before you set out it is essential that you know the name of your parish. At the Public Record Office, a step-by-step guide and colour-coding system is provided to help you find the census returns you are looking for.

If you live in a town or city with a population of more than 40,000, you should look at the Table of Street Indexes, London Street Indexes or County Street Indexes. For smaller places, you will want the Place Name Index. The indexes will provide you with the reference number you need to track down the specific microfilm or microfiche. You then spool through the film or fiche using a reader until you find the folio number for your street. Once you have found what you want you can buy a photocopy, or a microfilm or microfiche of the relevant page or pages.

Census returns make fascinating reading, providing as they do details of the exact number of people who lived in the house, their age (approximate to the nearest five years for adults) and what they did for a living. You may be surprised that so many people lived in the house but the returns show that it was quite common for ordinary Victorian

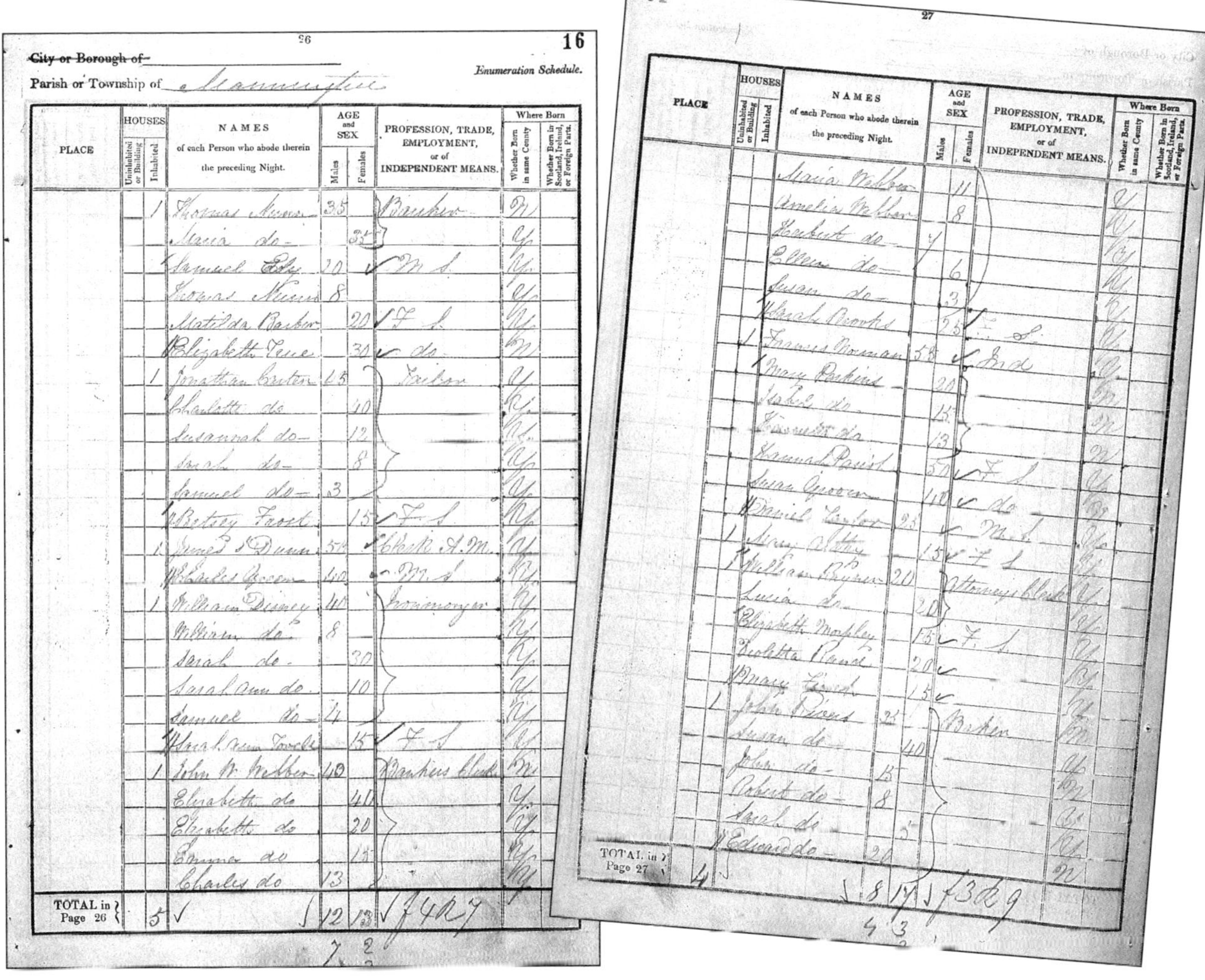

26 16

City or Borough of—

Parish or Township of Manningtree

Enumeration Schedule.

PLACE	HOUSES: Uninhabited or Building	HOUSES: Inhabited	NAMES of each Person who abode therein the preceding Night.	AGE and SEX: Males	AGE and SEX: Females	PROFESSION, TRADE, EMPLOYMENT, or of INDEPENDENT MEANS.	Where Born: Whether Born in same County	Whether Born in Scotland, Ireland, or Foreign Parts.
		1	Thomas Nunn	35		Banker	N	
			Maria do		35		Y	
			Samuel Eley	20		M.S.	Y	
			Thomas Nunn	8			Y	
			Matilda Barker		20	F.S.	N	
			Elizabeth [illegible]		30	do	N	
		1	Jonathan Curtis	45		Tailor	Y	
			Charlotte do		40		Y	
			Susannah do		12		N	
			Sarah do		8		N	
			Samuel do	3			Y	
			Betsey Frost		15	F.S.	N	
		1	James S Dunn	50		Clerk A.M.	N	
			Charles Green	40		M.S.	N	
		1	William Disney	40		Ironmonger	N	
			William do	8			N	
			Sarah do		30		N	
			Sarah Ann do		10		Y	
			Samuel do	4			N	
			Sarah Ann Towell		15	F.S.	N	
		1	John W. Webber	40		Bankers Clerk	N	
			Elizabeth do		41		Y	
			Elizabeth do		20		Y	
			Emma do		15		Y	
			Charles do	13			N	
TOTAL in Page 26		5		12	13			

27

PLACE	HOUSES: Uninhabited or Building	HOUSES: Inhabited	NAMES of each Person who abode therein the preceding Night.	AGE and SEX: Males	AGE and SEX: Females	PROFESSION, TRADE, EMPLOYMENT, or of INDEPENDENT MEANS.	Where Born: Whether Born in same County	Whether Born in Scotland, Ireland, or Foreign Parts.
			Maria Webber		11		Y	
			Amelia Webber		8		N	
			Herbert do	7			Y	
			Ellen do		6		N	
			Susan do		3		Y	
			Sarah Brooks		25	F.S.	N	
		1	Frances Norman		58	Ind	Y	
		1	Mary Perkins		20		Y	
			Isabel do		15		N	
			[illegible] do		13		N	
			Hannah Pond		50	F.S.	N	
			Susan Green		40	do	N	
			Daniel Taylor	25		M.S.	N	
		1	Ann Nottage		15	F.S.	N	
			William Byrne	20		Attorneys Clerk	Y	
			Lucia do		20		N	
			Elizabeth Mapley		15	F.S.	N	
			Violetta Pond		20		N	
			Mary Lincoln		15		N	
		1	John Rivers	25		Baker	N	
			Susan do		40		Y	
			John do	15			N	
			Robert do	8			N	
			Sarah do		5		N	
			Edward do	20			N	
TOTAL in Page 27		4		8	17			

***Above* FAMILY FORTUNES The 1841 census return for Manningtree High Street. This was an invaluable source of detailed information on who was living in the houses we were investigating. Number 38 was home to an ironmonger, William Disney, and his family. Meanwhile, number 40 must have been pretty cramped: the banker John Webber, his wife, servant and no fewer than eight children were living there.**

tradespeople and farmers to employ live-in servants (servants are usually abbreviated as 'F.S.' for female servant and 'M.S.' for male servant).

It is well worth going through all six available censuses because they may reflect a change in ownership, occupation or usage of the house. In some cases it may help you work out the date the house was built. If it is a Victorian house that appears in the 1871 census, for example, but not in the 1861 one, then the chances are that it was built in the intervening decade. However, you should still seek other evidence because anomalies do exist within the returns and it is possible that your house was missed one year or is listed elsewhere. For example, the census returns for Bidston provided no clues as to who lived at Church Farm in 1861 and 1871, but in 1881 it stated quite clearly that a Thomas Lamb occupied the farm with his second wife and their 14 children.

The census return above is a fine example of the depth of information that you can hope to find. We were investigating two neighbouring houses in Manningtree High Street, the first of which was next door to the site of an old chapel. In the census returns of 1841, the vicar, James Dunn, is listed along with his male servant Charles Green. Next door is William Disney, an ironmonger, with his wife, three children and a female servant. Meanwhile, the larger of the two houses was being occupied by a banker's clerk, John Webber, who, it says, was not born in Essex. He had a large family, including his wife Elizabeth, six daughters and two sons, as well as a female servant.

These sorts of details are immensely useful because they enable you to plot the genealogy of your house backwards into the past and forwards into the twentieth century. It is important to analyze every scrap of information because it could very well lead you on to another source of documentary evidence.

For example, the Manningtree census mentioned a banker called Thomas Nunn, who owned the bank in the High Street. Investigations revealed that Nunn later went into business with his banker's clerk, John Webber, to set up a bank called Nunn and Webber. This bank was later taken over by the larger London and County Bank, which itself went on to become part of the National Westminster Bank. The modern-day NatWest Bank keeps detailed records and was able to provide us with valuable details about the house in the nineteenth century. We were also able to track down original cheques from the bank going back more than 150 years.

WILLS AND PROBATE INVENTORIES

Wills can be a very valuable source of information and, if you are lucky enough to track down a probate inventory, you may find you have a wealth of detail that can tell you a great deal about how previous occupants of your house lived several centuries ago.

To start off with, you need the name of somebody who lived in your house and the date on which they died. The places to look are Somerset House in London, which holds records of wills proved since 1858 in England and Wales, and your local County Records Office or the Diocesan Registry, because the wills of ordinary people were generally proved in ecclesiastical courts. The indexes are filed alphabetically under the name of the deceased and according to the date of the will.

Considerable studies have been done on wills in different regions, for example, Dr F. G. Emmison's *Elizabethan Life: Wills of Essex Gentry and Yeomen*. Books like these often list the names of testators in an accessible form, so it is worth asking at your local library if such a book exists in your area.

On first reading, wills may appear to be a daunting wall of almost incomprehensible legal jargon, but do not be put off. If you go through it methodically, you should be able to produce your own transcription. We have taken a fine example of an early-eighteenth-century will that we discovered during our investigation in Bidston, Merseyside, which shows the best way to go about sifting out the information you are seeking.

Wills vary greatly in length. Ellin Wilson's will of 1703 (shown opposite) is a full example, although it does not have a separate inventory. The writing is not easy to read and the words do not flow off the page, but it is well worth battling your way through the whole document

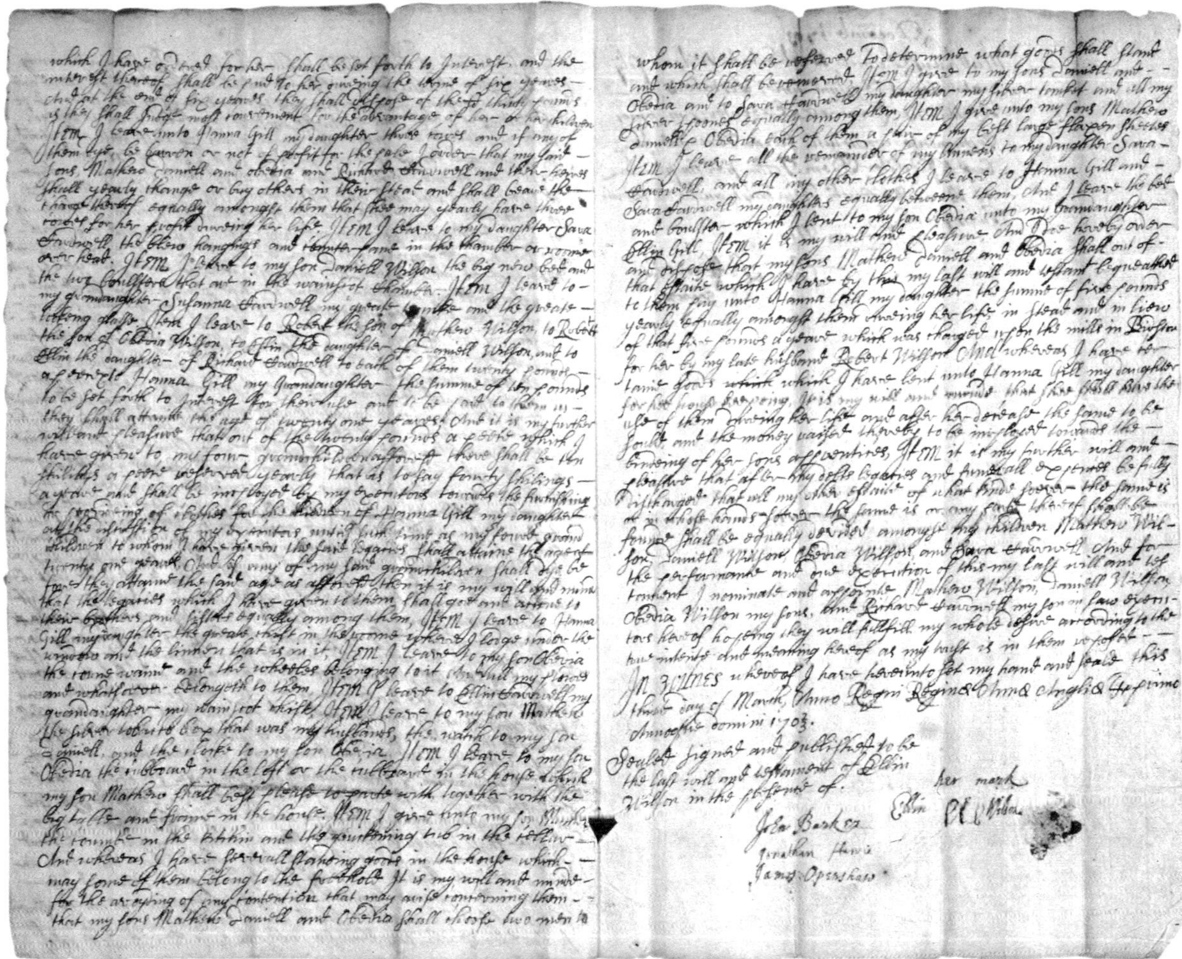

ELLIN WILSON'S WILL
This will, written in 1703, proved very enlightening to the survey on the Bidston house. Wills generally give you information on people associated with a house and an indication of their social standing. They often mention rooms and contents and other valuable information on the house. When the writing is impossible to read, seek professional help from an archivist.

because it will help to get a feel for the person and for how your house was furnished and lived in.

The will starts with a clear statement of Ellin Wilson's sanity: 'In the name of God amen I, Ellin Wilson of Bidston in the county of Chester, while being aged and infirm of body but of sound and perfect disposeing memory…'

It is then down to business: in this case, the money she is leaving, because the farm itself had already been left to the two eldest sons by her late husband, Robert Wilson. Ellin Wilson shared out several hundred pounds between her nearest and dearest, which was a considerable sum of money for a yeoman farmer at that time:

> *I give and bequeath the said hundred pounds unto Sara Cardwell my daughter and the summe to be kept at interest and the interest thereof to be paid yearly unto Sara Cardwell my daughter during her life…*

Further sums were left to her son, Obadia, and to her various grandchildren. Reading through the will, you are left with an impression of a strong woman who knew what she wanted and intended to get it from beyond the grave. In the will she left £50 to her granddaughter, Elizabeth Gill, but there were conditions attached:

> *It is my further will and pleasure that, except shee shall marry to the content and satisfaction of Mathew, Daniel and Obadia my sons and Richard Cardwell my son in law, that twenty pounds of the said fifty which I have ordered to be set forth for her use shall be taken from her and set forth for the use of Ellin Gill and Ester Gill my grandaughters.*

The beginning of any will tends to be formulaic; where it gets really interesting is when it moves on to the carve up of the possessions. In some cases, this is done as a separate inventory, but for Ellin Wilson it was included in the will itself. Ellin bequeathed high-value household objects, like wardrobes, beds and tables, and her personal possessions to different members of the family:

> *I leave to my daughter Sara Cardwell the blew hangings and counter-pane in the chamber or roome over head. Item I leave to my son Daniell Wilson the big new bed and the two boulsters that are in the wainscot chamber. Item I leave to my grandaugther Susanna Cardwell my greate trunke and the greate looking glase.*

Ellin had clearly amassed a substantial amount of property during her lifetime. This new sense of wealth and possession was typical of the rising middle classes during this period. Insights into early-eighteenth-century society aside, the will also answered an architectural puzzle. We had been unable to prove when the cellar was created until we came across this entry in the will: 'Item I give unto my son Mathew…and the quickening tub in the cellar'. We already knew that the original house did not have a cellar: now we had definitive evidence that the cellar existed in Ellin Wilson's lifetime. (Incidentally, the quickening tub was used for brewing, so as well as providing us with a crucial piece of the jigsaw, it also helped us to visualize the way the family lived and boozed three centuries ago.)

You will be lucky to find a will as revealing as Ellin Wilson's. However, you might be even luckier and track down an inventory. An Act of Parliament of 1529 during Henry VIII's reign required that a probate inventory, or a list of all the possessions of the deceased, be compiled if the total value was more than £5. These inventories sometimes mentioned the separate rooms of the house. You can work out the size of the rooms and what they were used for by their contents. Inventories can be a welcome bonus if you are becoming increasingly frustrated by the patchy nature of early records, not least because the earlier the inventory, the more detailed it is likely to be.

The precursor of the will was the 'inquisitones post mortem', which can be found from the thirteenth to the seventeenth century. These documents were only needed if the death of a landowner with property or position was of interest to the king which, sadly, ruled out the majority of the population.

TAX RETURNS

Tax returns from the seventeenth to the nineteenth century have bequeathed useful records to modern house detectives and we recommend that you try to find these documents for your area.

Hearth tax

The hearth tax was collected between 1662 and 1689, and records of who paid what can be found at your County Records Office. To make any real headway with the tax returns you really need the name of the owner of the house to start with.

The number of hearths or fireplaces somebody had reflected the size of their house and their wealth. For example, William Taylor, who lived at Church Farm, Bidston in Merseyside, was recorded in the 1663/4 hearth tax as having three hearths.

However, it is wise not to jump to conclusions from these readings. There was a hearth tax listing for Manningtree dating from 1662. The house had a towering chimney stack with six shafts, which, logically speaking, should serve six hearths. However, this turned out to be a classic red herring. On the listing, a man called Taylor was the only person who paid for six hearths. It would have been easy to assume that he was our man, but architectural evidence suggested otherwise.

On close inspection, the stack was merely a decorative status symbol and there were just two hearths. From other sources we had established that the owner of the house about 30 years earlier had been called Richard Edwards. In 1662, there was a Robert Edwards, possibly Richard's son, listed as having two hearths, so in all likelihood it was he who lived in our house. This is a good example of why you should always seek corroborative evidence.

Window tax

The window tax was in force between 1696 and 1851 and returns provide details of the name and address of the taxpayer, the number of windows on which tax is payable and the amount collected. This can also be an important architectural clue: if, for example, there are more windows now than there were then, it may indicate that the house has been extended. However, there could also be another reason: windows filled in to avoid tax could have been opened up once the tax was abolished!

Land tax

Some land tax returns can provide you with a date for when your house was built, as well as a complete list of its occupants between 1692 and 1831 – if you are prepared to put in a lot of work. Land tax was introduced during the reign of William and Mary to finance a war against France and was levied on houses, land and tithes. You should be able to find the returns in your County Records Office.

However, there is one crucial problem: the land tax records show a list of names parish by parish, but there is no mention of individual addresses. If you have a name already, you should be able to locate it and then painstakingly follow the records back year after year looking for changes in ownership.

COURTS OF QUARTER SESSIONS

Quarter Sessions documents can turn up some invaluable leads and cover a large swathe of history from the sixteenth century to 1889, when the system was effectively replaced by County Councils. Magistrates for the courts fulfilled administrative functions, as well as trying civil or criminal cases, and this is reflected in the wealth of documentary material which includes deposited plans, petitions, local complaints, letters and land taxes. The magistrates clerk generally kept a minute and order book to record decisions.

Before you start going through the records with a fine toothcomb you should already have some names and leads. You may be lucky and find that your local Records Office has typed out Quarter Sessions material or even published part of the records.

ECCLESIASTICAL AND MANORIAL ESTATES

If you have come across evidence that your house once belonged to a manor or a religious order you could be onto a winner as far as the documents are concerned. Three of the properties in the television series were blessed with excellent records: for the two farms in Bidston and Dunsby Fen, there were wide-ranging estate archives, while for the former vicarage in Ledbury there was a wealth of ecclesiastical sources.

ARCHIVAL EVIDENCE Detailed documents from the Charterhouse archive enabled us to trace the history of Dunsby Fen Farm in Lincolnshire. The extract from an accounts book (above) provided a useful clue as to the amount of money invested in the farm. A deed (left) from 1771 referring to the division of the Dunsby estate into individual farms gave us a starting point for our inquiry.

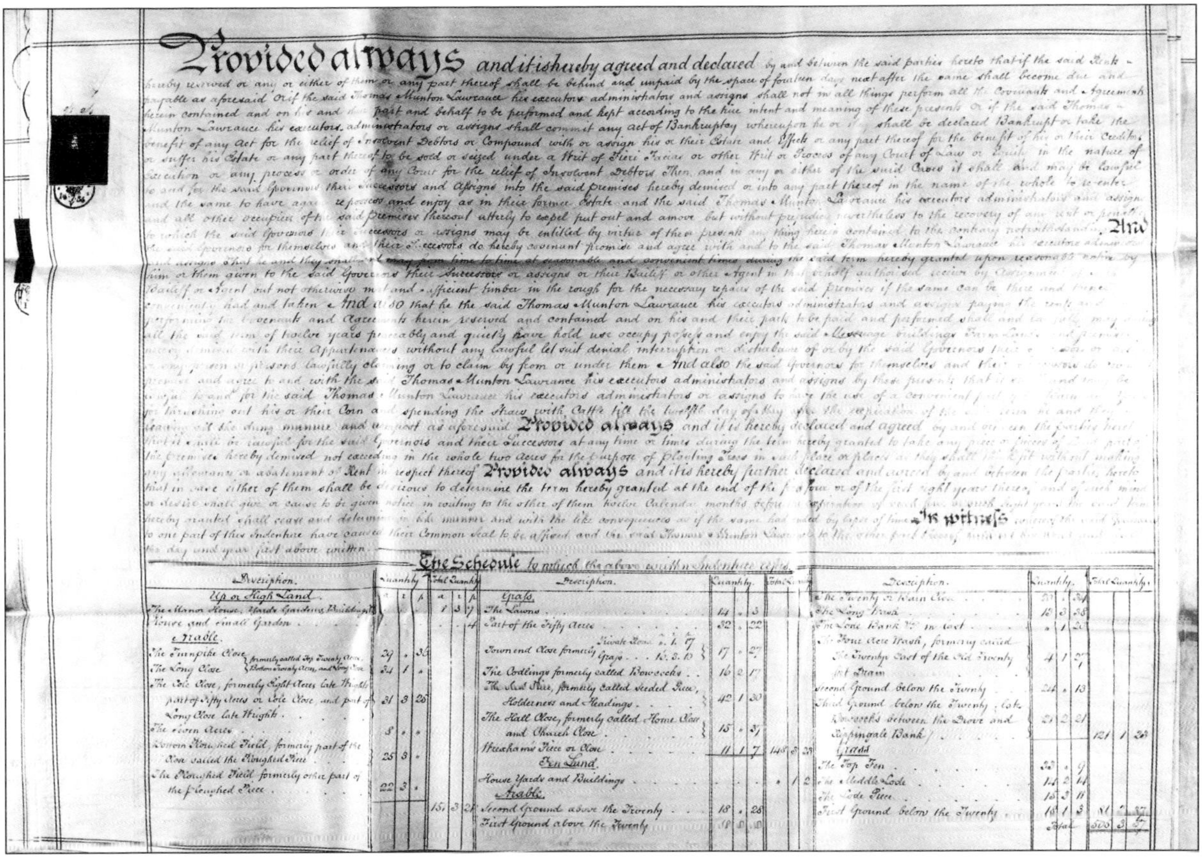

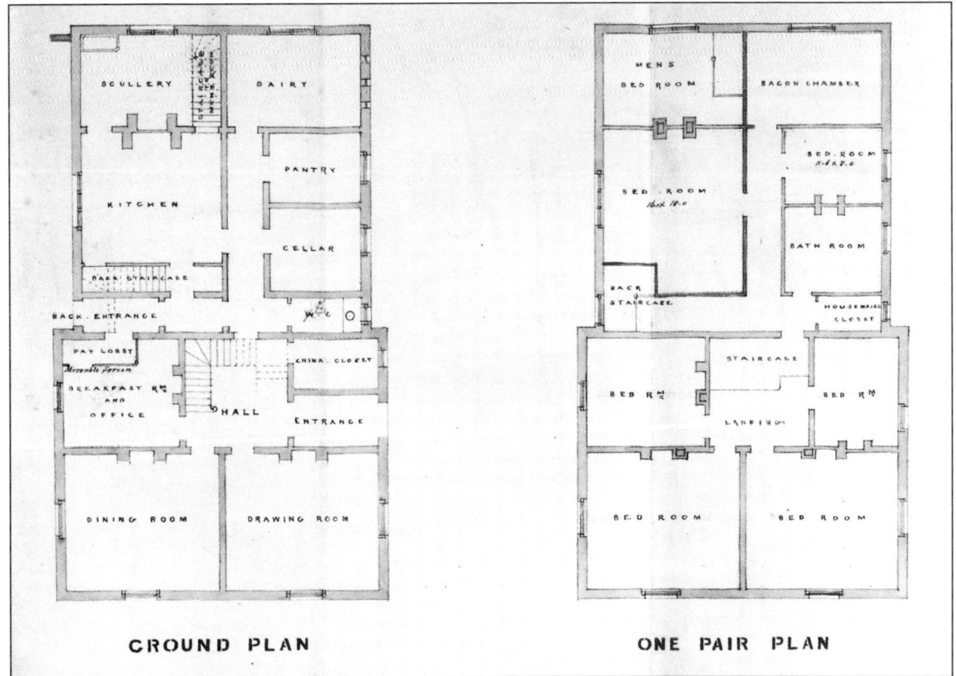

Above A nineteenth-century lease of Dunsby Fen Farm to the Casswell family, which we found in the Charterhouse archive.

Left An 1872 plan of Dunsby Fen Farm drawn up by London architects for the Charterhouse estate. The actual house did not follow the plans to the letter.

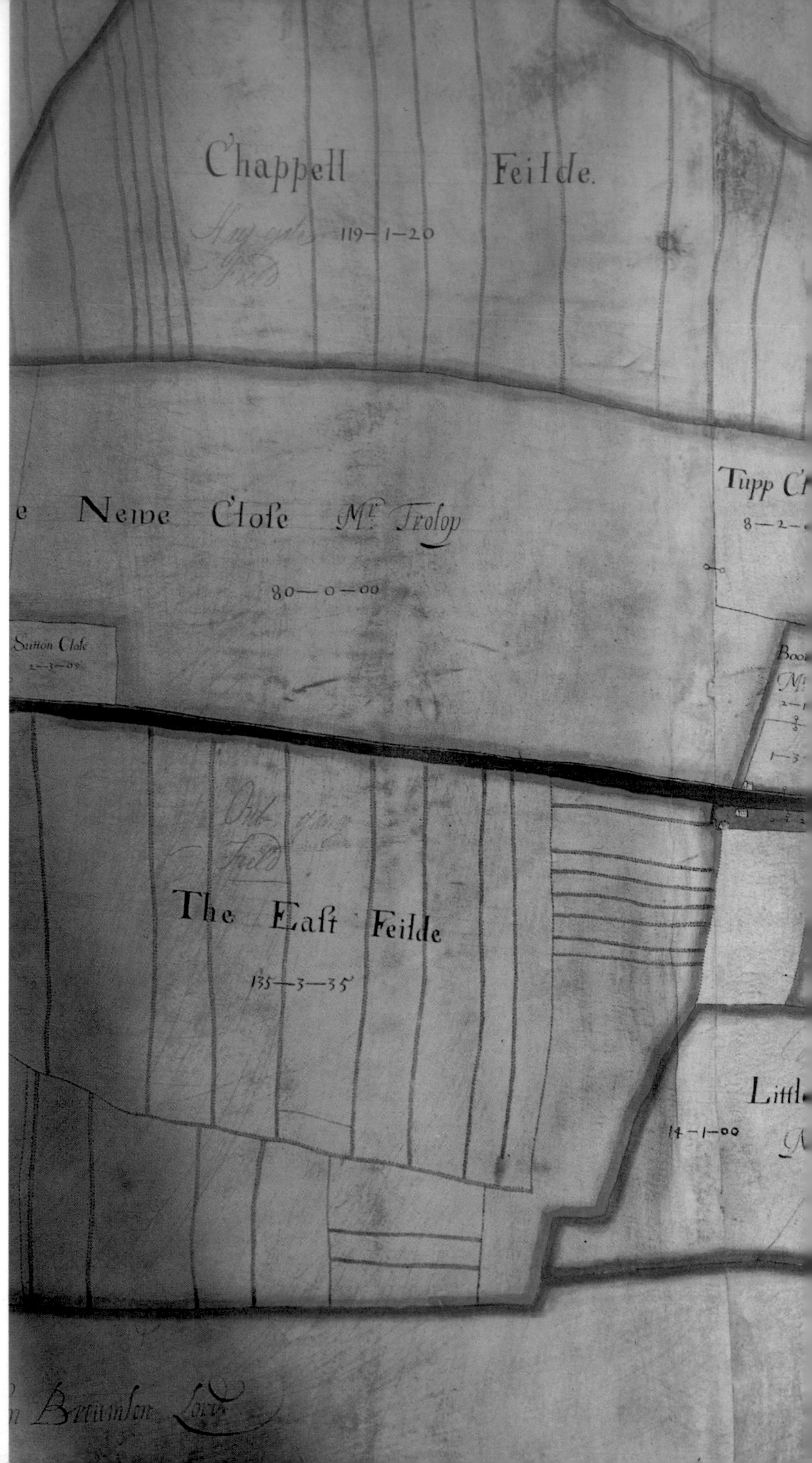

THE CHARTERHOUSE ESTATE MAP
This parchment map of Dunsby Fen in Lincolnshire dating from 1646 gave us an accurate picture of the fen-edge area. Although it showed there wasn't a farm there at this time, it is important to look at all maps as they can help narrow down the period during which the house will have been built. In the case of Dunsby Fen Farm, later evidence showed that the farm had come into existence around 1771. Interpretation does not come easily with such maps. It is helpful to have later maps for comparison with guidelines such as field patterns and boundaries.

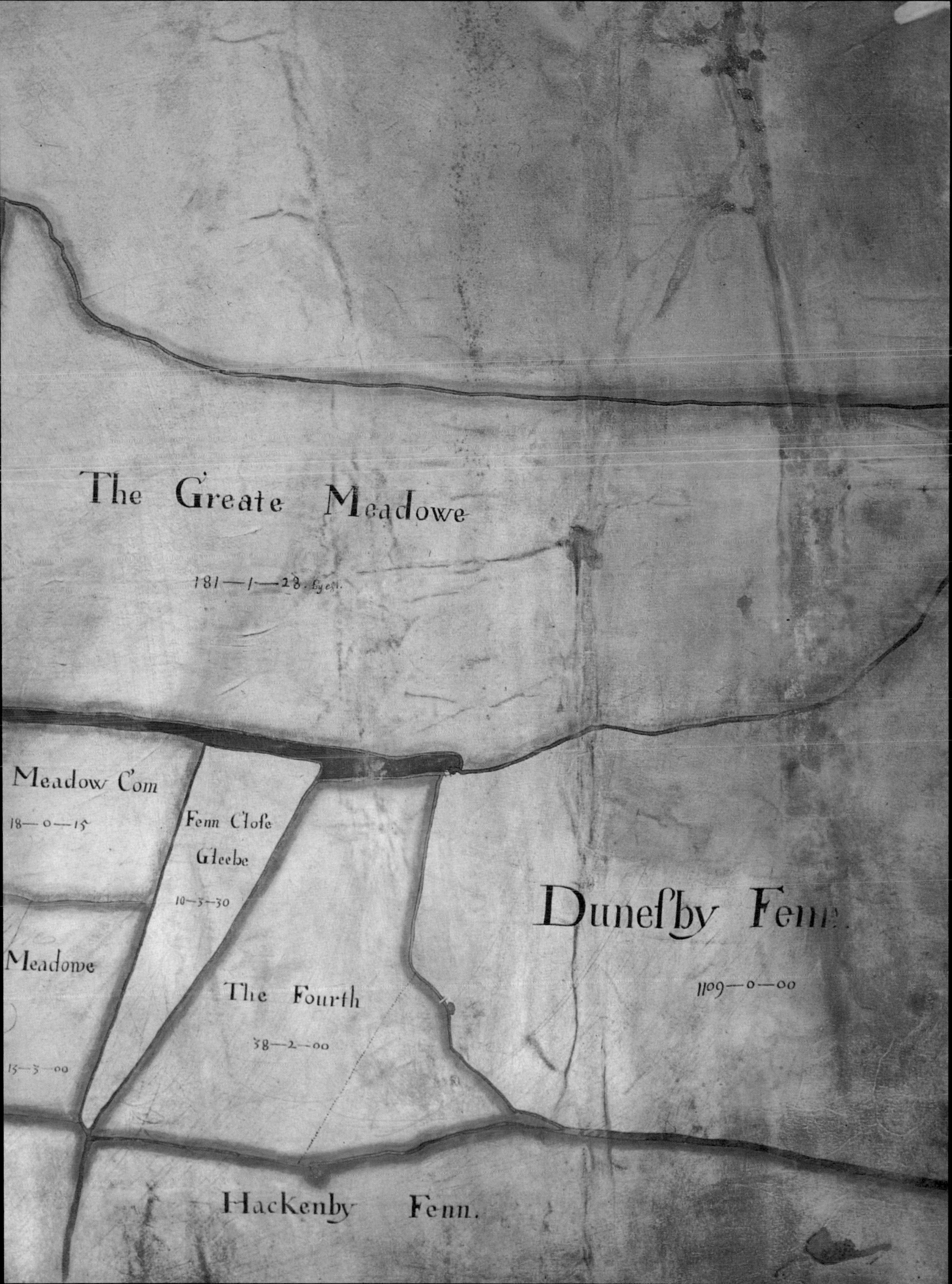

The Greate Meadowe

181—1—28. Pyes.

Meadow Com

18—0—15

Fenn Close Gleebe

10—3—30

Meadowe

15—3—00

The Fourth

38—2—00

Dunesby Fenn.

1109—0—00

Hackenby Fenn.

Manors

As far as manors are concerned you should be looking for deeds, farming leases, accounts books, maps, plans for buildings, rentals, mortgages, surveys and valuations, which describe accommodation and fittings. When family estates were sold, detailed catalogues of the property were produced.

The records of manor courts can also be valuable. In Manningtree, a manorial rental from 1628 provided us with the name of the owner of the house at that date. If estate records are not held in Records Offices, they could still be held by the estate or company, a land agent or a solicitor. Some basic detective work should enable you to track them down without too much trouble.

Religious institutions

The Church and other religious institutions, including guilds and monasteries, also kept comprehensive records covering the administration of almshouses and hospitals, the management of estates, the overseeing of leased property, the maintenance of church buildings and the moral state of congregations. The sort of documents to look out for include *glebe terriers*, which are inventories of church land dating from 1571 onwards; account books; surveys of the diocese (which usually followed a bishop's visitation); wills, which were proved by episcopal clerks until 1858; petitions to the Church Commissioners; court books; minutes of meetings and correspondence relating to the area.

Church records can provide rare insights into life in the past. The bishop in his courts would pass judgment on property disputes and give his verdict on sexual 'incontinence', adultery and theft, so if you suspect the person who lived in your house was a bit of a rogue he may well be mentioned in ecclesiastical court records. Bishops also registered the houses where dissenters were allowed to worship and it was through this that we found out that Church Farm, Bidston, had been a meeting place for non-conformists in the 1690s.

Diocesan records are normally held by the local cathedral, while provincial or archbishopric archives are kept at Lambeth Palace (for Canterbury) and at the Borthwick Institute of Historical Research (for York). The Church of England's Record Centre in London holds estate muniments for the Church of England. There are also records of non-conformist churches held by their main offices. Some ecclesiastical records can also be found in County Records Offices.

PARISH RECORDS

Parish documents are a goldmine of local colour and detail. They can normally be found in County Records Offices and diocesan archives. The basic parish registers include details of births, baptisms, marriages and deaths. In some cases, the name of the person's house is noted, especially if it is a farm. However, you normally need a name to start with.

If you do, and you know roughly when the person was living, you will be able to put precise dates to one or more of those four key events in their life. Knowledge of when a person died is absolutely essential if you are to track down their will, for example. Other clues may emerge: you may discover the maiden name of a spouse, which will provide another name to explore in other documents. In the television programme about Church Farm, Bidston, the parish register revealed that the owner of the farm, a Robert Wilson, had been a religious non-conformist because his children could be baptized only after his death in 1698.

Churchwardens' accounts can be equally revealing. In the sixteenth and seventeenth centuries, churchwardens had far-reaching powers: they were keepers of the bylaws and adjudicated over questions of access and disputes about land. If you have time, it is worth ploughing through their accounts because you may recognize a name or even a property that is mentioned. Among the other useful parish documents are vestry minutes and assessment rolls from the sixteenth century; poor relief accounts from the seventeenth century; militia books and muster rolls; parish constables' reports; the Great Poor Law Statute; local petitions and records of bishops' visitations. As is so often the case, you really need to know the name of the person who was living in your house if you are to benefit from these records.

EARLY DOCUMENTS

Researching early documents can be rather a hit-or-miss affair. Often, they are sporadic and too unspecific for the purposes of house detectives; occasionally, however, they can be an absolute revelation. The earliest documents are Anglo-Saxon charters, which date from about 590 until 1066. They are written confirmation of oral grants of land made by kings to the Church and lay retainers. Unfortunately, they are of limited value as far as vernacular architecture is concerned, because there is scant reference in them to actual buildings.

The next document of any note is the Domesday Survey, which was ordered by William the Conqueror at Christmas 1085 as a detailed inventory of who owed tax, or *danegeld*, to the king. The *Domesday Book* is split into *Little Domesday*, which covers the eastern counties of Essex, Norfolk and Suffolk, and *Great Domesday*, which takes in the rest of the country. Unfortunately, while the book is very good on institutions and general settlements, it lacks the details desired by house detectives. It is kept at the Public Record Office in London.

As you enter the Middle Ages, much of the useful archive material is connected with religious institutions and trade guilds, the local manor or estate and courts. The sort of documents you will come across are manorial court rolls, which are concerned with all aspects and disputes of medieval village life; hundred court rolls, shire court rolls and royal court rolls, which deal with rights of land; lay subsidy rolls, which are records of royal taxation on movable property, and manorial extents, which are the extent of the deceased's manor and estates and usually in the form of long lists of property including land, buildings and furnishings.

Most of these documents date from about the thirteenth century and continued until the seventeenth century. They are written in Latin, French or an early form of English, so you may need to ask someone at the county archives or local library for help.

WHAT'S IN A NAME?

Names of houses and roads can be very misleading and, as evidence, should be handled with great care. Names are liable to change over the centuries and often reflect the affectations of any given period. In the same way that a datestone above a door is likely to be a later addition, the name may commemorate a victory in a battle or be intended to conjure up romantic images of the past or just be something with a nice ring to it or a whimsy of the owner.

It is a relatively recent innovation to name or number a house: in the past, houses would normally be referred to by the names of the owners, for example Wilson's Farm. Be particularly wary of the snobbery of a former owner who decided to add the sobriquets 'manor', 'house' or 'hall', and also of the use of the word 'cottage', which is another common misnomer. In the traditional sense of the word, cottages were small, humble abodes; it is only in more recent years that it has taken on a quainter meaning.

Take the case of Mulberry Cottage in Swanage, which was featured in the television series: the name is a twentieth-century one, given to what was formerly Springfield House when it was split up. The name Springfield House gave us a clue that there was a stream nearby and, in fact, we later found that it flowed directly underneath one side of the house. There are times when a name *can* be helpful!

Street names, which are liable to change as well, can sometimes reveal that a mill or an old church had once existed in a road or may provide a clue as to the name of an estate owner or building developer.

NEWSPAPERS

It is possible to find a story relating to your house in an old newspaper, but you will need a strong lead before you can track it down. Notices of house sales were often published in local newspapers: these can be detailed and provide you with just the sort of information you are looking for, but you will need a rough date for the sale to start with. Searching through old newspapers without any clues is a thankless task and, frankly, a waste of time.

Another way you can use newspapers is by putting in an advertisement to track down former owners of your house or their surviving relatives or perhaps even servants. In the television series, we did this and contacted three grandchildren of the man who built the house at Fulwood near Preston almost a century ago. It is worth bringing this human dimension into your investigation because it helps to bring the past to life. Rather than reading words on a page, you will be entertained with stories that have never been written down and will tell you much more about what the former owners were really like. Family members may also have old diaries, photograph albums and documents relating to the house.

THE INTERNET

It may seem strange to surf the information superhighway when you are trying to find out about who lived in your house hundreds of years ago. However, with more and more people coming on line, the range and depth of information is extraordinary. You will be amazed at the sort of things that enthusiasts around the world put on the Internet. For example, during our detective work in Essex we did a search for Manningtree on the Internet. It came back with more than 40 entries, including a short history of the town and a list of the wills of Essex yeomen, gentry and merchants from the second half of the sixteenth century. This information came all the way from New Zealand, where somebody had painstakingly copied out the details from a book.

The Internet is also an efficient way of tracing genealogical information which can help you build up the family tree for your house. As with any research on the Internet, the more information you have, the better, when it comes to searching for the names of former occupants of your house. Even when you locate what you are looking for, the genealogical files tend to be so large that it takes a long time to download them.

The other way to use the Internet is to post a message in the appropriate newsgroups section, explaining what you are doing and what you are trying to find out. You may, for example, try to find descendants of former owners of your house, in the same way that you would if you placed an advertisement in a newspaper. The difference here, though, is that it is cheaper and the reach is potentially much greater. Even if this fails to yield any concrete leads, it may well put you in contact with other house detectives who you can share your experiences and frustrations with.

Local history on the Net

The *Victoria County History* also has a page on the Internet which provides a quick and easy way of finding out if the volume for your area has been completed. The address is http://www.sas.ac.uk/books/15-vch.htm.

Contact details of all the organizations mentioned in this chapter are given in Useful Addresses, pp.220–221.

DON'T GIVE UP!

You may feel that the documentary research is a daunting task and that there is a mountain of material to plough through before you get somewhere. Do not be put off though. You will be pleasantly surprised by how easily some of the evidence comes together and how quickly you are able to find names. Statistically, your house is likely to be nineteenth century or later, which means that the records will be fairly comprehensive and easily accessible. If your house is older, you can carry out your research at your leisure and, if necessary, eke out the difficult-to-find clues over months or even years. Ultimately you can decide how far you take the investigation: the main thing is to have fun while you do it.

MATERIAL WITNESSES

Overleaf
AN ELIZABETHAN WINDOW
The vertical bars (mullions) and the horizontal bars (transoms) show refined workmanship here at Moot Hall, Elston in Nottinghamshire, indicating wealth. The wallplate stretching across the window and the wall is moulded at the edges and has a frieze of beautifully carved grapes and leaves. The area of studwork (the vertical timber-framing) has been infilled with a herringbone pattern of brickwork called nogging, which is rarely contemporary with the timber-framing.

Building materials can be a very valuable source of evidence for house detectives, but you will need to research building traditions in your own region before coming to any firm conclusions. It is also important to be aware that your house may be built of a variety of materials depending on how and when it was modernized.

TIMBER

From the Middle Ages right through to the seventeenth century, the majority of houses in lowland areas were built around a solid framework of local timber. Timber had many advantages: it was cheap, quick to procure, adaptable and could be reused. Its main disadvantage was that it was flammable and, after the seventeenth century, this was one of a number of reasons why it declined as a principal building material in many regions. Timber also became more expensive, partly because supplies were stretched by the growing demand from ship building and partly because other materials came into fashion.

How many surviving timber-framed buildings there are in Britain today is hard to say as lots of them go unrecorded, encased by later brick or stone buildings. Of the six houses investigated in the television series, three were timber-framed; however in two of those the original structure was well concealed.

It would be fair to say that the timber-framed houses that are still standing were well-built, good-quality buildings, probably home to merchants, yeomen and only the most successful peasant farmers. Most people would have lived in cheaply built timber constructions or traditional mud buildings that generally only lasted for a generation.

ASSEMBLING THE FRAME

There are two main forms of timber framing: *cruck-framing* and *box-framing*. The crucks were curving single or jointed timbers that came down from the apex of the roof, delivering its weight to the ground in one long sweep. The box-frame relied on *plates* (horizontal beams) set at the top and bottom of upright posts to give them a box-like rigidity (see Chapter 4, pp 89–93).

Most surviving examples of medieval timber-framed houses are oak, since that was the most durable wood to build with. It was cut green and gradually became as hard as stone, lasting indefinitely. How-

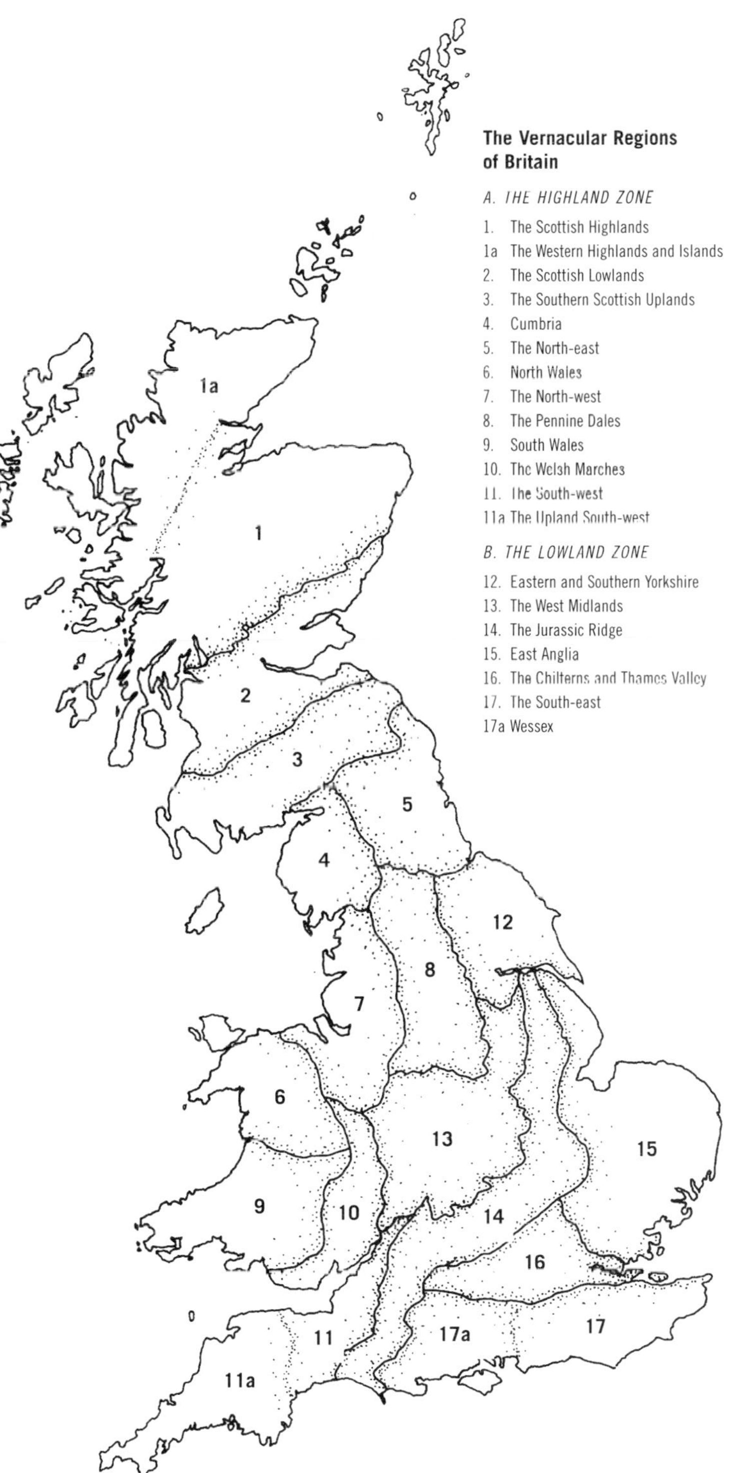

ever, lower-quality houses were built of elm, chestnut and willow, which were cheaper and more widely available than oak but less durable. Few examples of these survive.

Timber-framed houses were prefabricated in the woodland, where trees were specially cultivated for building. Unseasoned green trunks were felled and split to make planks and beams. These were cut to size and smoothed with adzes, and *peg and mortise* holes were gouged out with augers, a hand tool used for boring holes. Often the individual timbers were numbered with Roman numerals to create a kit that was then transported to a different site to be erected.

The carpenter's mark or numbers can provide a useful clue, but the main problem with dating timber-framed buildings is that they can be moved and the individual parts reused at a later date. When studying them, always be on the lookout for evidence such as unused peg or mortise holes that indicate the timbers have been moved.

Infilling

The gaps between the timber walls or panels were generally infilled or covered with cladding material. In some cases, the whole of the timber frame was completely concealed; in others, virtue was made of the timber's decorative potential.

Traditionally, the panels were filled with *wattle and daub*, which, because it could be easily removed without affecting the structure, could be replaced in such a way as to hide the original frames (see 'Rendering', p.77). This is what makes it hard to count the number of medieval houses in Britain: it is highly likely that

there are still early walls and timbers concealed behind brick, stucco, plaster and stone walls. The panels themselves varied depending on local taste and fashion: close *studding* (non-structural vertical timbers) was one popular way of showing off your wealth, as were elaborate patterns in the studwork.

DISGUISES

As wood supplies became scarcer and more costly, the timbers used in houses became less substantial. This was not something to show off about and whole timber frames were covered up. A variety of methods were used at different times in different areas. In rural south-east England, especially Kent, a technique known as weatherboarding, which consisted of covering the whole house in wooden planks, was used in the eighteenth and nineteenth centuries, as were brick tiles. Mathematical tiles, which were designed to imitate brickwork, were popular in south-eastern towns around then. If you are thinking of exposing a timber frame, ask yourself first whether this was ever intended by the builders of the house.

BRICKS

Bricks are very revealing and, in combination with other clues, can help build up a wider picture for the house detective. Their shape, size and colour are all important, as is the style in which the bricks are laid. However, there are significant regional differences and it is impossible to generalize about when different types of bricks came into common usage. Also, bricks can of course be added to an existing building, which may prove misleading. They are

Different styles of cladding

WEATHERBOARDING

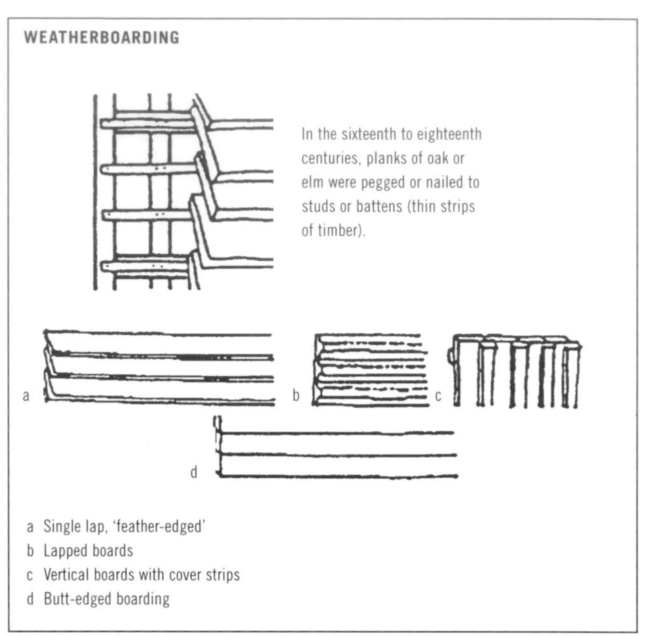

In the sixteenth to eighteenth centuries, planks of oak or elm were pegged or nailed to studs or battens (thin strips of timber).

a Single lap, 'feather-edged'
b Lapped boards
c Vertical boards with cover strips
d Butt-edged boarding

TILE HANGING

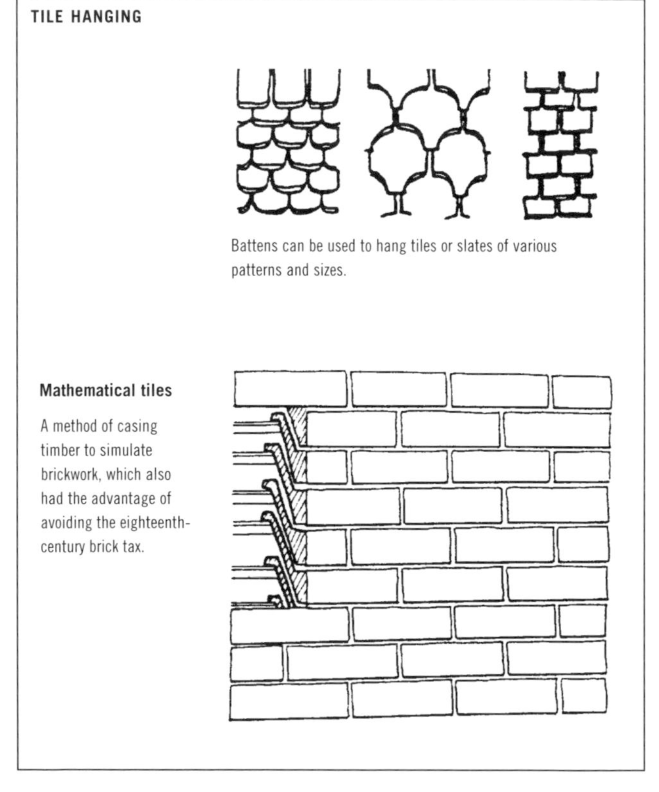

Battens can be used to hang tiles or slates of various patterns and sizes.

Mathematical tiles

A method of casing timber to simulate brickwork, which also had the advantage of avoiding the eighteenth-century brick tax.

best thought of as providing circumstantial evidence; nonetheless they may just be a key piece of the jigsaw.

History

The earliest known bricks in Britain were made by Celts, but these tended to be soft and fragile. The Romans were able to produce a brick of a higher quality, but they took their expertise with them when they left Britain. Roman bricks, which were narrow and resembled tiles, were later reused from the ruins of Roman buildings by the Anglo-Saxons and their Norman conquerors over several centuries.

Later, bricks were produced by Flemish immigrant craftsmen as early as the thirteenth century, but this had little or no impact on vernacular architecture. It was not until the second half of the sixteenth century that the brick made a widespread comeback. Brick buildings began appearing in the south-east from about 1560 and during the next 50 years they were introduced into Berkshire, Nottinghamshire and other regions.

These bricks had great status value and were expensive, so they were used sparingly on the parts of the house that could be seen, notably gable ends and chimney stacks. Wealthy people splashed out and encased entire timber-framed buildings in fashionable brick, some of which were beautifully moulded for maximum effect. We encountered an example of this in Manningtree (see Chapter 7, pp.178–185).

The brick revolution did not hit some regions, including Wales and the Pennines, until the nineteenth century and brick was never widely used in the Scottish Highlands. However, in most regions brick took over gradually as the most popular building material, supplanting timber-framed and cob buildings even at the cheaper end of the scale.

Brick was durable and easy to work with: increasingly, it became competitively priced, especially in areas where stone and timber were in short supply. Initially, it replaced wattle and daub as infill in timber-framed buildings and it became fashionable to lay the bricks in a herringbone pattern.

The single most important event in the decline of timber and the popularity of brick was the Great Fire of London in 1666, which exposed the dangers of having densely packed timber buildings. Brick was fireproof and the ideal material for rebuilding the devastated capital. It became the main building material until 1784, when the first brick tax came into force. By this time stone had taken over as the material chosen by the discerning, which spawned the fashion for covering brick façades with stucco to give the impression of stone.

Colour

Early brick production was localized, limited to wherever the necessary clay loams existed. The colour and texture of these bricks depended on the content of the local clay. In Lancashire and Staffordshire, for example, bricks were bright red because of a high iron content, while in south Wales, Surrey and Berkshire, bricks were black because of manganese in the clay. White and grey bricks, which contain lime but no iron, were common in numerous regions, including East Anglia, Oxfordshire and Hampshire. Wherever elements of chalk or sulphur occurred, as in the Thames Valley, the bricks took on a yellowish hue. As you can see, regional variations were extensive and it may be worthwhile turning to local experts for advice.

The precise shade of the brick also depended on where they were placed in the kiln, which, in the sixteenth century, was shaped like a ridge tent. The bricks in the middle received the most intense heat and invariably came out dark blue or almost black, while the bricks on the outside were a much lighter orange colour. This is why the bricks on a lot of Elizabethan Tudor buildings are a mixture of different colours: a useful clue in itself. As brick buildings became more widespread the bricks became more uniform in colour.

The colour of bricks was also subject to the vagaries of fashion, especially after the transport revolution of the early nineteenth century, which meant that bricks from different parts of the country could be moved quickly and cheaply. From the sixteenth to the early eighteenth century, red brick was popular. The Georgian period was marked by a new taste for grey, brown or yellow bricks, which were closer to the colour of fashionable stone, although red bricks were still being used, often for decorative purposes, on the external corners of buildings. Yellow bricks were also widely used in London, but by the second half of the nineteenth century they fell out of fashion because they were associated with working-class housing.

Improved transport during the last century meant that different colour bricks could be combined decoratively and stylishly. For example, many simple Victorian terraces built of yellow bricks were embellished by courses of red bricks running above, around or below the windows in tasteful patterns. There was also a vogue for elaborate patterns of different coloured bricks, most notably in railway junction towns like Reading and Crewe.

Dating bricks

Measuring bricks can provide a useful clue to their age. Before the middle of the sixteenth century bricks were thin, only about 2 in (5 cm), but gradually increased in size to around 3 in (8 cm) in 1784 in direct response to the introduction of the brick tax, which was levied on the number of bricks not their size. The tax was repealed in 1850.

Early bricks were moulded or handmade, sometimes using a crude 'pat-a-cake' method, and before 1620 they had to be laid in a thick bed of mortar. Irregular-shaped bricks are often a good clue that they are pre-eighteenth century, but this is not a hard-and-fast rule because poorly made bricks certainly existed after that period.

As production methods improved and bricks became more regular in size and texture, less mortar was needed between courses and the bricklayer's work became neater. By the middle of the last century, most bricks were machine-made and more regular, making them easy to distinguish from their earlier counterparts.

Bonding evidence

The way in which bricks are laid or bonded is also revealing, because although style changed with time typically there was a time lag between regions.

Early vernacular brick buildings weren't bonded in any consistent pattern, but English bond – which, oddly, had its origins in France – emerged around 1560 and was popular until 1720. This had

SHAPED GABLE
'Dutch gable' is a popular term for such a structure – although some people like to call them 'curly gables' and historians refer to them as 'shaped gables' – because the introduction of this form of gable seems to have been a two-way exchange of ideas between England and the Netherlands. They appeared in the sixteenth century and were very popular in the first ten years of the seventeenth before beginning to decline. This house is in Kent.

alternative courses of *headers* (bricks laid headwise) and *stretchers* (laid lengthwise). Another pattern, known as English garden-wall bond, consisted of one row of headers with up to seven courses of stretchers and was most common in Wales and northern England.

By the eighteenth century, Flemish bond, which originally alternated headers and stretchers in the same course, began to take over. Up to five stretchers were laid for every header in a later variation on the theme. In some areas, plain header bond was preferred. However, with the development of cavity walls in the last century headers became superfluous because metal ties were used to link the two sides of a wall. As a result, stretcher bond came into its own.

STONE

Stone has been used to build houses of all kinds for thousands of years. Polite buildings like churches and castles have always held stone in high esteem. However, at the vernacular level stone tended to be used only in the regions where it was found and was, in many regions, originally dry-stone or clay bonded. These tended not to survive. In some areas of western England, Scotland and Wales, where it was widely available, stone was the most common building material. But stone masonry developed more slowly than brickwork on a national scale and only really became widespread from the seventeenth century onwards.

Stone houses that have survived from the Middle Ages are by definition good quality. As a rule, they would have been built from stone dug from shallow quarries or salvaged from the ruins of old

Stonework

Irregular types

a Compact irregular
b Mountain limestone
c Coursed rubble
d Snecked
e Coursed
f Cement rendering, peeled to reveal coursed rubble

Note: all stone or brick (or modern breezeblocks) can be rendered

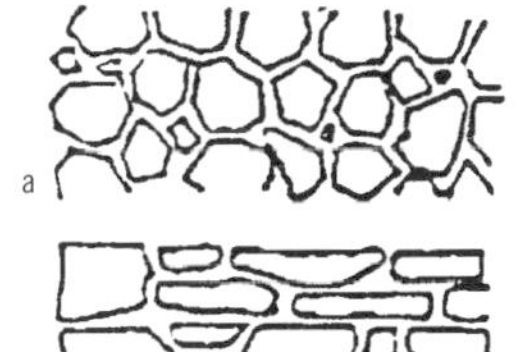
a

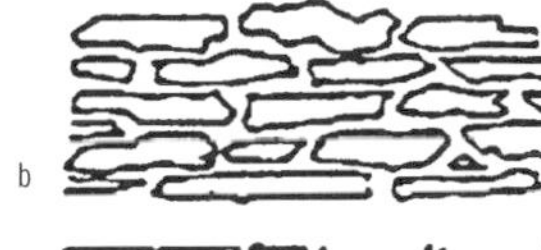
b

c

d

e

f

Regular types

Regular means a tool-shaped stone. A thin, flat stone applied to present a big surface area is called an ashlar.

a Uniform stonework, or ashlar
b Dressed stone with coursed infill
c Uniform with thin mortar courses
d Quoins – corner stones, often cut to give a decorative look

a

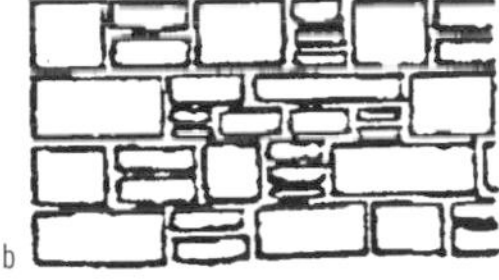
b

c

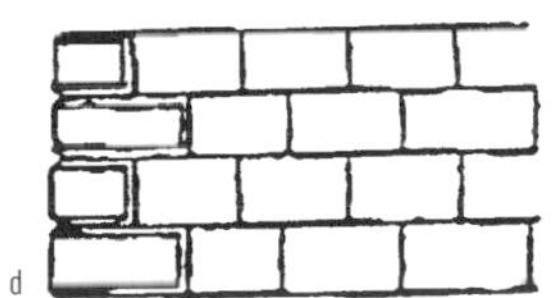
d

Rusticated stonework
Found principally on expensive housing developments and estate property

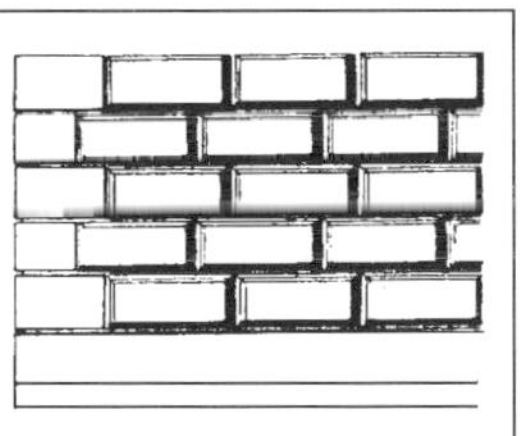

Natural types

Cobbles, pebbles and flints

a Coursed – cobbles are 80-230mm, pebbles less than 80mm
b Coursed – same uncommon shape
c Coursed with brick-dressing
d Knapped flint with stone-dressing-flints are squared off on five sides (front edge and four sides) to form a pattern
e As with d above, but overlaid
f Natural flint with stone courses
g Patterns of knapped flints with stonework (flushwork)

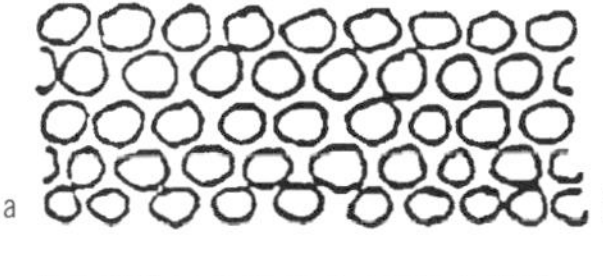
a

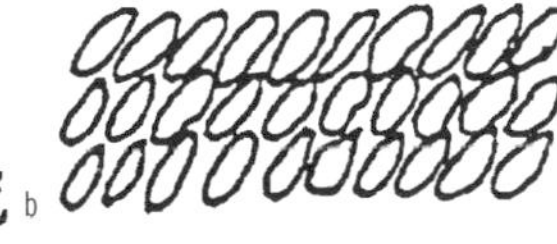
b

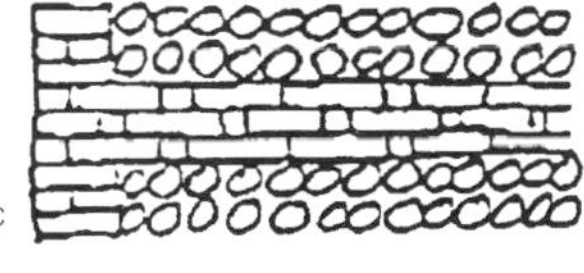
c

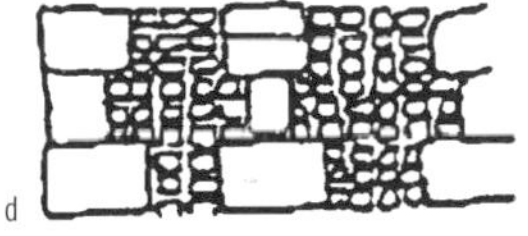
d

e

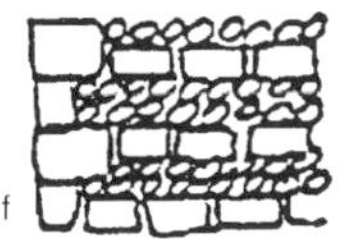
f

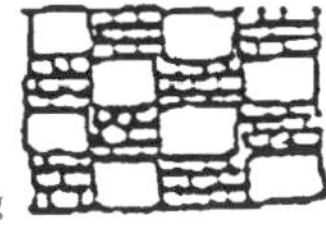
g

castles, churches or other buildings. This has led to one of the classic red herrings for house detectives: stone masons' marks on reused stone. You may find yourself believing that you live in a twelfth-century stone building, simply because somebody in the sixteenth century built part of their house with stone taken from the ruin of a monastery dissolved by Henry VIII in the 1530s.

Types of stone

Britain has a plentiful and varied supply of stone, which has contributed to the impressive collection of vernacular buildings in this country. From the sixteenth century, small local quarries were springing up wherever rock outcropped to help fill the gap in building supplies left by a depleting stock of timber. The regions where stone was most readily available were north and west of the 'Jurassic Ridge' (region 14 of map on p.65).

Stone buildings are widespread in these areas, but there is great regional and even local variety. Hard-wearing igneous rocks, like granite, are most common in the west of Britain, including Cumbria, Devon, Cornwall and Scotland. These come in a range of different shades, depending on their precise composition. Perhaps the most popular igneous rock for building, granite, can be recognized by its coarse grain and the presence of small coloured crystals in it.

The principal sedimentary rocks used for building are sandstones and limestones. The strongest sandstone is Millstone Grit, found in the southern Pennines, which is used in Yorkshire and Derbyshire. However, limestone is more widely used because it can be easily worked and comes in a variety of colours. Oolithic limestone, which consists of a mass of small calcium carbonate spheres, provides some of the best-known types of building stone, including the renowned Portland stone of Dorset, Bath stone and Lincolnshire limestone. During the television series, David Austin discovered a piece of local limestone at Dunsby Fen in Lincolnshire and was able to identify it with a little trick of the trade. He poured vinegar on the stone and waited. The vinegar underwent a chemical reaction with the calcium carbonate and bubbled, confirming that it was limestone.

Previous spread
A MEDIEVAL STONE-BUILT HOUSE
The garden view of a very famous building, the Old Post Office at Tintagel, Cornwall, which started life in the fourteenth century as a manor house. It has thick walls laid in courses of irregular stonework. Age has obviously wearied it, as the buttresses are twentieth century.

Regional variations

With stone more than any other material you need to be aware of what occurs naturally in your area. Here's an example to show how difficult it is to generalize.

Wiltshire County Council carried out a survey of building materials used for pre-1840 buildings and divided the county up into no fewer than five distinct areas. The areas show a clear split between what is generally referred to as highland and lowland Britain, stone-built houses lying to the west of the boundary. Dating a house by the style or thickness of its stonework generally requires the help of local experts and the *Wiltshire Buildings Record* gives very specific guidelines. In the area of the county with the best limestone around Corsham and Bradford-on-Avon, houses from the sixteenth century have walls about 26 in (66.5 cm) thick. By the nineteenth century, the thickness had been reduced to 19 in (48 cm) or less and the stone had a much more refined finish. This sort of highly specialized information can be priceless.

The northern part of Wiltshire benefits from the same supply of fine Jurassic limestone as the Cotswolds, which enjoys a reputation for well-built stone buildings from the top to the bottom of the social scale. With the taste for well-proportioned classical façades during the Georgian period, quality stone was in demand. In nearby Bath, the elegant Georgian crescents, squares and terraces are built with local stone. The blocks were smooth and rectangular and ideal for the taste of the day because they could be laid in a regular fashion, giving the houses the desired sense of symmetry.

Where this was not possible, brick or rubble stone buildings were rendered with stucco to obtain the desired smooth effect. This was also achieved by using the artificial Coade stone which was being produced from the second half of the eighteenth century, or, more recently by cement (see Chapter 4, pp.112–113).

In areas without supplies of local stone, flints, which are found within chalk deposits, were used for building. These were tough, but came in a mass of mostly small and irregular shapes – known as cobbles and pebbles – that required a substantial amount of good-quality mortar, and often needed to be combined with bricks or other larger stones. Flint was not used for ordinary houses until the sixteenth century and was normally rendered over. In the eighteenth and nineteenth centuries, flintwork was valued for its decorative qualities.

These geographical differences mean that masonry walls vary considerably. There are, however, a number of general rules. The bulkiest stones were generally used at the base of walls and the next size down tended to serve as corner stones, or *quoins*, which are a common feature of stone and brick buildings.

MUD OR COB

It may be surprising, but there are a considerable number of houses in some parts of Britain built of clay, *cob* (a hard-wearing mud 'concrete'), *wychert* (a type of earth and chalk found in Buckinghamshire) or even turf. The cob buildings of Devon are probably the best example, but there are houses with earth walls in Leicestershire, Cumbria, Buckinghamshire, west Wales and southern Scotland.

The building technique is simple: local earth or clay was mixed with straw and manure, allowed to dry and placed layer after layer on the wall. Clay houses were generally built in areas where there was a lack of timber. The most humble of homes in the twelfth and thirteenth centuries were built of mud, but few of these have survived. Most of those that still exist were built in the eighteenth and nineteenth centuries when there was a demand for inexpensive housing and a lack of cheap materials.

From the outside, it is difficult to guess that these houses are made of mud because they have been rendered over with lime plaster and in some cases colourwashed. They can sometimes be recognized by the rounded corners of their walls if brick or stone quoins are not used. The surfaces are often irregular, and if some of the rendering has come away fibrous material can be seen.

RENDERING

Different types of rendering have been used over the centuries to give houses a more attractive finish, to hide

SOPHISTICATED RHYTHMS Consummate craftsmanship and skill in working stone is demonstrated in this Georgian terrace in Bath. The pattern of windows, coupled columns and horizontal entablature and cornice create visual harmonies.

cheap building materials and improve their ability to withstand the weather.

Daub

One of earliest forms of render was *daub*, a mix of earth, manure, sand and straw that was used as infill in timber-framed buildings. It would be tightly compressed around an open, basket-like woven framework of slim withies – pliable willow branches – known as *wattle*, hence the term wattle and daub. Limewash, a thin mixture of slaked lime and water, would generally be used as a finish. From the fourteenth century, lime plaster, a paste made from slaked lime, began to be used to render rubble-stone walls and to cover timber buildings.

Pargeting

In some areas, especially East Anglia, ornamental plaster-cement rendering known as *pargeting* was fashionable in the sixteenth and seventeenth centuries. It was often used to cover timbers, the most common decoration being simple repeat patterns, known as stick or combed work, that covered large areas of wall. More complex heavy-relief designs, including birds, flowers and other motifs, were created from moulds. Few original examples survive, but you may have seen the style reproduced in this century, or the Victorian equivalent, stamped work, which used Portland cement.

Other forms of rendering

Rendering became used increasingly to imitate fine *ashlar stone* – a facing or veneer of neatly dressed stone blocks about 2–3 in (5–7.5 cm) thick, immaculately applied to the outside of load-bearing walls. For several centuries the main ingredient continued to be lime. In the late eighteenth and early nineteenth century, a number of alternative rendering materials appeared on the market, including Liardet's cement (1773), Parker's Roman cement (1796), Aspdin's Portland cement (1824) and stucco, which was popular until 1850 when it began to be viewed as cheap and nasty.

The later Victorian period saw more terracotta and artificial Coade stone being used for rendering and decorative mouldings. In the north and west of England, a mixture of lime and gravel, known as *roughcast*, was literally thrown at walls to cover rubble walls and help waterproofing. It was a relatively cheap and easy method and spread around the country in the second half of the nineteenth century. Pebbledash, a rendering of mortar with smooth pebbles, emerged as a popular coating for suburban housing from the early years of this century.

ROOFING MATERIALS

In terms of dating your house, roofing materials are less revealing than other materials because they tend to be replaced more often as new alternatives come on to the market and fashions change. What was used depended on what was available locally, until the transport revolution made roofing materials available cheaply from elsewhere.

Thatch

Thatch is the oldest roofing material in this country and its use continued for centuries because it was light. Types of thatch varied with whatever was to hand, from long straw to nettles. However, it was also a fire risk, and from the thirteenth century onwards thatch was used less and less in towns – in London thatch was banned for newly built houses.

In some areas, wooden shingles were used instead of thatch but are rarely found today. They have the appearance of thick slates but on close inspection are made of wood. Tiles and slate took over as the main roofing materials, although thatch did enjoy a revival in popularity in the nineteenth century, by which time it had become a relatively expensive way to roof your house.

Many roofs that were once thatched now have modern tiles or slate. To check yours, study the steepness of the pitch: a roof that was originally thatched would typically be in excess of 50 degrees to ensure that water ran off as quickly as possible. However, it is virtually impossible to date a thatched roof because the thatch has to be replaced on a regular basis.

Tiles

The plain clay tile also has a long history in vernacular buildings, having made its first appearance in the south-east from about 1500. However, it was not until the late seventeenth century that these tiles became widely used in the north and west.

Old tiles tend to be curvier and less regular than later machine-made ones. They were held in place by pegs and were laid on a bed of hay or straw, which you can only see by going up into the attic. The production of tiles, as with bricks, was industrialized in the nineteenth century, making them flatter, smoother and more regular. There are later, convincing rustic reproductions which were popular with the Arts and Crafts movement in the

TERRACED HOUSES
Houses are not only about shape, design and materials, they are about people. Look closely at this industrial housing in Halifax, Yorkshire, and you will see how individuality can express itself.

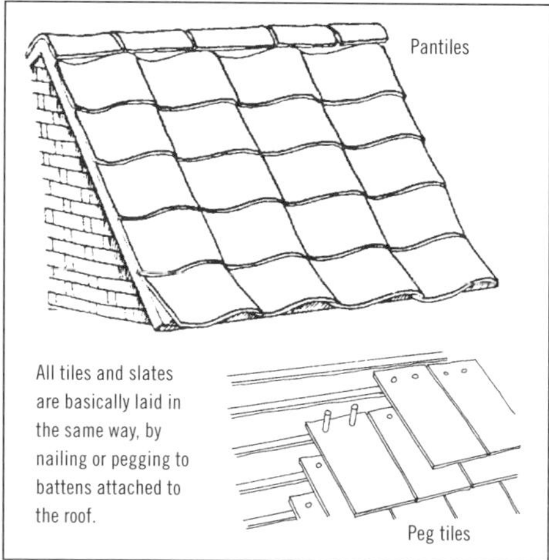

All tiles and slates are basically laid in the same way, by nailing or pegging to battens attached to the roof.

THATCHED COTTAGE
Thatch is the oldest form of roofing still used throughout Britain. In the earliest times any form of vegetable matter could be used but in recent times thatch has been made of water reeds and various types of straw. The tradition of thatching allows the thatcher to display his individual interpretation of the regional style. This cottage is in Great Dunmow, Essex.

second half of the nineteenth century and some are made in craft industries today. You would probably need expert advice to recognize the difference.

Pantiles, curved, almost S-shaped tiles, were popular in eastern counties from the seventeenth century. They were originally introduced to Britain by Flemish merchants and French Huguenots fleeing persecution and continued to be imported from the Netherlands until production started up in this country at the beginning of the eighteenth century.

Pantiles were very popular in areas where the clay was suitable for their production and they became an ideal alternative to thatch. Pantiles are mostly red in colour, but, like bricks, can be found in a variety of shades, including black, brown and yellow.

SLATES

Of all natural materials slate is the best suited to roofing because it allows for a flatter pitch. For centuries it was used only in areas where it was quarried: Wales, the

Previous page
SPOILED FOR CHOICE
A selection of houses descending one of the most famous hill streets in the country, Gold Hill, Shaftesbury in Dorset. It illustrates the individuality of the British: simply count the variations in roofing, windows, walls, and even the position of the doorways.

Left **FORMAL FAÇADE**
This very striking house is situated in the Northamptonshire village of Easton-on-the-Hill, a few miles from the western edge of Stamford. It belongs to the period known as Queen Anne and was built about 1700. The sash windows with their fairly thick glazing bars are typical of the period.

Lake District and Cornwall. However, following the improvement in transport during the Victorian period, slate became synonymous with the new building boom and in burgeoning urban centres rooftops glimmered with Welsh slate. The result was that by the 1890s slate had acquired a working-class image and declined in popularity in the twentieth century.

Stone slates of sandstone or limestone were used on better-quality houses in some parts from the Middle Ages, but were only used on ordinary homes from the seventeenth century. They were normally attached to the roof using wooden pegs or animal bones. The larger stones were placed at the bottom of the slope and lighter ones at the top for practical as well as aesthetic reasons.

Roofing became more sophisticated from the eighteenth century, when lead flashings and weatherings were introduced. Cast-iron gutters and drainpipes replaced their lead or timber counterparts in the last century.

FLOORS

It is a good idea to peel back your carpets to see what lies below. The materials can be revealing and the amount of wear will reflect how often people took a certain route within the house.

Earth

The earliest floors were no more than beaten earth, perhaps with a covering of straw or rushes. Unsurprisingly few of these have survived, the vast majority having been covered with other materials over the centuries. If you uncover what you think is an original earth floor, an expert may be able to identify it as medieval but there is no scientific way of accurately dating it. Any evidence will lie in the materials, like clay, lime or animal blood, used to bind the earth together.

Stone

Stone and brick have also been used for flooring over a long period, which means they are not a reliable way of ageing a house. Stone flagging was used by the Romans, but because the stone was laid directly onto damp earth the originals have invariably had to be replaced. The same is true for cobbling. From the beginning of the nineteenth century, solid floors were generally only found in service areas of the house.

Ceramic tiles

Ceramic floor tiles can be a useful way of dating a house. It was only from the seventeenth century that tiles were used for the ground floors of vernacular houses. In the eighteenth century, tiles were also used on upper floors of a house.

Before the Industrial Revolution, tiles were made of local clay and tended to be thick, plain and square. With the mass production of tiles a wide variety of shapes and colours became available and it was common for square tiles to be combined with triangles or chevrons.

The introduction of patterned *encaustic* designs (colourful ceramic tiles with a matt finish) from the 1840s, as part of the revival of Gothic or medieval crafts, effectively revolutionized floor coverings during the Victorian period. Mosaic patterns became popular for hall floors and there is a wide variety of designs. If you have an elaborate tiled floor in your house, refer to specialist books to help you date it.

WOOD

The other main floor material is, of course, timber. Early timber floors can be difficult to identify as they had numerous different types of joints, but there are a few straightforward clues to look out for.

Wooden pegs are good evidence of an early floor because metal nails and bolts were not used until the sixteenth century. Look at the joists: if they are large and irregular in shape and their broadest dimension is horizontal, they are likely to be pre-seventeenth century.

Floorboards tended to be about 1 ft (30 cm) wide and made of elm or any hard wood common to the area, possibly even the oak of previous times, which was the traditional timber used for floors. By the early eighteenth century, more and more pine was being imported from Scandinavia and the Baltics and floorboards were slightly narrower. By about 1800, pine had replaced oak as the main timber used for floors. After the timber industry was mechanized in the nineteenth century, floorboards became more regular.

GLASS

Until the second half of the sixteenth century, windows were generally unglazed. When glass was first used in vernacular houses it tended to be irregular in shape so the panes had to be small and were linked by lead strips, or *cames*.

You can recognize early glass because it is likely to have air bubbles and a slight tint. Curved glass is sometimes a good clue as to its age: it was popular for Georgian bow windows and continued to be used by the Victorians, but is rare nowadays. Bottle, or bull's-eye glass, is a common red herring: it is used in houses to give an 'olde worlde' effect. In fact, this type of glass was considered to be a waste product and not the sort of thing you would want to show off. Sheet glass was first introduced in 1773 but was not commercially available until about 1840, and this led to an increase in the size of window panes.

Before the nineteenth century, stained glass was found in only the most important houses and churches. However, during the Victorian period it became a common feature in the front doors, fanlights and hall windows of even the simplest of houses. Styles changed and enthusiasm waned after 1870, but stained glass continued right through the Edwardian period and did not die out until the 1930s. Again it is worth turning to specialist books to help you try to date any stained glass in your house.

A TRADITION TO CHANGE The sash windows with their slender glazing bars and their sash-boxes tucked behind the revealed, or set-back, brickwork indicate the early nineteenth century in this house in Fournier Street, London. The date is confirmed by the continuous line of the doorway. However, a glimpse of the neighbouring and abutting house tells us that the whole range dates to the early eighteenth century. The architraves of the windows and the coloured brickwork dressing the surround are the clues.

The Top Ten Innovations

	APPEARED	WIDESPREAD
1. The chimney	Late eleventh century	Late sixteenth century
2. Glazed windows	Seventh century	Sixteenth century
3. Bricks	Romans	Sixteenth century
4. Tiles	Twelfth century	1580s
5. Wallpaper	Fifteenth century	Seventeenth century
6. The semi	Late seventeenth century	Early nineteenth century
7. Vertical sash windows	1670	Early eighteenth century
8. Hot-water central heating	1795	1830s
9. Sheet glass	1773	1850s
10. Electric lights	1878	1890s

12
M. LUSTIG & Co
Manufacturers of
SUPERIOR

BUILDING A CASE

No one feature can date a house. One of the rules of being a good house detective is to remember that the tradition of building has always been to add on, alter and modernize – updating your property is a long-standing national pastime! Because of that, things are frequently not what they seem, and much of the evidence you unearth may be confusing, even conflicting. Even when you have discovered a genuine datable feature, remember that one is not enough to make a confident judgement; you need at least two in any one area.

To help you sift out the truth an appreciation of the history of vernacular architecture is one of the best tools you can have at your disposal. In this chapter we lay out the trail of historical evidence from the Middle Ages to modern times.

EARLY OUTLINE: THE MEDIEVAL PERIOD

Very few twelfth and thirteenth-century houses survive today. Those that have, such as Hemingford Grey Manor near Huntingdon and Boothby Pagnell Manor near Grantham, Lincs, are well cared for and well-documented. However, most medieval houses have been destroyed or demolished, either to make way for more modern buildings or because the materials had decayed.

Those that have withstood the passing centuries have usually been incorporated into later buildings. Timber-framed and stone houses dating back to the fourteenth century have been found, and indeed elements of construction going back even further. It is a joy to discover these. A fragment of an identifiable thirteenth-century stone wall may be found as part of an early-seventeenth-century brick wall in a house that, to all intents and purposes, is mid-nineteenth century. In cathedral precincts especially, it is common to find houses of authentic Georgian style and plan that have within them quite extensive Norman decorative features.

That said, only the houses of the more wealthy – minor lords, freemen farmers, merchants and tradesmen – would have stood a chance of surviving anyway. The supply of raw materials like stone, wood and lime was controlled by status and custom. Lords of manors kept a tight rein on the trees that could be felled for making the frames of vernacular timber buildings, and attempts to get round these restrictions were punished fiercely.

Inevitably, the lower echelons of medieval society would have had to get by in poorer-quality insubstantial buildings.

Sixteenth-century houses are, however, quite numerous, as by the later Middle Ages (up to about 1550), the manorial estates and courts had lost their grip on the countryside, allowing ordinary farmers more freedom. The aspirations of these upwardly-mobile 'middling folk' were expressed in their buildings, which became more substantial and closer in style to the gentry.

By the end of the Middle Ages, an increasing number of well-built and solid structures were being erected, hence the existence today of many more examples dating from the fifteenth and sixteenth century.

Basic Plan

The basic plan for surviving houses earlier than the mid-seventeenth century is rectangular. They were a single room's width but could have had a cross-wing running at a right angle to the main range. Most vernacular buildings of the later Middle Ages were timber-framed, working on the simple principle of supporting the weight of the roof on vertical posts. The basic structural unit of medieval buildings was the bay, the area defined and enclosed by the position of the principal posts of the frame and the roof beams that sat on them. These are not easy to identify from below as, from the later sixteenth century onwards, halls were reduced in size and second floors and ceilings were added. You are most likely to be able to spot a building's original bays in attics, where the old roof timbers may still be *in situ*. There were two basic types: the cruck-frame and the box frame.

Cruck-framing

Cruck-framing was a simple and ingenious piece of early engineering. A pair of large, generally curving timbers were placed together and joined by a horizontal collar to create an A-shaped frame that served as a combined wall-and-roof structure. In a more refined version, known as *closed truss*, a solid horizontal tie-beam was fixed across the pair of crucks. *Wallplates* – longitudinal timbers – ran the length of the building to support the roof rafters. The area between crucks (bays) tended to be about 16 ft

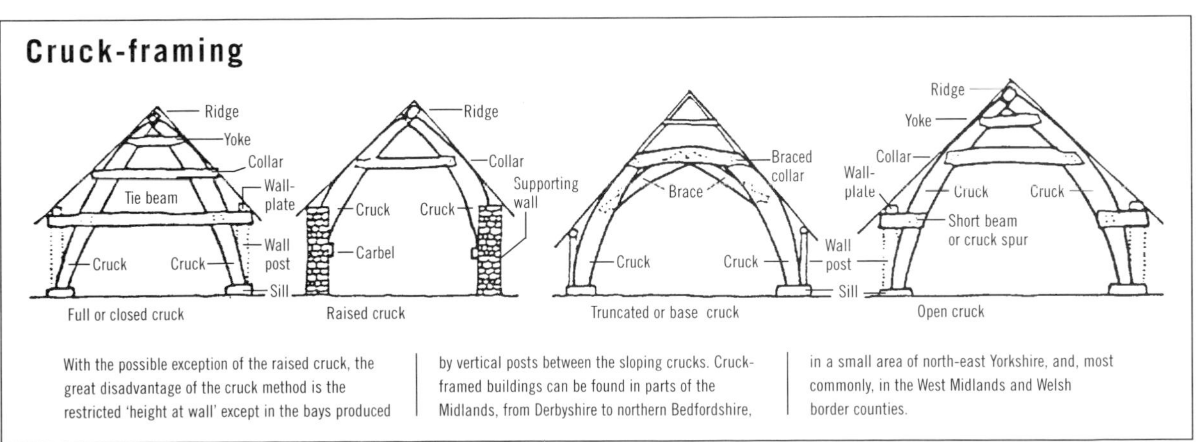

With the possible exception of the raised cruck, the great disadvantage of the cruck method is the restricted 'height at wall' except in the bays produced by vertical posts between the sloping crucks. Cruck-framed buildings can be found in parts of the Midlands, from Derbyshire to northern Bedfordshire, in a small area of north-east Yorkshire, and, most commonly, in the West Midlands and Welsh border counties.

TIMBERED BOX-FRAMING
There are two distinctively different forms of box-framing. In the West Midlands and Wales the predominant form is the panelled type (as shown here in this reconstructed house in the Welsh Folk Museum, St Fagans, Cardiff). Throughout the rest of the country, box-framing displays the vertical patterning of close studwork.

(5 m) long. A good way of visualizing a cruck-frame is to imagine a ship turned upside down.

Cruck-framed buildings date from the thirteenth century, but most of those that have survived are from the fifteenth and sixteenth centuries. They were particularly common in the north-east, the Midlands and Herefordshire. In the west of England it was normal practice to form each cruck out of two separate pieces of timber. This helped overcome the main disadvantage of the technique, which was that it relied on the availability of highly substantial timbers.

Box-framing

In the south-east, box-framed or square-frame houses emerged as the norm and went on to supersede the cruck-frame. Box-framed houses can generally be dated by the amount and size of timber they use. They were conceived as a series of boxes or bays: solid vertical and horizontal timbers were joined together with special joints to form a complex skeleton.

The main structural timber posts rising from the ground supported wallplates and the spaces between them filled in with non-structural vertical timbers called *studs*. The wallplates in turn held up an arrangement of principal rafters and *tie-beams*, which joined the feet of principal rafters in a roof truss. The roof, had a ridge piece at the apex and *purlins*, horizontal timbers running the length of the building that supported the common rafters. Braces were added to give the tie-beams or *collar beams* (horizontal beams linking rafters) greater solidity.

In the north it was common practice to insert a *king post* between the tie-beam

Box-framing and infilling

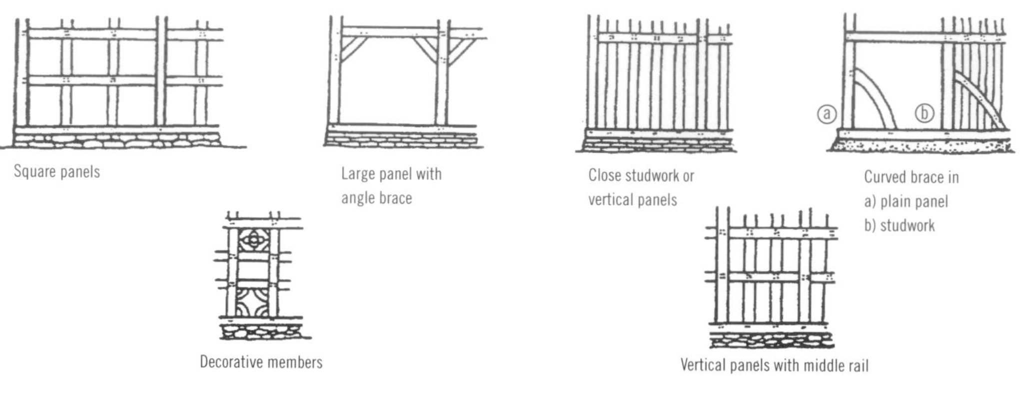

Square panels

Large panel with angle brace

Close studwork or vertical panels

Curved brace in a) plain panel b) studwork

Decorative members

Vertical panels with middle rail

Styles common to the Midlands and Western counties

Styles common to the Southern and East Anglian counties

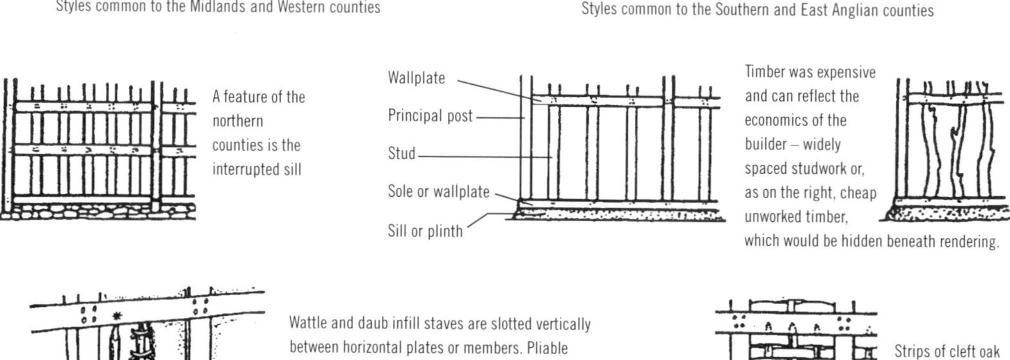

A feature of the northern counties is the interrupted sill

Timber was expensive and can reflect the economics of the builder – widely spaced studwork or, as on the right, cheap unworked timber, which would be hidden beneath rendering.

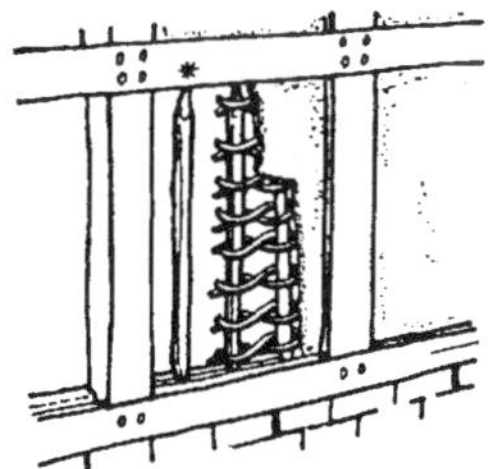

Wattle and daub infill staves are slotted vertically between horizontal plates or members. Pliable withies are woven in a basket-weave pattern and pressed down close to each other. Daub – usually a plastic mix of cow dung and clay – is forced tightly into the woven woodwork. The surface is finished with a coat of plaster.

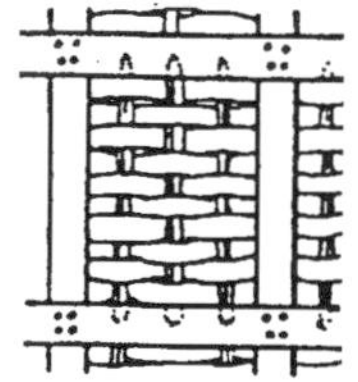

Strips of cleft oak make a tight, almost wind-proof surface to receive daub.

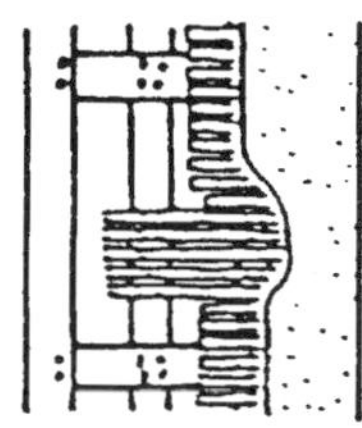

Plaster cladding – closely spaced laths are nailed to the studs and any specially placed vertical members, and then rendered over with plaster.

Brick nogging is the expensive alternative to wattle and daub.

The materials used in timber-framed building will vary according to local availability. In England, a wide selection of hardwoods was available with oak as the first choice. Other favoured woods are sweet (Spanish) chestnut, elm and, in the Fenlands, poplar, lime, hornbeam and even plum. Beech, various willows and imported softwood pine and fir were used for roofing and infill and interior fittings. Changes in the external appearance of wall surfaces could be caused by the desire to be modern or the need for protection from weathering by the elements.

Timber walling

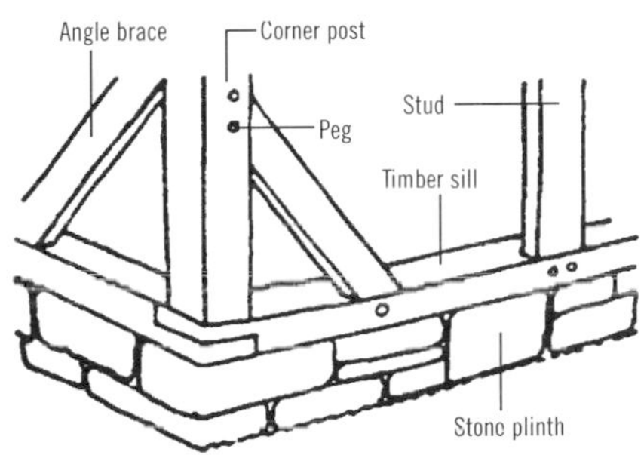

Detail at a corner showing the corner post resting on the sill and rising from it supported by angle braces. The sill is halved and pegged at the corner.

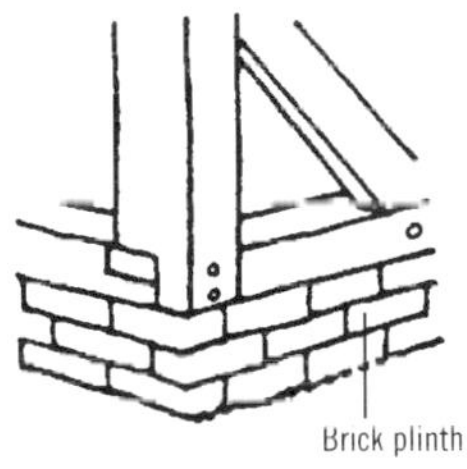

Here the corner post is halved into the sill.

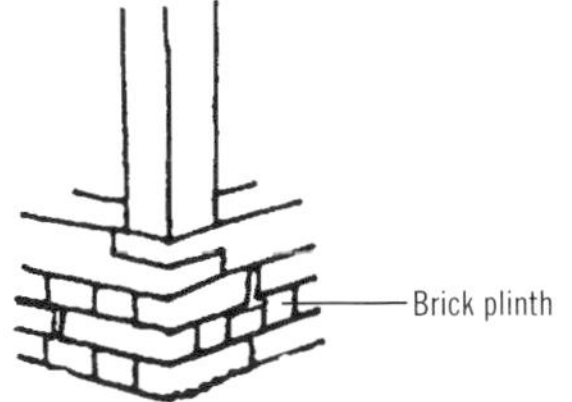

The corner post is rising from the sill. The studs and horizontal timbers hold the building together.

TIMBER-FRAMED WALL CONSTRUCTION AND INFILLING

Timber constructions vary considerably from region to region following a variety of patterns. Many timber-framed houses have been rendered over, hiding their structure. It is important to be aware of the local styles of building so that clues may be sought: for example, shadowy marks of the timbers beneath the wall surface or telltale bumps and lines pushing against the plaster-cement rendering.

and the ridge piece to give the building greater support. In the south-east this was more often achieved by fitting a horizontal collar parallel to the tie-beam and then joining the two with a *crown post*, itself supported by struts. Both box- and cruck-framed buildings could be widened by the addition of a second pair of wall posts outside the main posts. This created what was called an *aisle* along either side of the main hall – an arrangement we discovered at Church Farm, Bidston.

LIFE IN THE HALL

All later houses had a hall, which was of two or three or, rarely, four bays. Situated at ground-floor level, it was always the largest element of the building and was open to the roof. It lay at the heart of the medieval understanding of social organization and codes of behaviour and its origins can be traced back in Britain to late Roman times. The hall was the focus of family life, including dependants and servants, and it functioned as the heart of household activities such as eating, holding courts, cooking and even sleeping.

The earlier halls had open fires set centrally on the floor, the smoke rising up to the exposed rafters. Because the roof timbers could be seen, they were properly dressed and, occasionally, carved. Today, ancient roof timbers betray their age and original place by smoke blackening and scorch marks. However, by the later fourteenth century, hearths began to be sited next to the wall with hoods or smoke bays, a space in the roof allowing smoke to escape (sometimes found in timber-framed houses in the Home Counties).

At one end of the hall were the private apartments (*chambers* or *solars*), which

were reserved for the immediate family of lords or the head of household. They were often two storeys high and occupied one or two bays in a cross-wing. In higher-status buildings, the other end of the hall was often marked by small service rooms such as a buttery and a pantry, with a chamber on a second storey above. Many two-storeyed houses were jettied (see opposite) – buildings that employed a lot of these elements in a single integrated design were wealden houses which demonstrate a regional variation typical of south-east England.

Jetties

One of the most recognizable features of the earlier building period is the timber-framed jetty, whereby the upper storey or storeys of a house project out over the lower floor (York's famous medieval street The Shambles is an example).

Jettying can only happen in a timber-framed house because the walls rising from the projecting joists are in timber, with vertical posts resting on horizontal plates to give the load-bearing structure. If the timber used is of good quality and workmanship, it is likely to have always been exposed. Originally the timbers would have received a protective covering of limewash, which would have given them a silvery patina. Some historians believe that a water paint of lamp black or charcoal was used from the late sixteenth century to protect against the elements.

Above West Midlands and Wales in particular show the tradition of incorporating curved and straight braces within the box-framing. This farmhouse at Church Stretton, Shropshire, shows the commonly found modified form.

Above right Long-houses were low-cost houses found in many of the highland regions of England and Wales. From the outside, this example at the Welsh Folk Museum, Cardiff, could date from the late seventeenth to late nineteenth century, but interior details often reveal a much older structure.

The jetty

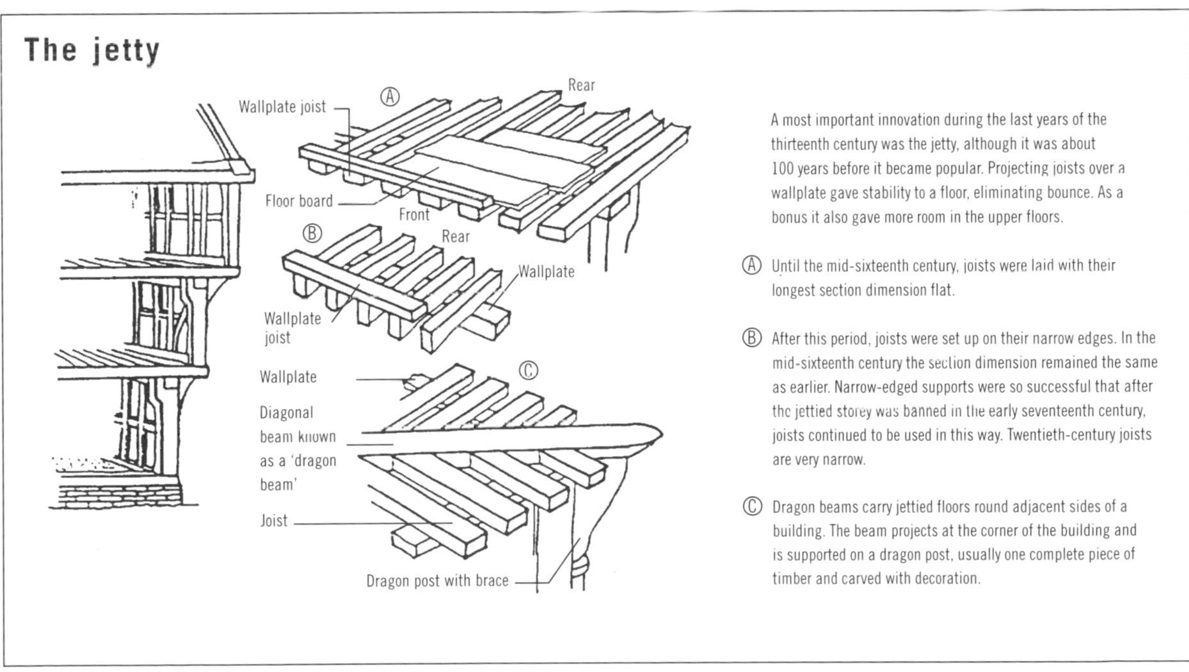

A most important innovation during the last years of the thirteenth century was the jetty, although it was about 100 years before it became popular. Projecting joists over a wallplate gave stability to a floor, eliminating bounce. As a bonus it also gave more room in the upper floors.

Ⓐ Until the mid-sixteenth century, joists were laid with their longest section dimension flat.

Ⓑ After this period, joists were set up on their narrow edges. In the mid-sixteenth century the section dimension remained the same as earlier. Narrow-edged supports were so successful that after the jettied storey was banned in the early seventeenth century, joists continued to be used in this way. Twentieth-century joists are very narrow.

Ⓒ Dragon beams carry jettied floors round adjacent sides of a building. The beam projects at the corner of the building and is supported on a dragon post, usually one complete piece of timber and carved with decoration.

Development of house plans until the early eighteenth century

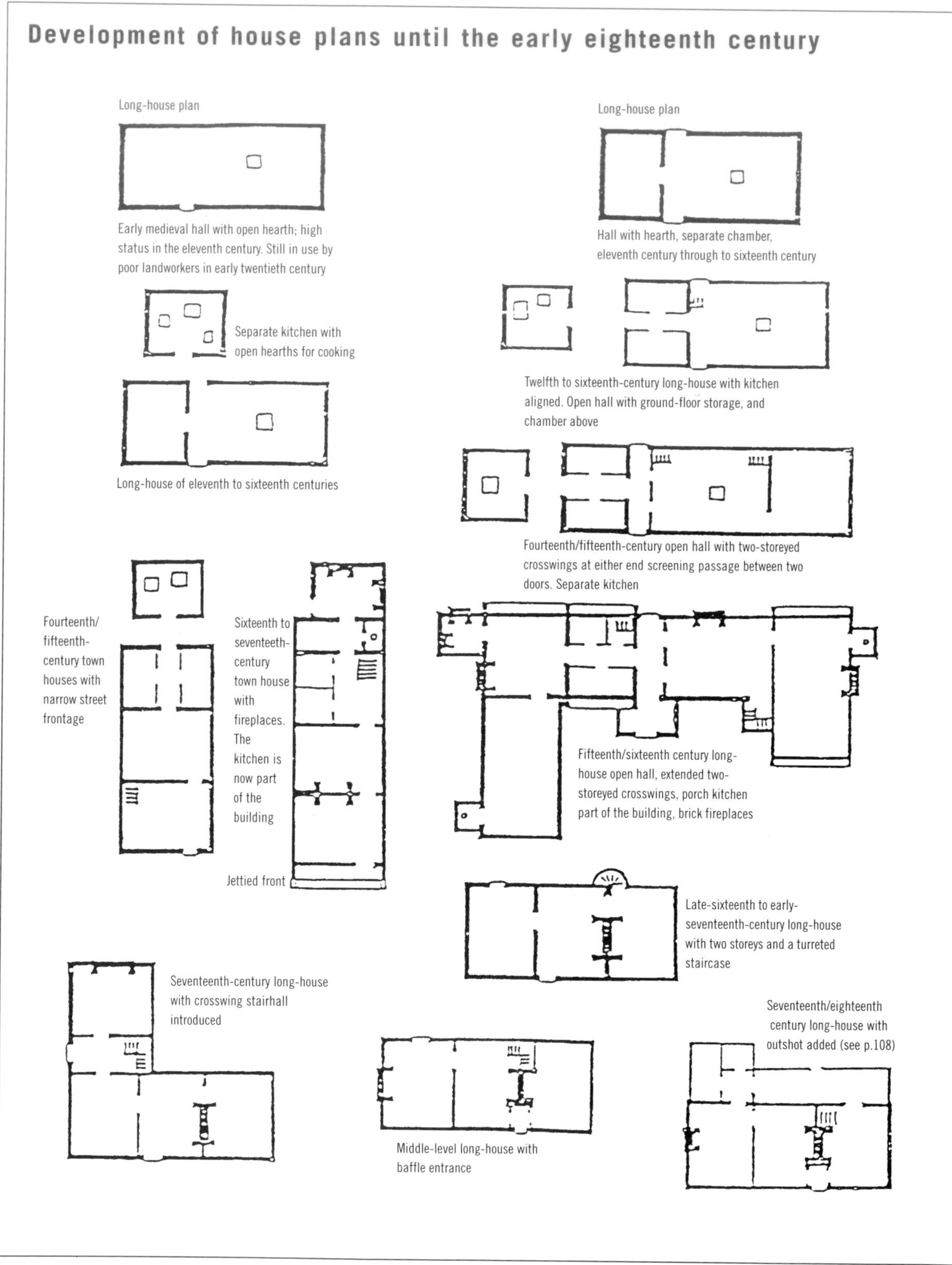

If, however, the timber is rendered over with a plaster cement, it may have been done at a time when exposed timber was unfashionable or because the timber was not all that good a quality.

Just why buildings were jettied isn't clear. The two main advantages are that it provided more floor space and that the projection acts as a cantilever, giving a more stable construction. It was a fashionable feature and it has also been suggested that a series of projections offered greater protection from rain damaging the walls.

Whatever the answer, the making of jetties lasted a long time. It was certainly used in the early fourteenth century and it lasted into the early seventeenth, until restrictions on timber and new ideas of house design put it out of fashion.

THE GREAT REBUILDING: 1550–1650

The transition from the Middle Ages to the early Modern era is marked by a sudden and very noticeable change in vernacular architecture all over Britain, known as 'the Great Rebuilding' (broadly, 1550–1650). This had two principal effects: new types of architecture and building techniques appeared and smaller buildings survived in greater numbers.

One of the main differences was that the size of the hall was reduced as the patterns of social life changed and houses became more private and subdivided into smaller rooms. The idea of the services end as a part of the operation of the hall disappeared and both storage and preparation of food were increasingly separated from the living areas, except in the smaller and more conservative forms of rural house. The hall space was on its way to becoming the living room and what we now call the hall, that is, the location of the entrance lobby and staircase.

This was aided by a growing preference – beginning as early as the later fifteenth century in south-east England – for second storeys to be built with continuous floors, thus preventing any of the ground floor, especially the hall, from being open to the roof. It was coupled with the increased use of hung ceilings that hid the roof timbers and provided new surfaces for decoration.

The greater emphasis on a distinctly different area on the second floor increased notions of privacy. For this and other reasons, the staircase to the upper floor became more emphasized as a social barrier, since it now clearly marked the entrance to the most private parts of the living quarters.

Fireplaces and chimneys, rare in vernacular buildings before the early sixteenth century, were added to earlier buildings and incorporated into the design of the 'new' types. These were usually built in stone and, increasingly, brick, and were placed in more and more rooms, getting away from the hearth's previously restricted situation in the hall.

Indeed, from the later sixteenth century onwards, there was increasing use of brick, stone and mortar; brick in the claylands of the south and east and stone in regions where it outcropped and was easy to quarry. Limestone, used in the production of lime mortars, was also more freely available and had a significant impact: walls that could be properly laid and mortared meant that the weight of roofs could be borne along their full length and

Above **TWO OF A KIND**
These two thatched-roof houses in Great Gransden, Cambridgeshire were both timber-framed lowland-type long-houses, single or 1½ storey, and quite possibly open hall with a hearth. Chimney pieces were introduced in the first half of the seventeenth century, when the further house was raised to a second storey.

Left **THE BEST OF (TUDOR) BRICKWORK**
As seen at the moated manor house of Beckley Park at Otmoor, near Oxford. High-fired bricks at the centre of the kiln turn blue-black; here they are displayed in the characteristic diaper pattern.

the need for the timber frame gradually began to fade away.

The pace of the Great Rebuilding differed from region to region, from generation to generation and from class to class, reflecting the major social and economic changes at the beginning of the capitalist era. Houses became bigger, more comfortable, more subdivided internally and more capable of showing the subtle shifts and nuances of status and wealth of their occupants, particularly among the growing rural and urban middle classes. A variety of different types of new buildings emerged: two of the most common are the *long-house* and *double-pile* houses.

Long-houses

Long-houses, which are single-span (one-room-width), are found throughout Britain. The term 'long-house', when used in reference to western or northern parts of the country, is essentially a building with a farmhouse at the upper end and an animal barn or byre at the lower, joined together under the same ridge-line, but separated internally by a solid wall.

Originally long-houses were a single-storey structure of timber and dry-stone or cob dating back to the eleventh or twelfth centuries. The earliest surviving examples, though, are from the sixteenth and seventeenth centuries. Although single-storey long-houses continued to be built in poorer areas like west Wales, northern Scotland and the south-west of England, they frequently had two-storey house ends. Some started out as only one and were later 'raised' by an additional floor.

Strictly speaking, the true long-house incorporates both house and byre, but buildings in areas outside of the highland regions also incorporated cross-passages with domestic rooms on each side. There is still a tendency for these three-bay dwellings to be known as long-houses.

The fireplace in the long-house, usually of *inglenook* type, is found in the main living room and tends to back onto the cross-passage, where it served both as domestic focus and cooking area, sometimes with a small in-built clay oven. Occasionally, however, the chimney was placed on an end wall, and sometimes there was a chimney in both positions. Staircases were often built into the space between the fireplace and the side wall away from the main entrance.

When chimney stacks were introduced into long-houses, front doors could open into a small lobby with the side of the chimney breast directly in front and the doors to the adjacent rooms on either side. This is called a *baffle entrance*. Staircases could be found in the lobby or on the other side of the chimney, although other solutions were found. Sometimes, the door would be one-third of the way in from the end wall furthest from the stack, opening into a corner of either the middle room or the end room. This is called a hall entrance.

Double-Pile houses

The double-pile or double-span house began in the middle of the seventeenth century as a gentry building. Instead of being linear and rangy, as the long-houses were, the shape became more boxy or square and was two rooms thick. Some builders achieved the double span by simply placing another house alongside an earlier one. Such houses had two gables at either end of the range with a valley between the roofs.

Its origin was in polite architecture as was the compact plan, which was itself influenced by the design of French châteaux and new architectural ideas seeded by the Renaissance movement in Europe. The essential effect of the compact plan on manor, merchants' and yeomen's houses was to produce a much closer, tighter layout of the rooms around an often elaborate entrance hall, of which the stairs would be an obvious feature.

VITAL CLUES AND WHAT TO LOOK FOR

THE SEVENTEENTH CENTURY

To be able to date a building, a house detective needs to be familiar with the elevations of this period. Bearing in mind the historical developments outlined above, a basic aid to remember is that the majority of these houses has a distribution of features – windows, door and chimney stack – that suggest three units. Stand back from the main range elevation and look for these. A giveaway of double-pile houses is when a side or three-quarter view shows the two spans where the gable-end roof is to be M-shaped.

Chimneys

Chimneys and their positions in the plan can be very useful clues. For example, in double-pile houses the position of the chimney along the elevation of the main range and within the plan of the house is a good pointer to early seventeenth-century details. The principal stack is likely to be in a 1:2 ratio along the front elevation. You can also find them centrally placed, and when you do there will be other features that point to the use of the house.

There is the chance that a chimney stack rising beside or off-centre to the roof ridge has been added to what was formerly an open-hall house. If the stack rises immaculately through the centre of the roof and looks from the outside as if it is sitting neatly astride the ridge, then it's more than likely that it was purpose-built, which is especially true of larger houses.

However, as we've already warned you, nothing is straightforward in the house detection business: that neat, ridge-clasping stack could be sitting on a new roof on an old house or even, as at Ledbury, pushed through an old roof on a redesigned house! Until you are happy and familiar with climbing around inside a roof-space, stick to the first two options, that is, a chimney stack in a modernized or a new house.

Fireplaces

As stone and, increasingly, bricks became more readily available, anyone who could afford it had fireplaces put in their houses, or had their new house built with fireplaces. These were wide and deep, forming the inglenook that always looks so attractive with its long, thick chimney beam forming the support over the hearth. Initially, inglenooks were built in service ends for cooking when the kitchen came into the house. However, not all seventeenth-century fireplaces were inglenooks.

The functional fittings of the fireplace can indicate the social level of the room or even the whole house. One clue to look out for is small niches or cupboards to one side of the back wall for keeping salt dry. If your fireplace was originally used for cooking as well as heating, there may also be a bread oven built into it.

Roofs

The shape, style and *pitch* of a roof can all be useful clues to dating a building. The pitch (steepness) of a roof depends partly on prevailing weather conditions, partly on the structural techniques used in the building and partly on the type of roofing material used.

In the Middle Ages, builders had a basic choice between two simple styles of roof. The most common was a *pitched* roof, which had a relatively steep angle of 50 or 60 degrees with a ridge running along the top and gables at either end The more complicated alternative was a *hipped* roof (see p.108), where the ends were also pitched at an angle. This type of roof, which was common in Kent, provided greater structural stability because the end slopes had a buttressing effect.

As the single-pile medieval house plan was superseded by double-pile houses, double-pitched roofs were built, but the gully between was a problem because it tended to let in water. Where slates or pantiles were available, a low-pitched single-span roof was a good alternative. Steep double-pitched roofs tended to go out of favour once improvements in transport meant slate was widely available.

As people wanted to make more use of roof spaces for storage and living accommodation, the shape of roof structures changed. A combination of a hipped and

THE COMPACT PLAN
Up until the seventeenth century, practically all vernacular houses were built as a single span, just one room wide, and then added to or extended with crosswings. Around the middle of the century, double-span, or double-pile houses came to be placed under one continuous roof producing a compact plan. Thorney Hall, near Peterborough, is of this type. Designed by Peter Mills, it rightfully comes under the heading of polite architecture, except it is quite a small house in a setting of buildings that have developed since early medieval times. Note the mullioned and transomed windows that have survived conversion into sash.

gable roof became popular, because it gave more height in the roof space and allowed the insertion of a window in the gable end.

The invention of the *Mansard* roof by a French architect, François Mansart (1598-1666), was an important breakthrough. This type of roof, which has a double slope, made it more practical to convert attic space into living quarters, and was a common feature in larger Georgian houses where servants slept in the loft (see illustration, p.108).

Internal proportions

Before the early seventeenth century, vernacular houses were built with open halls and low-ceilinged chambers. Around 1640 it became popular to have higher ceilings and to build in two storeys, though the one-and-a-half were still common in worker's houses and cottages. One option was to build a new house with ground-floor rooms about 7 ft 6 in (2.3 m) high. Another was to strip the house down to its skeleton timber frame, insert a new wallplate and raise the old plate that takes the joists to give extra height. A third was simply to dig out the ground and lower the floor. In the latter case you will step down into the house when entering, so consider this possibility straight away.

Dormer windows

As second storeys began to be built, instead of being open to the roof the upper floor often had a third storey created as an attic. The cheapest way to light it was to use the old method of putting windows high up in the gable ends.

Then, in the second quarter of the

Roof construction

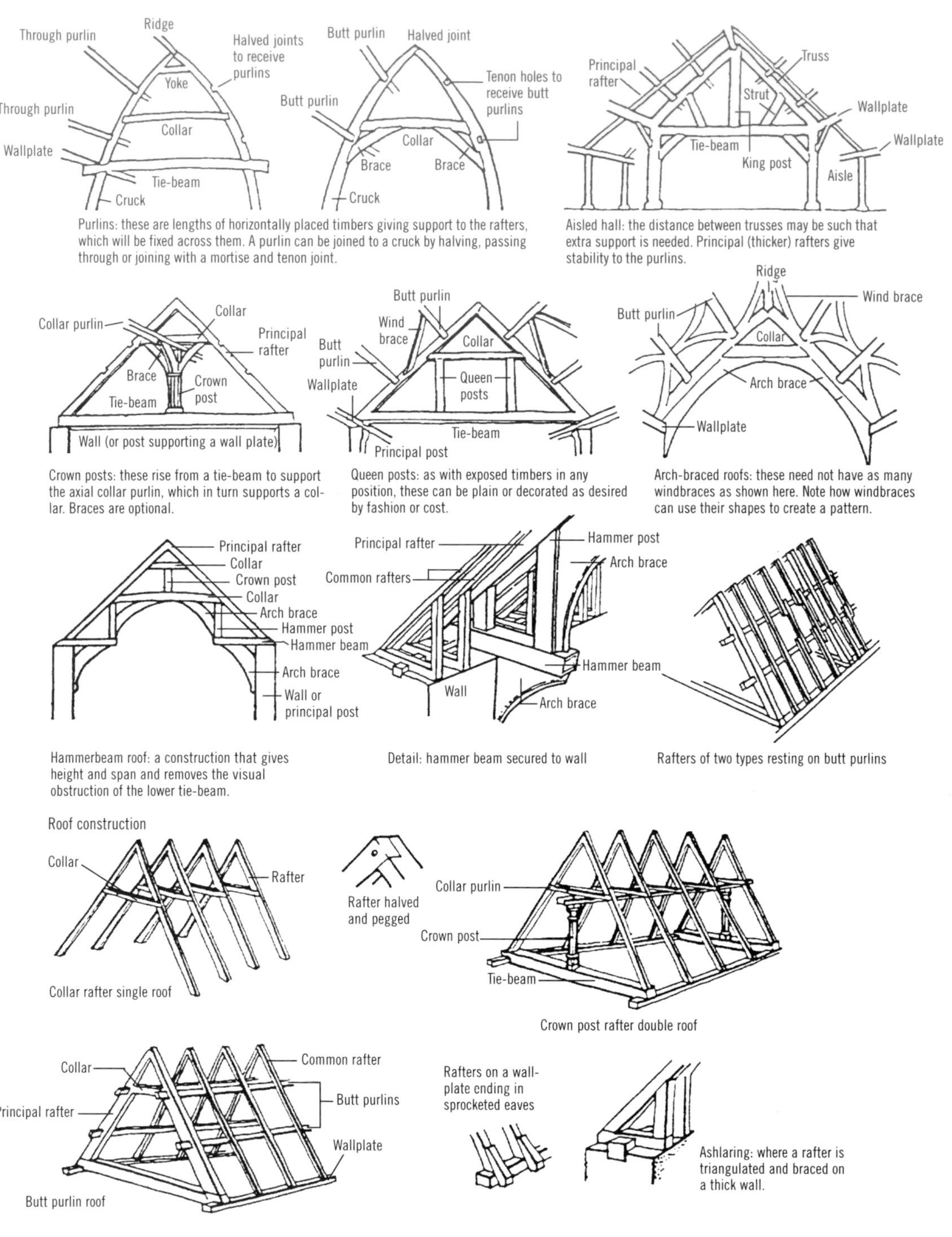

Purlins: these are lengths of horizontally placed timbers giving support to the rafters, which will be fixed across them. A purlin can be joined to a cruck by halving, passing through or joining with a mortise and tenon joint.

Aisled hall: the distance between trusses may be such that extra support is needed. Principal (thicker) rafters give stability to the purlins.

Crown posts: these rise from a tie-beam to support the axial collar purlin, which in turn supports a collar. Braces are optional.

Queen posts: as with exposed timbers in any position, these can be plain or decorated as desired by fashion or cost.

Arch-braced roofs: these need not have as many windbraces as shown here. Note how windbraces can use their shapes to create a pattern.

Hammerbeam roof: a construction that gives height and span and removes the visual obstruction of the lower tie-beam.

Detail: hammer beam secured to wall

Rafters of two types resting on butt purlins

Collar rafter single roof

Crown post rafter double roof

Butt purlin roof

Rafters on a wall-plate ending in sprocketed eaves

Ashlaring: where a rafter is triangulated and braced on a thick wall.

seventeenth century, a new innovation arrived from France. A smaller, neater variation of a type of window structure that had been used in Elizabethan times, it was called a *dormer* window and fitted into the slope of the roof. The earliest form of dormer rested on the upper wall-plate at the eaves in the manner of the sixteenth-century side gable, carpenters being reluctant to insert the extra weight into a hole in the roof-supporting rafters. However, as the century progressed, so did their confidence, and dormer windows gradually moved further up the slopes of roofs.

Dormers are particularly characteristic of the larger double-pile houses and compact plan houses, and it is not unknown to find two rows of them, one above the other, after the Flemish fashion. In more upmarket houses and polite architecture they may vary in roof shape and can be flat, triangular (the most common) or segmented, giving them a gentle curve.

Timbers

The size of timbers and how they are laid can all help date a house. A simple rule of thumb is that the thicker they are, the older they are. In practice, that rule is best kept for joists and rafters. Up to about the middle of the sixteenth century, joists were roughly 5 in x 4 in (127 x 100 mm), and laid with the greater dimension horizontal. Around the middle of that century someone turned a joist around 90 degrees and found that with the greater dimension vertical it was more stable.

One of the best places to date timbers is in your roof space. Until the seventeenth century, rafters tended to be wider and shallower. Later, both rafters and joists got slimmer and deeper – down to 3 in (76 mm) or slightly less in their narrowest dimension.

In earlier buildings, the timbers are likely to be native to this country, such as oak or elm, while from the end of the seventeenth century, soft woods, particularly pine, were being imported from Scandinavia and became more common.

You should beware of stories that the timbers in your attic were salvaged from shipwrecks. These tales are mostly complete fallacies because it would have been very hard to use seasoned timbers again, especially if they had been hardened at sea. You are more likely to find salvage from other buildings which had been knocked down.

If the underside of beams or other timbers are carved or chamfered it would suggest that they were designed to be exposed. If a considerable amount of the sharp corners of a beam have been cut away, it is likely to be sixteenth century or earlier. As time moved on, chamfers became smaller.

A principal load-bearing structure that developed with the advent of the chimney-piece was the sturdy *axial* beam, which extended down the central axis of a house supporting the floor above. Although they appeared in the sixteenth century, they weren't widely used until the seventeenth. They came to replace the tie-beams, extending across the width of the room, that had existed to support upper floors from earlier times. If the width of a room required an extra-wide tie-beam laid across the axial beam, the tie-beam would be halved so that it clasped the longer axial at the point where they met.

Staircases

In the earlier vernacular houses, staircases could be placed in any one of three positions: the opposite side of the chimney breast to the door, against a side wall towards one end of the main range, or in a compact, separate stairhall or turret attached to the outside of the building.

In compact plan/double-pile houses, where staircases were important features, *balusters* – the vertical timbers supporting a handrail on a staircase – were turned with well-proportioned mouldings and often had carved and decorated shafts. In the larger houses, staircases arose either from the entrance hall or from a hall of their own. In middle-sized houses, the staircase position aped the big houses, but on a less imposing scale. Smaller houses generally used what can be thought of as a room unit as a stairhall, which means that about a quarter of the house plan was given over to a staircase and landing.

As staircases required the services of a skilled joiner and were expensive, some houses would still have to make use of a ladder or a simple, open-stepped frame. Elaborate staircases had, since the sixteenth century, been constructed in wood or stone; however many vernacular houses would have had simple cylindrically-turned posts and balusters.

Windows

In the medieval tradition windows were longer horizontally than vertically and not always glazed. Less affluent homes might have had horn or vellum, or perhaps nothing more than shutters. Where there was glass it may have been changed several times. However, there are still an amazing number of windows that have survived, particularly from the early seventeenth century, mainly in stone or brick, though some timber frames can also be found.

The window surrounds had moulded inner edges developed from the chamfer, which is where the sharp corner was removed at a bevilled angle. This surface remained plain, or had a slightly indented line around its edge, or was shaped, when in stone or wood and moulded, when in brick, to create a curved section known as *bolection moulding*. These were used to decorate the edges of many features, such as axial and chimney beams and stone fireplace surrounds.

Windows were divided into two or three *lights* (openings) by wooden or stone uprights known as *mullions*. Each light would be vertically hung with a wrought-iron frame with leaded strips, called *cames*. These secured the pieces of flat-moulded glass (known as *quarries*) or square sections cut from higher-quality cylindrical blown glass. The former would generally show a scattering of impurity bubbles and light scratch scars of fine sand.

Today, most earlier window glazing will have been replaced, but the proportions and the surrounds and mullions remain unchanged. Originally, not all of the windows need necessarily open. Usually it would be a small part of the casement that opened from vertical hinges.

Not every compact plan/double-pile house went in for the latest style of window, which was still a casement but now with the longer sides vertical. Although sash windows, which slide up and down vertically, were first recorded

RINGING THE CHANGES
This house in Burford, Oxfordshire, has emerged from an earlier building and then received further modernization. The evidence begins with the lower eaves and higher roofs that extend from either side of it, hinting at a medieval building. The main period displayed by the house is early eighteenth century, as can be seen in the proportion of the sash windows with their projecting architraves. However, the doorway, with its eighteenth-century architrave, is set uncomfortably close to the edge of the façade. It intrudes into the vertical line of the quoins, or corner stones. The dormer windows are probably nineteenth-century modifications of earlier windows.

29

Types of roof

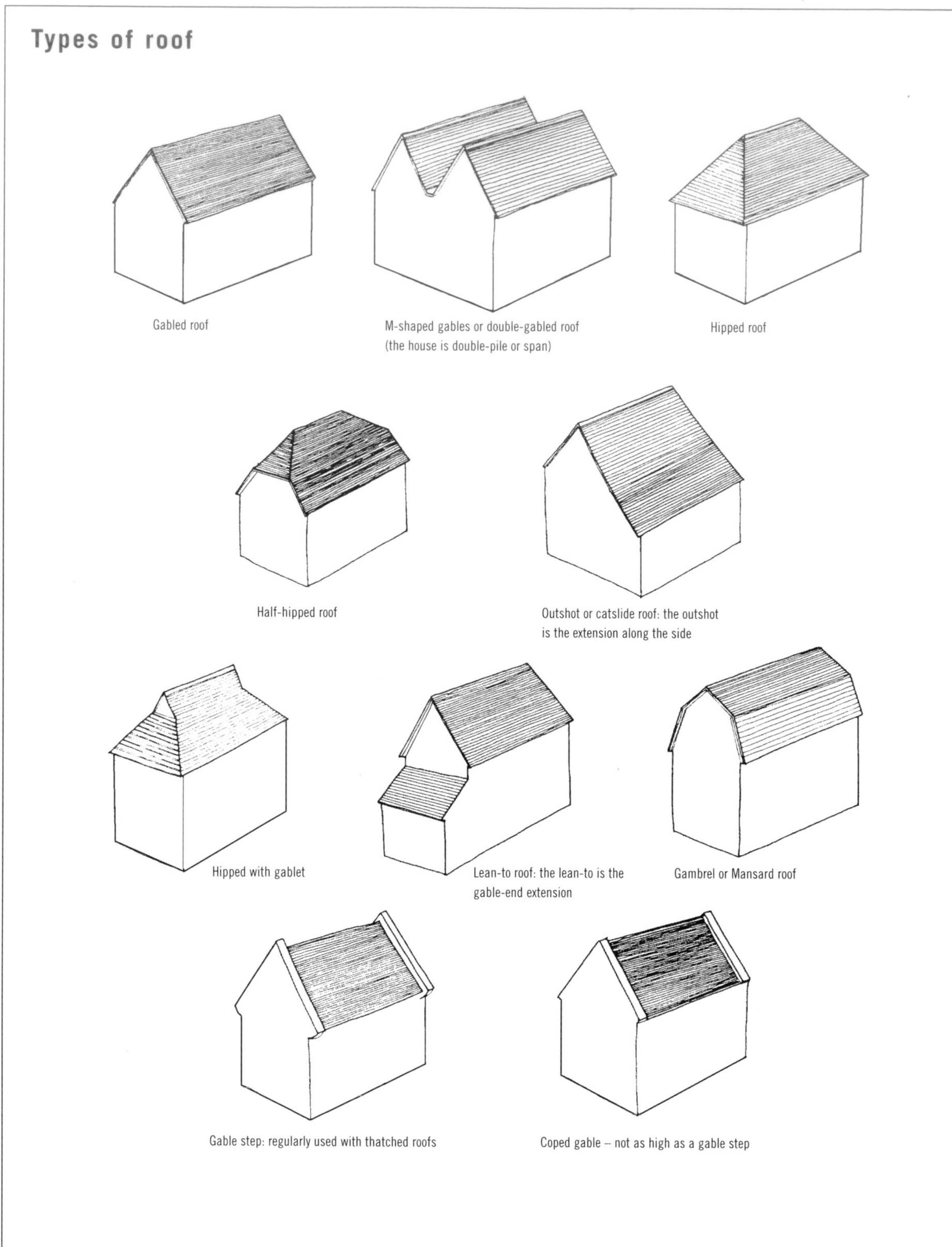

Gabled roof

M-shaped gables or double-gabled roof (the house is double-pile or span)

Hipped roof

Half-hipped roof

Outshot or catslide roof: the outshot is the extension along the side

Hipped with gablet

Lean-to roof: the lean-to is the gable-end extension

Gambrel or Mansard roof

Gable step: regularly used with thatched roofs

Coped gable – not as high as a gable step

in 1685, it seems likely that they had been around for five to 10 years before.

Doorways

The principal doorway may also have had a hood or canopy above it partly supporting the moulded frame around the door – the *architrave* – with curved console brackets. The underside of the hood was decorated with either a shell design or panelling. The hoods were commonly segmented or flat, the more elaborately decorated triangular pediment becoming popular from the eighteenth century.

LATE SEVENTEENTH AND EARLY EIGHTEENTH CENTURIES

This is the period sometimes called Restoration and then William and Mary, which leads into Queen Anne. These titles are given to many of the smaller houses because the feature styles of the grander and polite houses had such a strong influence on the vernacular.

The features of these houses at the different levels of society remained much the same as those discussed above. The front elevation was symmetrical, or very close to it. The roof swept up very steeply and was commonly hipped, curving out at the eaves in a projection that made an obvious impression. The roof edge had an extra curve to it, induced by a *sprocket* – a slender wedge-shaped piece of timber – on each rafter. The chimney stacks often appeared very tall and, as a result, looked somewhat top-heavy and incongruous.

Sash windows were very much the fashion, the glazing bars that supported the panes of glass being fairly thick and substantial, although they got more slender as the eighteenth century progressed. Like all wooden windows they weathered badly and were often replaced in the latest fashionable style.

At this time the wooden surround of the window – also called the *architrave* – clasped and projected slightly from the brick or stone wall, especially if it was a modernization inserted into a timber-framed wall. In a brick building, the lintel and edges of the windows were often emphasized by bricks of a slightly different hue to stunning effect.

EIGHTEENTH-CENTURY GEORGIAN

By the end of the seventeenth century, all traces of medievalism had gone. The single-span property had all but disappeared, except for the smaller labourer's or farmworker's cottage, a lot of which have survived intact or have been incorporated into extended houses.

Some of these smaller houses were one-and-a-half storeys high; others, two. They were always thatched and the front elevation consisted of a more-or-less centrally placed door with windows on either side at both levels, though the upper ones were sometimes dormers.

Very small houses were so tiny that they just had a door and one window on the ground floor and a single window high in the gable end. The ground-floor room would have been a combined kitchen, living and sleeping room, the single attic room approached by ladder or very steep stairs.

The importance of symmetry

For other houses built at this time, it is the influence of the Renaissance that really began to show. In any detached building, symmetry was essential. In terraces and small ranges symmetry was not possible and a slight stroke of artistic licence had to be used in order to make things seem to balance to the eye. Complete harmony of features produced the required result.

The very much grander town house, when positioned in a terrace, had the same problem. Such houses often had a narrow frontage which, coupled with the large reception space fashionable at that time, necessitated an offset front door. In such cases sheer elegance of features provided the visual pleasure.

Roofs and chimneys

During the century, the pitch of a roof became less steep to about 30 degrees at the eaves. The Mansard or double-pitched roof introduced during the mid-seventeenth century remained in fashion.

Chimney stacks were placed in symmetrical positions as they emerged through the roof or beside gable walls. Sometimes the fireplace or kitchen range was not directly below the stack, forcing the flue to move through contrived angles which were not evident within the house. Fireplaces often incorporated niches rather than bays.

Façades

In many houses, the facing wall rose to turn the dormers into a third storey; others put in dormers but hid them behind a parapet, keeping the servants quarters out of sight. Parapets – positioned at, or later added to the front wall where it meets the roof – bestowed status on a building, but brought their own problems: if blocked by blown debris, they caused damp.

Whether the eaves are exposed or not, the top of a façade wall was decorated with one or more horizontal courses representing vestiges of, and sometimes complete classical *entablature*. A simple projecting course is usually referred to as the *cornice at eaves*. The classical decorative mouldings found in a cornice were either a course of *modillions* (brackets or scrolls) or *dentils* (tooth-like blocks), or motifs such as egg and dart (in which a half-egg shape alternates with a dart shape). An elaborate entablature might have included the lot.

They were built in brick, stone or wood. If they are in wood, the house is likely to date from the very early part of the century, since from around 1705 external wooden cornices in towns were banned as a fire hazard. Window and doorway architraves, or surrounds, which had clasped and projected slightly from the wall surface, were banned for the same reason.

Stonework

Brick and well-dressed stone were the external materials for house walls. It was fashionable to dress, or emphasize, features such as windows and doorways in a brick-built house in contrasting stone, for example, using edging lines of creamy-white limestone against the mellow reds and buffs of brickwork. Such contrasts enhanced the architraves around windows and doors.

The name given to stonework at the corner of a building or a feature such as a porch is *quoins* (pronounced 'coins'). The term is also given to brickwork that has been given the same decorative

FINE FACING
Hall Farm, on the edge of Chelmsford, Essex, has a well-balanced symmetrical front that is classically eighteenth century. All the features date to around the 1720s, including the dormers, the projecting cornice at the eaves, the architraved windows and the impressive doorcasing.

emphasis through a slight projection at a corner. Stone quoins also decorated an ashlared building.

When stone was used with stone, another method of treatment was to carve textures, random forms or worm-like patterns into the decorative feature. Random forms were simply described as textured, while the worm-like pattern is known as *vermiculation*.

The lower part of house walls had projected regularly over the centuries from timber ground-sills (the joists forming the lowest member of the timber frame) to be slightly projecting courses in brick or stone called *plinths*. The edges of stone blocks or ashlaring were given a chamfer or bevilled edge that catch the light to form a linear pattern. This decoration is termed *rustication*.

Windows

Windows in the principal elevations of a house were almost always sash. At their tops were *lintels*, which were essentially decorative – the constructional lintel lies unseen behind the brick or stone facing. At the base of the windows were the sills (or cills) which were made of brick or stone. The window frames were in wood, as were the glazing bars which, as we've already noted, became more slender as the century progressed and were decorated with very fine moulding.

The proportion of the principal windows showed slight variations in that they appeared a trifle narrower in some early houses than later. The number of panes in these was 12. The glass was nearly always crown, that is, when a nodule of molten glass is spun into an enormous disc, cooled, and the thinner, outer portions are cut into squares for glazing the windows. Contrary to popular belief, the centre of the disc, the 'bull's eye' was not actually used but thrown back into the melting pot to be heated up again.

Towards the end of the eighteenth century, some windows of principal rooms were made a little wider to permit more light to enter. The number of panes increased to 16 and sometimes more.

A window shape that occurred in the larger house from around the 1720s was the Palladian or Venetian window. This window was in three parts, comprising a central round-headed window with a narrower horizontal-headed window on either side. It took its name from two sources: the Italian architect Andrea Palladio, who favoured it as a design, and Venice, where it was much used. At their best they appeared as a significant, eye-catching feature over the main door; however, they became an obsession with some people, who covered the entire front elevation of their house with them upstairs and down.

Doorways

Doorways were a great feature of the eighteenth century and looked extremely elegant. It was usual for them to be approached by a series of steps protected by wrought-iron railed banisters.

Doors were generally made from painted pine and had carved mouldings around their panels. These panels were usually in sixes: two small ones at the top, the two largest in the middle and two slightly smaller ones at the base. In the late seventeenth and early eighteenth century they were wider than in later times.

Fanlights appeared over doors at the end of the seventeenth century and became very decorative features with flowing patterns evolving from their glazing bars. Fanlights started off rectangular in shape, becoming semi-circular for the rest of the century. This, you might imagine, is a useful datable fact, until you discover that there was a return to the rectangle at the turn of the eighteenth century into the nineteenth!

New materials – and revivals

Stucco, a slow-setting plaster made from gypsum, sand and slaked lime, had been used, but under different names such as plaster rendering and pargeting, from the early sixteenth century. In the eighteenth century it became popular under its new name and was used for different reasons.

When the brickwork was not of high

quality, it could be hidden beneath a rendering of stucco which, by incising immaculately marked lines to a masonry pattern, simulated stone. This is called *false-ashlaring*. Sometimes, particularly when dealing with an upper part of a house wall, the masonry pattern was carried out with lines drawn with graphite. Specific textures could be achieved by mixing 'grog' (ground, fired clay), marble dust or powdered stone with the plaster. At the turn of the century and into the period known as Regency (1812–1837) stucco became very acceptable and indeed fashionable in its own right.

Artificial stones of various qualities were manufactured in the second half of the period. Probably the most famous of them was Coade stone, made from 1769, which was finer than stucco. The earliest attempts to make and market it by the men of the Coade family were not successful until Mrs Eleanor Coade took over the running of the business on part of the site later used by the Festival of Britain in 1951.

Early Coade stone was perhaps more closely related to stoneware pottery or refractory ware than the plaster-based composites. It was found in all kinds of architectural ornament – good surviving examples are in the doorways in Bedford Square, London. Its use extended into the nineteenth century when, in 1821, the firm was taken over by a cousin of the family, William Croggan, who expanded the business even more. The London operation finally ceased around 1858, when the moulds and plant were bought by a firm at Stamford in Lincolnshire.

Wood, like stucco, also underwent a revival. Although front, rear and side walls were built in brick, load-bearing interior walls were constructed of wood. The supporting structures within the basic frame of the house would be of slender studs and braces that bonded the fabric together. This bore little resemblance to the earlier timber-framed construction, and though it was obviously sound, was much slighter and not particularly attractive. Nonetheless, many people expose these eighteenth-century timbers with pride…

Overleaf

A LINE OF ELEGANCE
The refined, upmarket town planning of the eighteenth and nineteenth centuries is usually associated with Bath or Brighton, not these elegant Regency houses in Toxteth, the homes of Liverpool's commercial and professional families. Columned porches with their curled Ionic capitals and elaborate entablatures are arc de triomphes setting off the well-proportioned sash windows with their sharply defined lintels.

Social function and design

The plans of Georgian houses were variations on the themes of social use and functional service. Ideally, the residents used the first floor as a *piano nobile*, the principal floor for the reception rooms where guests were entertained. Apart from increasing the comfort of living, the new houses had a strong social function, particularly among the established upper classes and emergent upper-middle classes. The house began its social statement with its external appearance and continued it with its interior.

The main staircase, with its gracefully turned balusters and elegantly moulded banister, or rail, would bring visitors up from the stairhall to a landing, from which doors led into the salon and dining room and other reception rooms in the larger house. Each room had another door that would give access to the adjacent room and, in turn, all the other rooms, depending on the size of the house. Another staircase, smaller and more confined but still admirable, would complete the social requirements of this floor. The second staircase had to have a degree of charm about it because not

169

only would the servants use it, but visitors too, so it would play its part in the social circulation of the house. A very big house would have had separate stairs for the servants.

The ground floor of a merchant or professional gentleman's house would have at least one room for carrying out business. It could also have had a dining room, though there may be one upstairs, and a bed-chamber. Again, there would have been bedrooms used in the receptions on the *piano nobile*. But this is a description of a rather grand house; the majority of middle-level houses were used in whatever way suited the occupants.

Basements provided space for kitchens and storage but once again there were variations – many houses had kitchens on the ground floor. The attics provided accommodation for both servants and children.

THE URGE TO REFASHION

Walls in the principal rooms were capped by moulded cornices, which may have had a frieze of classical motifs, tiny dentils or a course of *anthemion*, a floral design consisting of honeysuckle or palmette. A rough rule for dating is that the decorative forms are more ebullient at the beginning of the eighteenth century and more restrained and refined from around 1760. However, the nineteenth century used both styles.

It is not uncommon to find seventeenth-century long-houses that have been given the eighteenth-century treatment. A house would be stripped down to its timber-framed skeleton. The floors would be removed and the wallplates that had supported them raised by the addition of shorter studs on a newly inserted wallplate. The floor joists were then set back into their old positions on the now raised wallplate, and, hey presto, the ceiling was not only higher but more fashionable.

This method of raising a ceiling could be applied to either or both storeys. During the operation, chimney-pieces could be taken down and new or remodelled fireplaces and chimneys assembled in modern positions. A central room could be divided in two, so that one half could become the stairhall. The staircase could be made *the* feature, a joiner being permitted to display his skill with a repeat pattern of three types of exquisitely turned balusters. The old casement windows could be replaced with sash windows in the now higher walls, or if, say, one floor had not been raised, then a truncated form of sash window could be made for it. The outer walls could be rendered over or even cased in brick.

All this obviously depended on how much money the owners could afford. Any really wealthy person would have either knocked down the old house and built a new one on its site, or passed the old one on to someone else in the family and had their new house built in the most fashionable style on a different part of their estate.

NINETEENTH CENTURY

The earliest style of the nineteenth century was Regency. Although, strictly speaking, the country was headed by the Prince of Wales for the nine years between 1811 and 1820, the style that bore the name of his title began in the 1790s and lasted until the 1830s, just before Victoria became queen. At the same time houses of all sizes were being built that continued to be known as Georgian. There is a current tendency to think of the Georgian period as being solely eighteenth century, and this concept receives an element of encouragement from estate agents, who refer to some houses of the early nineteenth century as being in Georgian style.

The Scottish influence

It is often said that Scottish architecture from medieval times to the eighteenth century was more influenced by the French rather than English mainstream development, a view that is supported by many of its buildings. However, a number of England's most influential architects of the eighteenth century came from north of the border. The flower of Scotland's contribution to innovative building in England included such names as Robert Adam, Colen Campbell and William Chambers, two generations of architects that brought more unified styles to the whole of the United Kingdom. The turn of the century, for example, saw terraces of up-market town houses of similar classical grandeur from Cheltenham to Edinburgh, and from Harrogate to Dublin.

Regency hallmarks

Regency may be described as the ultimate development of the refinements of late eighteenth-century work. The stark plainness of regular, subdued-coloured brickwork or stucco contrasted with features such as doorcases, windows and eaves of sharp and immaculate linear quality, although the elaborate chimney-pot shapes were on the point of being 'over the top' with their contrived shapes and mouldings.

Windows in general were a little wider than in the previous century. They were revealed with little of the outer framework showing and the glazing bars were slim and delicate. Sixteen panes of glass were very common. The lintels, whether in brick or defined in stucco, extended sharply outwards to acute angles.

Curved, bow-fronted houses were common, bow-window bays sometimes extending to the top of a three-storey elevation (though more regularly only to two). Equally popular was the arcaded front of arched recesses which extended along the front of a house or a terrace. These recesses, which took the windows and doors, could be at either one or two storeys' level.

Another feature of doorways in the first half of the nineteenth century was the *tent porch*. It consisted of an ironwork frame decorated with a lattice design in the side panels, surmounted with a metal-panelled hood that swung down in a curve out from the wall like a tent canopy. Cast-iron balconies and window-boxes added further decorative patterns against the plainness of the walls.

Roofs were pitched as low as 30 degrees at the eaves which, at their most fashionable, showed a considerable projection out from the wall and were supported by shaped brackets. In complete contrast, by around 1840 eaves were reduced to almost nothing and the roof hardly projected at all.

As before roofs were hipped, this time in cool blue slate from Wales, Cornwall and Leicestershire. (Transport had been

BERKELEY HOUSE

A SELECT TRIO
Three houses from a very long terrace in Bristol, a development of town houses dating from the commercial successes of the port in the early nineteenth century. These are large houses with four storeys and basements. They are in smooth stone ashlar on the upper floors and rusticated on the lower. A feature of these three is the dark-coloured rendering on their lower half which contrasts rather unhappily with the natural stonework. Their decorative appearance is compounded by their fanciful cast-iron balconies painted in white. The rest of the range is three storeys high, plus dormers and basement and in the natural stone. (Our three have been altered and added to and require little detective work!)

improving, with better-constructed turnpike roads, an increasing number of canals and modernization of the trading links with the sea, allowing building materials to move more easily and cheaply between regions.)

Middle-class mores

The basic elevation and plan remained very much in the manner of the eighteenth century. The social side of the home remained important, so reception rooms needed to be kept as up to date as possible.

The concept of the *piano nobile* declined during the first half of the nineteenth century as a result of a division in the middle class. The well-to-do professional and merchant class that had come to the social and economic fore during the eighteenth century – the nouveau riche spurned by Jane Austen as 'improvers' – now spawned a second middle class of 'white-collar workers' from the ranks of management.

One significant class-based change that took place in the 1820s was the introduction of the corridor on the principal floors. No longer did people, particularly servants, have to go through room after room when moving about a house. Privacy had arrived for the upper classes. The influence came from the functional advantages of corridors in smaller houses, where a large number of people, both family and staff, had to live in fairly confined conditions. It was one of those rare cases when the lesser house created a fashion that was adopted by the greater. However, what was really the corridor behind the front door of these large houses became known, rather grandly, as the hall.

Flushed with success

Water closets were introduced into houses in the 1770s when a London watchmaker, Alexander Cumming, patented the S-bend water trap. In 1778, Joseph Bramah produced a valve that permitted a flushing control, which remained the principle of the WC for decades.

The new-fangled contraptions were much welcomed and appreciated, but were placed in partitioned closets in the corner of rooms and cupboards created on corridors without the practical thought of ventilation.

Fortunately, in the 1870s, a system was created upon which all modern toilets are modelled: Twyford's washdown closet. Water was always present in the curve of the lavatory pan and the flush was more efficient thanks to ballcocks, valves and ventilator pipes. However, the privacy of the bathroom had yet to arrive.

Revivalism

Apart from Regency, the early nineteenth century produced other polite styles in architecture. Where Regency was a natural progression and modern development from what had gone before, the other styles were concerned with modern adaptations from past periods.

Gothick, Elizabethan and Jacobean harked back to 'the good old days' before the industrial revolution and the bucolic joys of 'Merrie England', while the Greek revival was a statement reminding designers how far the Arts had degenerated from the original sources.

These themes were demonstrated on a grand scale in public buildings and private houses. They became the source of inspiration in the designs of houses cov-

Nineteenth-century turning points

The nineteenth and early twentieth centuries witnessed major advances in housing conditions and a whole range of legislation and inventions that revolutionized the way many people lived. There were advances in heating and lighting, better sanitation and improved transport. Here are some of the key dates:

1807 National Heat and Light Company set up.

1810 Pall Mall becomes first street to be gaslit.

1820s Cast-iron pipes begin to replace wooden ones. Gas meters become available.

1832 Development of plate glass.

1839 Steam-powered multicolour printing by roller invented: very influential for wallpaper manufacture.

1840s Glazed stoneware pipes first used.

1848 Public Health Act creates Public Boards of Health which could make local laws and went on to be highly influential.The threat caused by unhealthy urban living conditions was at last on the agenda.

1850s Damp-proof courses introduced.

1851 Great Exhibition: 10,000 exhibits displayed.
Repeal of windows tax.
Repeal of glass tax.
Repeal of brick tax.

1852 Synthetic dyes introduced (aniline dyes made from coal tar; mauve was the first).

1860 10,000 miles of railway track already laid. Paraffin (petrol-based) oil lamps appear – Argand burner.

1869 Gas-powered geysers are used to heat water conveniently.

1875 Public Health Act: influential and efficient legislation on WCs, sewers, water supplies, etc.

1883 Working Men's Trains Act – a step towards working-class suburbs.

1885 Incandescent gas mantles introduced – twice as bright and not as sooty. Two million gas consumers registered.

1890 Penny-slot gas meters introduced.

1903 First garden city, Letchworth, is built.

1910 Most new houses have electricity.

1919 The Addison Act introduces publicly funded housing for the working classes.

Right **MINERS' HOUSES**
Domestic architecture is so full of contrasts. Here in County Durham in the mining village of Chopwell a row of tightly packed houses are stepped down a steep hill. Each building is the home for two families. Note the pattern of doors and windows: they may be lacking in decorative features but the importance of window sills and doorsteps is clear in this society. Of the five chimney stacks in this range only one still displays a weather-hood instead of a chimney pot.

ering the rest of society throughout the century and up until 1939.

VICTORIAN AND EDWARDIAN HOUSES

The Victorian and Edwardian periods (1837–1910) saw the development of a multiplicity of styles. The shapes and designs of features and decorations borrowed from many periods and sources, both European and further afield.

Houses that had previously reflected status by size and the level of modernity now reflected class by stylistic divergence. The poor lived in plain houses derived from the Georgian terraced and detached homes, and the middle and upper classes lived in more elaborately designed houses that portrayed status by their size, decorative features and position in the environment of the developing town or city.

An example is the Enclosure Acts of the mid-eighteenth to mid-nineteenth centuries, which provided farmers with the opportunity to position their home actually on their 'estate' in the manner of the gentry, who had been able to do it for centuries. Some of the farming families who waited until the second half of the nineteenth century before building their elaborate piles certainly proved the old adage that an Englishman's home was his castle.

VICTORIAN VALUES

Some of the very recognizable features of the period were the angled or square window bays rising one or two storeys and topped by a parapet, a balustrade, crenellated battlements or a half-roof rising like a turret top and abutting the main roof.

A CATALOGUE OF DESIGN
As industry and commerce progressed throughout the nineteenth century, it divided and sub-divided society into different layers, particularly among the still-emerging middle class. These houses in Stafford Terrace, Kensington, would look like industrial workers' tenements if it were not for the incredible display of decorative garnishing on the outside. All the dressings are compounds of stone in the manner of Coade stone. There is a marvellous selection of features: dormer windows with segmented pediments behind a balustraded parapet, a regal cornice, flat windows with architraves, flat windows with pediments, balconies, porches and the most powerful of angled-bay windows, all bursting with brackets, balusters and beading.

As for materials, brick was the most common, thanks to the ever-developing railway system, and blue slate became even more popular. If a region had easily accessible stone it was used, but some areas did not start using locally quarried stone for general low-cost housing until there was an excess produced by modern industrial processes. This certainly happened with the Purbeck stone in Dorset and the ironstone measures in south Wales, and may have happened elsewhere.

The 'Battle of the Styles'

The British 'High Victorian' style grew out of numerous revivals of earlier architectural styles. The classical style continued to have its devotees throughout the nineteenth century, but many of the people responsible for the building boom of this period were bored with the regularity and plainness of the Georgian style – particularly the rows of Georgian terraces – and longed for more colour and romance in architecture. Although many of the new industrialists – the nouveau riche – felt comfortable with reinterpreting the classical, many more favoured the more flamboyant mock-Gothic, which seemed to express and display, in architectural details, their success and also linked their new-found status with some mythical medieval lineage.

This 'battle of the styles' between the classical and the Gothic was particularly evident in public buildings – notably in the decision in 1836 to rebuild the Houses of Parliament in the Gothic style, in contrast to the Foreign Office, which is classically inspired. This 'battle' was fought in many towns and cities throughout Britain, particularly in buildings such as hospitals, town halls, museums and schools.

The clash of styles filtered its way through the different levels of architecture, affecting first major country houses and suburban villas and later whole estates. The academics argued that Gothic was more 'pliable' and the classical too 'rigid'. However, most of this was lost on the large number of speculative builders who were responsible for the vast majority of vernacular buildings. They borrowed happily from many styles: often incorporating in the one house details from Gothic, Greek Revival, Tudor, Elizabethan, Rococo and Italianate.

Continental drift

The 1830s saw the development of Italianate features in low-cost houses, such as terraces ending with little square-towered or pavilion-like buildings, round arches and classical motifs. Often the door surrounds were decorated with plain pilasters with stylized leafy capitals, from which arose an arch in brick or rendered cement. They were always very simply done, but based on the elevation of an Arc de Triomphe!

During the century, doorways became recessed to form small porches. The porch itself became decorated with stone or artificial stonework or designs in terracotta. This form continued to be used so often and in so many ways over subsequent years that it eventually became a cliché of suburban design.

Medieval motifs

Old English is another style found at all levels of building, from exclusive detached properties to semi-detached double dwellings and terraced houses. Here the influence on features was medieval, motifs appearing in doors, windows, bays, gables and chimney stacks with a hotchpotch of results.

Innocent, angled-bay windows of suburban streets were capped with castellated parapets, while projecting rainhoods extended above windows in Tudor fashion. The detached house of the village doctor gained turrets with pointed arched windows rising menacingly into the sky; gables were decorated with mock-timber framing and others were shaped and garnished with motifs developed from Jacobean strapwork designs.

Seeing the light

Some important dating features occur with windows. The removal in 1845 of the duty on glass resulted in more windows appearing in middle and upper-level housing (low-cost houses did not have enough wall space for any more).

At about the same time, technical improvements in the making of plate glass allowed for larger panes to be made. The Great Exhibition of 1851 featured the new glass and from then on houses from all periods had glazing bars and small panes replaced with large sheets of the latest window glass. This is particularly noticeable in the professional districts of towns, where one-time town houses have been turned into offices with modern glass below and upper storeys in the earlier multi-glazed form.

Another significant date is about 1880, when sash window frames were strengthened at their corners by slightly extending the vertical stiles to form curved horns.

Redbrick

Red brick became a status material throughout most of the country in the last quarter of the nineteenth century and from then onwards through the Edwardian period. It looks its best in detached and double dwellings; rows and rows of terraced houses, even when the total redness is relieved with stone-coloured dressings, look incredibly boring. In a region where clays produce another colour, the local material is used for three-quarters of the house and imported red brick used on the street façade. (Perversely, some areas with red brick, such as parts of Leicestershire and Lincolnshire, import another coloured brick for the house fronts.)

The whole range of this style is called Redbrick, though a significant type of house within it is more commonly called Queen Anne. The dominant appearance of the Queen Anne house was taken from the compact plan image of the late seventeenth and early eighteenth centuries, both in England and the Continent, and of course they featured the red bricks. These houses can look very attractive with white painted features contrasting with the warm red brick.

Some of the distinctive decorative features and details are: shaped brackets supporting sprocketed eaves, balconies and porches; bellied oriel windows (a bay that does not rise from the ground); vertical ribbing or shafts on walls and the corners of chimney stacks; scroll-shaped pediments in terracotta over windows that have aprons beneath them; sash and mullioned windows, and stained or painted glass in many and various parts of the windows.

SUBURBAN HERITAGE
As the nineteenth century moved into the twentieth century, architects and designers looked for themes and visual ideas to celebrate the new century. Revivalism had brought them into the nineteenth century and so, with great inspirational thought, it took them into the twentieth, albeit differently. Although the styles had separate titles such as Redbrick, Queen Anne and Old English and became part of the Arts and Crafts movement of the 1880s to 1930s, they all mingled from time to time. Here is a typical house in red brick but displaying sixteenth-century chimney stacks and seventeenth-century barge-boarding at its gables and the plan of a medieval manor house in the Old English style, as well as a late twentieth-century conservatory.

The less expensive Redbrick house modifies its features to suit the purchaser's pocket.

ARTS AND CRAFTS STYLE

The Old English and Redbrick styles of the last quarter of the nineteenth century produced a less flamboyant and altogether quieter and more retiring version of themselves. The Arts and Crafts style, which began as early as 1885 and continued into the 1930s, was purposely created by its exponents, yet the appearance of the houses suggests a gentle emergence from them: whereas the Redbrick has a vertical feel to it, the Arts and Crafts tends to spread in an additive manner.

It produced some quite small houses and has a rural look, even when found in an urban suburb. Typical Arts and Crafts cottages of the early twentieth century had a combined kitchen and dining area, and a sitting room. There were small storage closets, and an attached, outside toilet. Upstairs there were three bedrooms, two of them smallish (nowadays, one of them is the bathroom). Their influence on the design of twentieth-century middle and low-cost housing is obvious, though most of the Arts and Crafts houses were designed for the comfortably off.

The general appearance sought was of the antique. They demonstrated a preference for existing materials rather than a change to new, other than favouring pebbledash as a rendering for outer walls. Plain tiles were preferred to slate, although pantiles were also popular; casements replaced sash windows and doorways sheltered beneath porch hoods supported on wall brackets.

GARDEN CITIES AND LOCAL COUNCIL ESTATES

The ideal for improving the lot of the industrial workers and their families was promoted by a number of philanthropic industrialists at the end of the nineteenth century, although it was the twentieth century before they came to fruition. The garden city scheme was conceived by Ebenezer Howard in 1898 and his book, *Tomorrow*, inspired the setting up of the movement. The aim was to provide homes in pleasantly designed houses built in an amenable environment with space and fresh air. Each house had a front and back garden and overlooked or was near to an open green area.

Letchworth was the first of the garden cities in 1903, although the first garden suburb had been built much earlier: Bedford Park, London, began in 1877 to designs by Norman Shaw. Industrial residential areas had also been built at Port Sunlight in 1888 and at Bournville, Birmingham from 1893.

GARDEN CITIES
The idea of improving houses for the working class developed from Ebenezer Howard, and people like him, from the 1890s. These houses in Hampstead Garden Suburb evolved from the designs of Barry Parker and Raymond Unwin in the early 1900s, following on from their work at Letchworth. Here the style is restrained Old English and set such an example to suburban houses in general that in years to come it may even be called timeless.

The designs for these houses followed the themes introduced by the Arts and Crafts movement. The general elevations were of late medieval or early-seventeenth-century proportions applied to semi-detached houses, but with the features of chimney stacks, windows and doors placed in the formal functional positions required by smallish dwellings.

The introduction by the British Government of the Right to Buy Act in the 1970s has meant that most estate houses purchased by the former tenants are now displaying the individuality of ownership. Whereas there had been strict controls on the appearance of such houses, they now have as many different doors and windows, extensions and garages as can be extracted from planning departments. They have also joined the late twentieth-century's Age of the Conservatory. These will be the next houses for house detectives to work on – perhaps sooner than you might think!

CHANGING DISGUISES

Style features allow a householder to show off his or her wealth and, due to the regularity with which they were modernized, should be viewed as corroborative rather than outright evidence. During the television series we witnessed this in Manningtree, where a sixteenth-century owner had built a huge, imposing chimney stack, the ultimate status symbol at the time. In another example at Fulwood near Preston, a self-made man built his own house and decorated it with all the latest wallcoverings, mouldings and stained glass.

In both cases original features have survived, but all too frequently original panelling, windows, fireplaces, wallcoverings, doors and even staircases have been ripped out and replaced with the latest style on the market. However, there is a chance that you will find evidence of an old window or door that has been blocked in, or even remnants of old wallcoverings, so a knowledge of how style features developed is crucial.

One of the keys to successful detective work is recognizing features and being able to tell when they were put in and whether they were part of the original house. In the eighteenth century, many existing houses were 'Georgianized' – given classical proportions, sash windows and a portico door – so be aware of reproductions and imported features.

You should also assess the standing or status of the room when looking at style features. The best rooms in a house, the drawing room or a principal bedroom, had the most money lavished on them in terms of elaborate friezes, fine cornices and elegant fireplaces. As the function of different rooms changed, you may find the best-quality features turn up in surprising places. Large rooms can be divided up into smaller ones and converted to other uses, but evidence of the original room is not always completely erased. The pecking order for interior features even applied to toilet seats: in plush nineteenth-century houses, the family toilet seat was made of highly polished walnut or mahogany, while the servants had to make do with a plain 'scrubbable' in white pine.

This chapter is a summary of the main developments affecting the principal features of a house, so you may find you need to refer to other more specialist books to help you put a precise date to any one detail. If you are planning to restore your house, you will want to look in more depth at the styles and fashions of the period you are aiming for in order to give your rooms an authentic look.

WINDOWS

Strange as it may seem, most early windows did not have glass in them. Although glass was being produced from the thirteenth century, only the windows of the wealthy were glazed before Tudor times because glass was so expensive. Early windows had shutters on the inside and you can sometimes find evidence of where they were attached. Alternatively, openings were covered with vellum or parchment, waxed paper or cloth stretched across a wooden frame.

Early windows were small and basic with vertical stone or, more often, timber mullions separating the lights or individual openings. The mullions helped to support the lintel above the window and also prevented uninvited guests from climbing through. Square mullions were typically set at a diagonal to allow more light to pass through, an effect that was also achieved by putting in splayed reveals, that is, the vertical sides of an opening in a wall for a window (or door).

GLAZED WINDOWS

Glazed windows did not appear in some regions until the seventeenth century, but by the Elizabethan period glass was becoming more widespread. The glass itself came in small diamond or lozenge shapes known as quarries, which were held in place by lead strips or cames.

In wealthier households, mullioned windows became taller and more impressive. Horizontal *transoms* (bars) were used to separate the lights and give the windows greater solidity. People were increasingly at pains to decorate their window frames with tracery and the impression was completed by setting them off in a Tudor arch or a late-Medieval depressed arch. Projecting brickwork, known as *rainhoods*, and other decorative weather moulds above a window were a common feature in the sixteenth and seventeenth centuries. This style developed into a continuous string course in brick or stone extending at the line at the top of windows. A string course should not be confused with a *plat band*, which is a series of two or three courses of brick projecting at the height of each storey.

MULLIONED WINDOW The style of this window is late sixteenth century. Only one of the casements opens and it has been hung vertically to open on hinges. Above the window is a projection called a rainhood or label. An early-sixteenth-century window would have had a slightly arched head.

CASEMENT WINDOWS

A key development in ordinary houses in the sixteenth century was windows that could be opened, or casement windows, which took the form of iron or wooden casements fitted into existing window openings. In the following century, glass became more readily available as production developed in the north-east and north-west of England, with the result that quarries increased in size and the frames of the casement windows were made bigger.

Crown or spun glass, which was blown and spun out into a flat disc, also appeared on the market at this time (see

SACK

Left **PANELLED WALLS**
These can be either partitions, dividing one room from another, or coverings to load-bearing walls, as can be seen here at the sixteenth-century Moseley Old Hall near Wolverhampton. Note that there is structural studwork above the plain panelling.

Chapter 3, p.86). Surprisingly, much seventeenth and eighteenth-century spun glass survives today – you can recognize it by its slightly curved surface and the presence of tiny air bubbles.

Sash windows

Another big turning point came at the end of the seventeenth century, when the new and fashionable sash windows began replacing casement windows. Thought to have originated in the Netherlands, sash windows became a staple of Georgian houses because they fitted in with the classical quest for symmetry. The earliest weighted sash windows had solid wood frames flush with the wall with grooves for the weights.

It was not long before these were replaced by boxed frames, in which the pulleys were set and the weights hung. In some areas, sideways-sliding sash windows, known as Yorkshire windows, were a popular alternative, especially in smaller houses.

The sash went on to become the dominant window design for two centuries or more, but there were enough changes in details to enable a house detective to differentiate between them. The earliest sash windows had many separate panes of glass and the glazing bars were very broad, nearly 2 in (5 cm) across. The window frames were built of local hardwoods such as oak, until softwoods, including fir and pine, were imported from the Baltics in the first half of the eighteenth century. Because these new woods were not as tough, nor as well thought of as oak, they were normally painted white.

Building legislation also affected the exact position of a window in a wall and can be a good clue as to when a window was put in. Because of the risk of fire, regulations were introduced in London in 1705 stipulating that window frames had to be set at least 4 in (10 cm) back from the front of the wall. This created a gap or reveal at right angles to the window which was likewise generally painted white.

At the same time in London, gauged brick arches were built above windows to

a

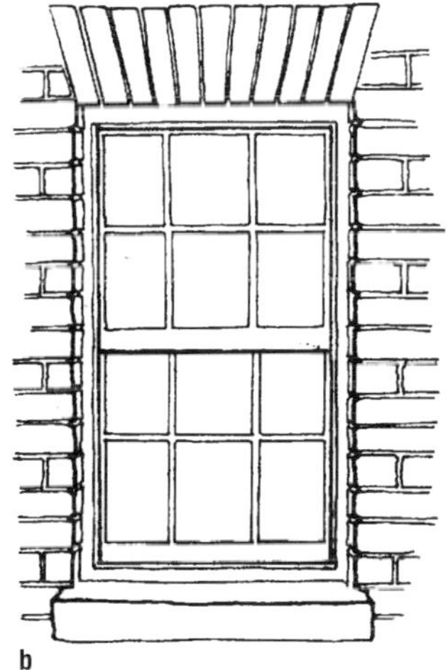
b

c

SASH WINDOWS
a. Early sash windows up to 1710 show an expanse of sash boxes down each side, joined at top and bottom by moulded strips that turned them into architraves flush with the wall surface. Thick glazing bars secured the panes of glass.
b. After 1705, when an ordinance required windows to be set back from the facing surface of the wall, architraves were partly obscured by the brickwork and glazing bars became slimmer.
c. From 1774, another ordinance had the architrave and sash boxes tucked almost out of sight behind the reveal.

replace the old (banned) wooden lintels. The glazing bars were becoming thinner and the number of separate panes was decreasing. However, in rural areas the changes seen in London did not come until later. By 1820, glazing bars were 1/3 in (1 cm) or less in width and the six-over-six type – six panes in each sash – had become standard.

Georgian style

During the Georgian period, window surrounds and frames in modest houses became embellished with classical details plundered from the design and pattern books being used by a new breed of speculative builder. The Venetian or Palladian window, which had been introduced into polite architecture by Inigo Jones a century earlier, began to appear in ordinary houses. The windows were generally square in shape and had three sections, the side ones being narrower than the central arched one. In town houses a higher first floor or *piano nobile* was fashionable (see Chapter 4, p.113) and the height of the windows reflected this. Both on the inside and outside, entablatures were added above the windows (see Chapter 4, p.110).

A dormer with horizontal sliding sash windows, commonly called 'Yorkshire sliding sash', but found everywhere!

From the middle of the eighteenth century the bow window, a shallow projecting window, became popular, especially for shopfronts, and was a feature in Regency houses. The *oriel window*, which projected from an upper floor and was supported on brackets, also came back in from the Tudor period. In larger houses the attic was used as living quarters, usually for servants, and different-shaped dormer windows were built into the slope of the roof, although these were sometimes concealed by a parapet (see p.110). Be careful, though, when trying to date a house by its dormer windows, because they were first used in the sixteenth century when open-hall houses were converted into two-storey buildings and became popular again in the nineteenth century.

It is also worth considering the impact of the window tax, which was introduced in 1696 and was not finally abolished until 1851 (see Chapter 2, p.55). In 1746 the cost of windows was further increased when excise duty was imposed on glass. In many houses from the eighteenth and early nineteenth centuries you can see evidence of windows that were filled in to save money. However, don't go jumping to conclusions: some windows were filled in for different reasons during other periods and others, which had been filled in, have since been reinstated. There was also a habit among Georgian builders of putting in fake windows, which were sometimes even painted, to achieve the desired sense of symmetry.

Bay windows

The nineteenth century was marked by a number of key developments in windows: the widespread use of plate glass; the adoption of arched Gothic styles and the emergence of the bay window in ordinary terraced houses. Plate glass first appeared in 1773, but it was not widely used until 1838 when polished sheet glass became available. This meant that fewer glazing bars were needed and four-paned windows became the norm from the middle of the nineteenth century, often replacing older windows with numerous panes.

NINETEENTH-CENTURY WINDOWS
a. Early-nineteenth-century Regency style bow window with 12-pane sash windows.
b. Gothic window in an ogee curve. There are two vertically hung casement openings.
c. A sash window revealed (set back) from the exterior wall. The large panes of glass are post-1851 when such glass was first marketed, and shaped horns at the ends of the vertical frames have to be later than their introduction in the 1880s.

a

b

c

The new windows had the advantage of letting in more light but they were also less solid. During the 1880s, the side frames of windows were extended to finish as shaped horns to make them stronger. Gothic influences led to there being more arched and pointed windows, but it is the bay window that is most commonly associated with the Victorian period. The style goes back as far as the Elizabethan and Jacobean periods, but was generally found only in smart houses. Country houses and urban villas from the middle of the eighteenth century tended to have substantial bays linked to the house by a moulded cornice or continuous parapet.

A century later, bay windows started to become commonplace in ordinary urban terraces. These were more angular and less curved in shape than their earlier counterparts, but efforts were still made to decorate the surrounds with mouldings of flowers, leaves, serpents, birds or animals. A building act of 1878 can help house detectives date bay windows. The act stipulated that a bay was not to extend more than 3 ft (almost 1 m) from the front of the house and was not to take up more than 60 per cent of a house's total frontage, so it is worth taking some measurements and hoping that the builder stuck to the rules.

Twentieth-century developments

Sash windows continued to dominate in the early twentieth century and, by this time, they generally had just one large pane in each half. The plate glass sash later developed into the modern picture window, a large window with a single pane of glass. The long-lasting habit of putting shutters on the inside of windows began to die out at this stage. However, large flat windows were not ubiquitous: during the 1930s, casement windows with leaded lights were particularly common in suburban mock-Tudor homes. Some of these were decorated in what appears to be stained glass but was in fact painted glass.

Left
ANGLED BAY WINDOWS
A typical bay could be brick or stone. The horizontal lines could represent coloured brickwork or stone mouldings.

Below
GOING TO GREAT PANES
Interior view of the decorative windows with leaded lights and coloured glass in the Edwardian house at Fulwood, Preston.

DOORS

Doors, like windows, were also liable to be replaced as designs improved and fashions changed. For this reason, you would be very lucky to find an original door dating from the Tudor period or earlier; not because the doors were badly built, but because, as the point of entry to a house, it was essential that the door looked the part – and that, inevitably, meant modernization. You are more likely to find old doorframes or even doors hidden away in a part of the interior that is rarely seen by visitors: in the series we discovered a late-medieval doorway between the kitchen and scullery in Church Farm, Bidston.

DOORS AND DOORWAYS Over the centuries doors changed from being crude and heavy to being elegant and yet substantial enough to do their job. This was very much due to improvements in the skill of carpenters and joiners.

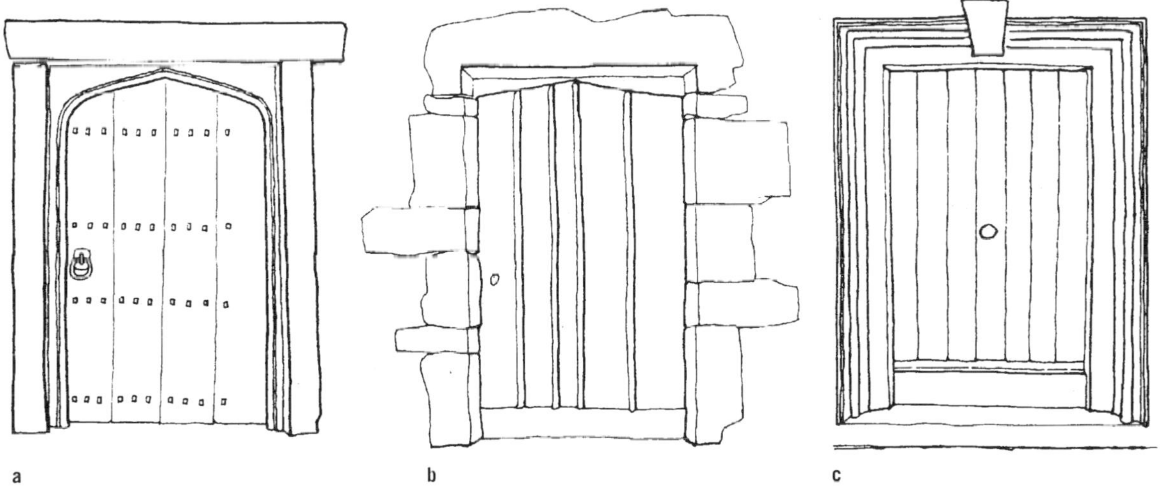

a. A fine fifteenth-century door set into a four-centred arched opening.
b. A sixteenth-century panelled door with decorative vertical ribs set into a crude stone surround. Only the lintel has carving that shows any refinement.
c. A seventeenth-century door with finely moulded architrave displays a sophisticated appearance not found in the other two.

MEDIEVAL DOORWAYS

Medieval doorways like the one in Church Farm were usually pointed, but with time the arch tended to become flatter. Early doors were short, stout, oak-built structures that tended to be hung directly to the walls on sturdy iron pins or in very solid timber frames. The simplest version, the batten door, was merely a row of heavy vertical planks fixed with wooden pegs or nails to a series of horizontal planks across the back. By the seventeenth century, doors in vernacular houses were generally square-headed or had a four-centred arch known as a 'Tudor arch'. These doors were built of lighter boards and were fitted in heavy wooden frames and had large locks.

PANELLED DOORS

A key innovation was the panelled door, which first appeared at the end of the sixteenth century and became widespread during the course of the seventeenth. The number of panels set in the frame varied with time, as did the amount of decoration on them.

Early panelled doors had two raised panels and were moulded or carved to suit florid Baroque tastes. By the late seventeenth century, Renaissance influences were coming to bear on doors and the number of panels increased to six, eight or even 10. However, it was the six-panelled door that became the norm throughout the eighteenth century, a design in which, typically, the top two panels were smaller than the lower ones.

With cheaper softwoods being imported from the Baltics, even the more modest houses could afford panelled doors. In some smaller houses, four-panelled doors were preferred because they were more in proportion with the building. The panels were generally sunk into a rebate – a rectangular recess – and better-quality doors also boasted discrete moulding around the edge of the panels.

Door surrounds

When you are trying to work out the age of a door, the style of the doorcase and surround can provide you with useful clues. Tudor doors tended to have a protruding stone or brick course, known as a *label*, above exterior doorways to prevent water running straight down the wall and onto the door.

Geometrical mouldings surrounded doors in the seventeenth and early eighteenth centuries, but it was the classical style that had a more long-lasting influence. From the mid-eighteenth century, doors were surrounded by pilasters or columns and had a horizontal entablature across the top. Inspired by the new pattern or design books, triangular or curved pediments and a wide range of ornamental details including keystones were popular, even for modest houses, creating a rather grandiose look.

MAKING A GRAND ENTRANCE
Classical influences are shown in the decorative details and the symmetry of these five doorways. Every single feature costs money and so all these elaborately decorated doorways are symbols of success and status.
a. Late seventeenth century – the scale of the whole doorway is larger than the eighteenth-century forms that were to follow. Even cheaper, plainer doors of this period had a greater width.
b. This early-eighteenth-century doorway has fluted columns rising to very stylized leafy capitals that support a segmented arched pediment decorated with a series of carved classical motifs. The fanlight glazing is defined by torch-shaped bars into a ray of pointed arches.

Fanlights

Fanlights above doors first appeared in about 1700 and were a practical and stylish way of getting light into the hallways of houses (see Chapter 4, p.112). Over the centuries fanlights came in a variety of different styles and, from a house detective's point of view, this can provide valuable evidence.

Early fanlights had wooden glazing

bars but these were later replaced with wrought iron or lead. By the end of the eighteenth century, fanlights were being mass-produced in a variety of designs, from straightforward fans to spider's webs and loops, while in the early nineteenth century, fancy heart or honeysuckle motifs were popular.

Porches

Porches can also be dated, but you must beware that they are not later additions.

c. A mid-eighteenth-century doorway with the actual door set back beneath an open triangular pediment to form a porch.
d. Doorway from the second half of the eighteenth century with the door and fanlight set into a continuous arched opening. It is framed between pilasters with ionic capitals that support a horizontal entablature that has a triangular pediment rising from it.

was in fashion. A series of Buildings Acts in London in the eighteenth century meant that timber was used less and less for facades and the surrounding brick or stonework became the focus of ornamental work.

Victorian doorways

There were further developments in the size of doors and the style of their surrounds during the Victorian period. In towns, the advent of villas led to wider

The porch evolved from the need to protect a doorway from the weather. Initially, a short lean-to roof on posts or brackets was used to keep off the wind and rain. By the turn of the eighteenth century this had evolved into a flat classical doorhood, supported by console brackets and often beautifully moulded or carved. A century or so later, the rather less practical ornamental cast-iron or trellis porch

e. A cast-iron porch with a curved canopy of thinly pressed metal sheeting creates a decorative fretwork of patterned shapes as it stands at the top of railing-lined steps. Here the style is mid-nineteenth century.

doorways with windows on either side. By this stage, porches were commonplace. The mechanization of door production led to thicker, heavier doors and the classical requirement that a door's height should be twice its width was not as strictly adhered to as before.

Many upmarket new houses had a raised ground floor above a basement and the front door was reached by climbing a

DECORATIVE DOORS
An added refinement to late-nineteenth-century door panelling was the insertion of figurative and organic decorations. These designs could be carried out in a composition plaster such as anaglypta, or thin sheets of moulded metal.

flight of steps. The Gothic style also proved influential and coloured brick or carved stone were used for both door and window surrounds. The wood was grained artificially to imitate oak and add to the sought-after medieval look.

From the middle of the nineteenth century, the building boom in the new suburbs brought a new arrangement for doors in terraces. Row after row of new housing was being put up for artisans and workers following a pattern of window/door, door/window, window/door, etc, right along a street. Some terraced houses were purpose-built as flats and had two doors side by side on the ground floor.

By the end of the century, even the most modest houses had tiled paths leading to a small arched or pointed porch supported by a column. The top of the column was often decorated with a variety of mouldings featuring monkeys, snakes, fruits, flowers etc. Most doors by this stage were of the four-panel variety and had a rectangular window above them, often in stained glass, to allow light into the hallway. By the end of the century, it was fashionable for doors to have stained glass panels built into them. The designs ranged from the subtle colours of the Arts and Crafts movement to the curvilinear Art Nouveau patterns at the end of the century.

Door furniture

Until about 1700, door furniture – for example, the strap hinges characteristic of batten doors – was made of wrought iron by a local blacksmith. Early external doors had no handles and were kept closed at night by a wooden latch on the inside. A basic iron latch then became common until it was superseded by the brass rim lock in the mid-seventeenth century. In the late eighteenth century, cast iron became widely available and began to replace wrought iron.

Door knockers were first used around 1700 and were made initially of wrought iron or brass and decorated according to the prevailing taste. By the eighteenth century, their use was widespread. Animal heads and dolphins were popular, while an S-shaped door knocker was common in Georgian times.

On the best doors, keyholes came with elaborate escutcheons (a plate surrounding the keyhole) while decorative finger panels, usually rectangular plates of brass, were used to prevent the paintwork from marking.

Brass was not widely used for knobs and knockers before the nineteenth century. Even during the Regency period, cast iron was preferred. It was not until Victorian times that houses were lavishly adorned with brass knobs, by which time bells with pulls were beginning to replace knockers. The most common bell pulls were circular knobs set into a brass dish.

Letterplates, or letterboxes, first appeared in 1840 when the penny post was introduced. They can be distinguished from their modern-day counterparts because they were smaller and fitted vertically down the centre of the door. House numbering was introduced at the same time and for the same reason: the numbers were either carved into the door or were made of brass with spikes on the back to keep them in place.

DECORATIVE PORCHES
Artificial stone, such as Coade stone, was first developed in the late eighteenth century, and ever since all manner of compositions have been developed. This is typical of a doorway in which intricately crafted foliage designs are used in panels and capitals.

CHIMNEYS

The chimney has been around for about 900 years, but was not a common feature in vernacular houses until the sixteenth century. Before then, fires were lit in the centre of the main room or hall and the smoke escaped through the roof or a smokehole (see Chapter 4, p.93). This tradition persisted in some rural areas of Scotland until the end of the eighteenth century. There was a reluctance among some people to accept chimneys, which were considered to be unhealthy. It was believed that a daily intake of wood smoke was good for you!

The Romans were thought to have used a basic form of chimney but it was not until the Norman conquest that a 'built-in' wall fireplace and simple tunnel flue system was invented. Few of the early chimneys that have survived are totally original because most have been restored or repaired over the years. Lantern-style chimneys, which had openings for the smoke beneath a conical cap, were a feature of the thirteenth century, but few of these still exist. Fire was a major problem with early chimneys and legislation was introduced in the fourteenth century stipulating that chimneys must be built of stone, brick or plaster and not timber.

Stacks of money

The golden age of the chimney really began in the fifteenth century and continued

into the sixteenth century, by which time ordinary homes were provided with chimney stacks. The development of the chimney directly influenced the way houses were built and how people lived in them. The open-hall plan was no longer necessary and second storeys could be added throughout the house. Some early chimney stacks projected out from the end of a gable wall, but were later incorporated into the wall itself, while others were placed in the centre of the house.

Merchants and wealthy farmers used chimneys to show off their status and Tudor chimneys are renowned for their fine moulded brickwork. Builders exploited the decorative quality of Tudor bricks, which came in many different colours: oranges, reds, blues, purples, browns and blacks. By the end of the sixteenth century, the shafts themselves were finely crafted in a variety of shapes: spiral, octagonal, fluted, hexagonal, fluted, circular and rectangular of course. The stacks themselves were tall, imposing and well proportioned, and sometimes boasted numerous shafts with their brickwork caps joined together.

STACKS CAP A BUILDING
Improvements in brick-making from the late fifteenth century saw chimney stacks move from being functional and status symbols to functional and decorative features. Some, the poorer cousins of these striking chimney stacks, always remained basically functional.
a. The late-fifteenth- and sixteenth-century stack often appears as a cluster of angled shafts, some plain, some decorated. However many shafts rose from the stack, it would be unusual for more than two to have flues actually rising from fireplaces.
b. A refinement occurs during the second half of the seventeenth century. This example is typical of a popular type with its rectangular stack decoration with an arched pattern.
c. Perhaps the most common was this purely functional type of stack, to be found from the seventeenth and early eighteenth centuries, which rises to a slightly splayed top. Nowadays they can be found sporting chimney pots.

As a house detective you should be suspicious when you see a considerable number of shafts because some of these may be decorative and not serve any practical purpose. While the most elaborate chimneys sat proudly on top of manor houses or stately homes, the humbler homes of merchants or farmers also sported large flamboyant stacks that dominated the skyline.

Another useful guide to a house's size and affluence is the hearth tax, introduced by Charles II in 1662, which can even help you find the name of the house's original owner (see Chapter 2, p.55). However, you have to remember that the tax was levied on 'each fire, hearth or stove' and not on the chimney itself, so dummy stacks did not bear the tax. The tax itself was deeply unpopular and was abolished in 1689.

THE RELEGATION OF CHIMNEYS

By the late seventeenth century, chimneys were becoming smaller, both for practical and aesthetic reasons. Coal, which was replacing wood as the main fuel, could be burned in smaller grates, while Renaissance influence on building led to tall, slender, classically symmetrical shafts, sometimes with entablature.

As the Georgian period progressed, the chimney was relegated as an important design feature in house building and in some cases efforts were made to conceal stacks behind a surrounding balustrade or cornice. Georgian architects were keen to lose the central stack because it placed constraints on the internal layout and, worse still, ruined the symmetry of a house. For this reason chimneys were located at a gable end or were set above the eaves on external walls.

Chimney pots

By the late eighteenth century, ready-made chimney pots were being produced, which improved the circulation of air and helped inefficient flues clear the acrid smoke from coal. Previously, slits in the stack were designed to let the smoke escape and, from the sixteenth century, some stacks had pots or were capped with stone slates to help draw the fire. Long 'tallboys' chimney pots, up to 6 ft 6 in (2 m) high, were introduced in the late eighteenth century in an effort to create more draught and solve the problem of smoke.

d. Eighteenth-century chimney stacks are of elegant proportions, usually decorated at or near the top with projecting string courses with classical motifs. Here we have a course of modillions. Although constructed in brick they are often cased in a stone ashlaring.
e. Chimney pots, as we recognize them today, were created around the 1790s. They produced a better updraught and hopefully prevented too much smoke drifting out into a room. This stack is typical of the late nineteenth and first half of the twentieth centuries.
f. An example of a nineteenth-century stack in a Tudor revival style. The shafts with their decorative brick or terracotta work can look very authentic. However, the moulded caps at the top and the material quality of the bricks at the stack as it appears on the roof will usually give the game away. Decoration as shown here will confirm it as revival.

Victorian chimneys

As with other features, the Victorian period witnessed an eclectic range of chimney designs, ranging from tasteful and well-proportioned shafts to massive, simple stacks with many flues and Gothick revival masonry stacks. Some of the latter are difficult to distinguish from authentic medieval chimneys, but relatively few have survived because stone is not as fireproof or durable as brick.

Many Victorian chimneys were dominated by a variety of different chimney pots and galvanized cowls, or hooded tops, in weird shapes and sizes. The urban skyline became a forest of different chimneys and pots, as terrace after terrace stretched into the distance. In sharp contrast to this were the unique, fanciful chimneys found on the so-called *cottage*

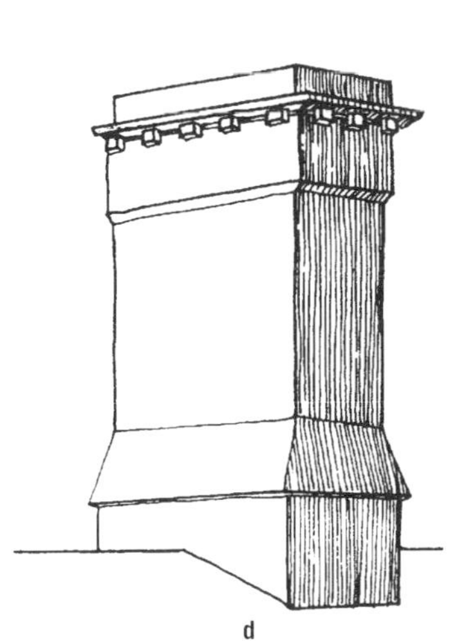
d

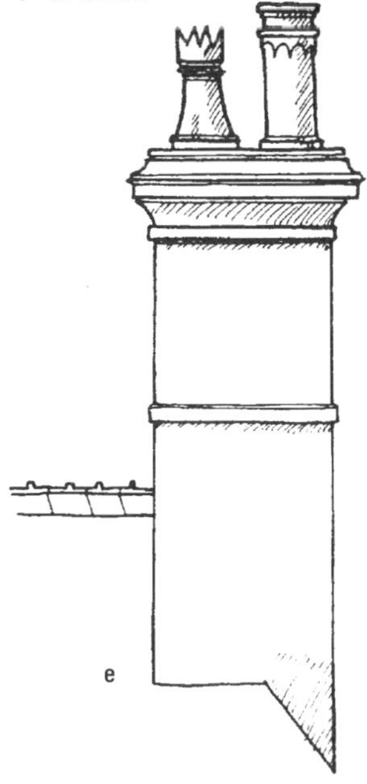
e

f

THE LIVING ROOM
In some large houses, working out the use of each room becomes an exercise in social expertise. However, in rooms such as this one displayed at the Tenement House in Glasgow, the whole business of living took place.

ornés, which were asymmetrical, rustic thatched buildings inspired by the Picturesque movement of the late eighteenth and early nineteenth century.

FIREPLACES

Fireplaces did not become a common feature in vernacular houses until the sixteenth century. The earliest ones were large with substantial stone or timber lintels that were sometimes moulded and shaped into a flattened version of a Tudor arch. As previously mentioned, they were usually located in the centre of the house because they were the only source of heat. Some early fireplaces were even built of timber in more modest houses, a very crude form of fireproofing being provided by a coat of plaster or mortar.

These fireplaces had to be large

EARLY CHIMNEY PIECES
A chimney piece generally refers to a fireplace that is either large or elaborate and dates before the mid-eighteenth century.
a. A chimney piece without much style, this is just a basic shape in local stone. The moulding on the side pieces date it to the early seventeenth century and we would expect to find, out of sight, a brick flue.
b. This brick chimney piece is the oldest of the three. It dates conservatively to the early sixteenth century and is comparatively small. Unlike the inglenook below, you would not want to sit in it! The back is curved and rendered over with a hard mortar, although many of this type reveal the brickwork.
c. A typical wide seventeenth-century inglenook, it has a central area backed with a herringbone pattern of high-fired, reduced, and therefore heat-resistant, bricks. There is a ledge to support firedogs and cooking equipment and a niche for a salt cupboard. Recesses on either side allow for sitting or for the storing of logs.

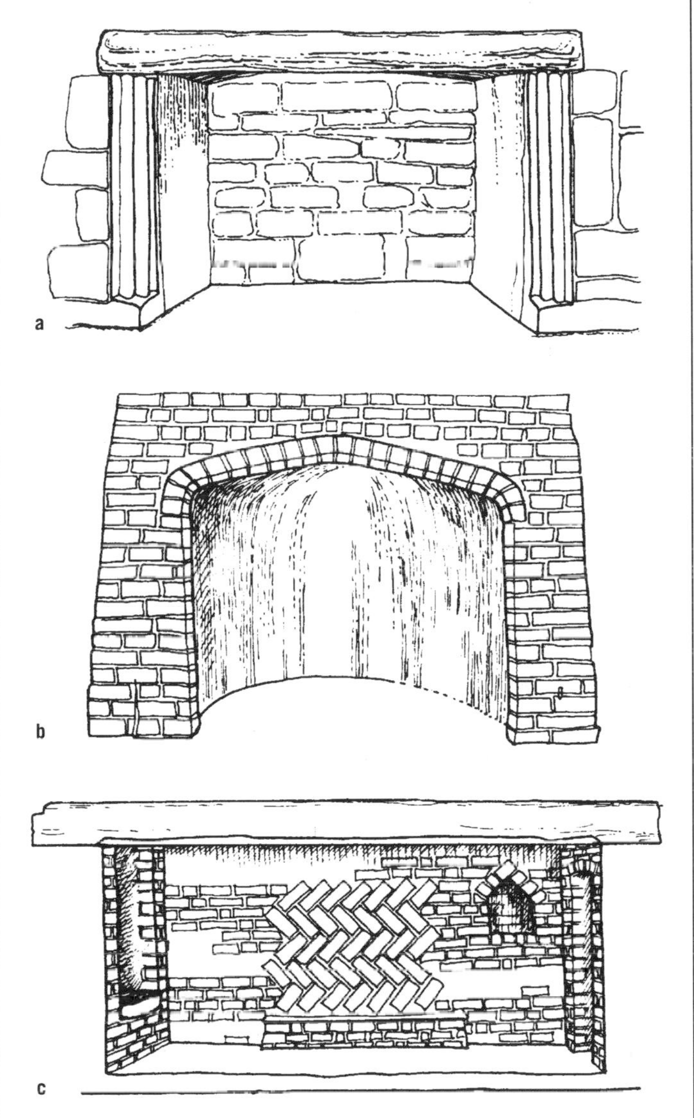

enough to burn huge logs, which were placed in a pair of raised iron bars called *firedogs* and they would generally have had an inglenook, which was almost a room in itself where people could gather snugly around the fire and avoid draughts. Expansive hoods were often set in the wall above the fire and supported by either *piers* (solid vertical masonry) or a stone lintel bracket.

Sometimes a bread oven was built into the wall around the fireplace, but if you discover one of these you should check the brickwork to ensure that it is not a later addition. Take heed also that inglenook fireplaces are not necessarily early features: in some rural areas the inglenook was still common well into the nineteenth century and the style also enjoyed a revival after the First World War.

Later chimney pieces

HEATING AND COOKING
The decorative features on a chimney piece will reflect the style of the period. Earlier fashions in revival designs will be found, but then remember, no one datable feature confirms the date of a building. Successful dating requires a succession of supporting features.

a. Seventeenth-century chimney piece with refined stonework in bolection moulding (inset shows a typical section).

b. An early-eighteenth-century chimney piece with the mantle revealed as a decorative cornice. The frieze has a heraldic device with extending baroque leaf-shapes and the fire basket continues the leafy theme.

c. The classical form and motifs are continued through the mid-eighteenth century, but introduces elegance in proportion and more restrained decoration.

d. An Adam-style fireplace reveals the use of refined motifs, notably the honeysuckle, in linear patterns set in the spaces of panels. The fire baskets and grates of this type echo the themes.

e. A very plain nineteenth-century fireplace with wood or stone surrounds on a brick structure. It has a cast-iron hearth. A slight touch of the medieval is given by the spear-points and the smokehood.

f. A nineteenth-century kitchen range with surrounds in Coade stone or actual stone. Such chimney pieces can be large and wide; occasionally the range has been removed in the late twentieth century and the unit has been converted into an inglenook!

g. By the end of the nineteenth century it became popular to introduce tile surrounds. This one is early twentieth century and reflects the Art Nouveau style.

Changes in design

As a general rule, fireplaces became smaller as burning fuels changed and technology improved. Over the years, most early fireplaces have been replaced by an up-to-date version. We encountered this at Bidston in Merseyside, where an inglenook fireplace had been filled in with no fewer than five different designs over the centuries.

The two main factors that influenced the relegation of chimneys in the late seventeenth century – coal and classicalism (see pp.140–141) – equally affected the hearth, resulting in smaller, more refined and sophisticated fireplaces that had a central role in achieving the desired symmetry in a room. Early Georgian fireplaces tended to have columns or pilasters on either side and classical pediments in the place of a mantelshelf. Those in wealthier houses were built of marble or carved stone, while in ordinary homes imitation Coade stone, plaster and even painted wood was used for the surrounds.

Likewise, the location of fireplaces also changed because the old-fashioned central chimney ruined the classical proportions of a house. Fireplaces were placed at the four corners of a house or inserted into a gable wall.

Improvements in the design and efficiency of fireplaces in the late eighteenth century meant that the hearth was able to become still smaller. The Rumford fireplace, which threw more heat back out, encroached further into the room and had an angled back and sides. Mass-produced marble and cast-iron fire surrounds also became widespread in Victorian drawing rooms.

The nineteenth century brought considerable developments in terms of style: from the genteel and compact Regency look through to the imitation of the medieval Gothic style and the fashion for more heavily ornamented fireplaces at the end of the century. From the 1860s, tiles were introduced into the cast-iron inserts on either side of the fire and tiled hoods were also common. You should be able to identify the tiles by referring to specialist books and put a date to them, with the proviso of course that they are original to the house. Art Nouveau tiles from the turn of the century are instantly recognizable by their graceful curving motifs.

Fireplace designs had evolved yet again by the late nineteenth century, the Arts and Crafts movement harking back to wide hooded hearths with stone frames and wood surrounds. Otherwise, the trend was towards ever-smaller fireplaces with surrounds in painted pine or slate, marble being increasingly expensive. In Victorian houses, the style of the fireplace depended on the status of the room. In the reception rooms, hearths were often grand in their ornamentation, while in servants' quarters and smaller rooms they were very simple, often with cast-iron surrounds that were frequently painted white.

Kitchen ranges

The eighteenth and nineteenth centuries also saw advances in cooking facilities in fireplaces. The kitchen range with a combined iron oven and grate first appeared in about 1770. In 1802, the closed range was introduced, in which the grate was covered by a hot-plate. This was superseded during the 1820s by the 'Leamington kitchener', which comprised two ovens and a water boiler. By 1815, a freestanding portable range, a forerunner of the twentieth-century Aga, had also been patented.

STAIRS

The earliest stairs were really just ladders, which were used to reach first-floor rooms in late-medieval hall-houses. Stone spiral staircases were built into walls or on the outside of buildings in some higher status buildings. The first wooden stairs as such appeared in the sixteenth century and were merely solid blocks of wood placed against a wall, with simple panelling on the open side.

As more and more houses became two-storeyed, turnpike or newel stairs developed: these were a stone or timber spiral that met in a central post or *newel*. These staircases were often inserted next to a chimney stack or built into the thickness of a wall. In highland areas, stone stair turrets, which projected from the façade, were a popular alternative. Steep spiral staircases continued to be built in small houses until the nineteenth century.

FRAMED STAIRS

A major development came in the late sixteenth and early seventeenth century with the emergence of framed stairs with treads and risers. These were much heavier than modern stairs and tended to be built of oak.

This breakthrough paved the way for straight-flight and dogleg stairs that had a 180-degree turn at a half-landing. Both of these types of stairs used the closed-string technique, that is, the treads and risers were framed into and hidden behind the strings, or outer framing

Early staircases

A variation on the theme of the ladder was to support triangular-sectioned blocks of wood and secure them to long stretchers of timber set at a suitable angle for a staircase.

Turreted staircases have the treads shaped from solid stone or wood and built out from the curving wall to be morticed or slotted into the central newel post. When carried out in brick, the operation requires the extra support of vaulting beneath the stairs.

members. The newel posts, handrails, balusters and capping to the strings were often elaborately carved and moulded. A circular acorn shape was a popular ornament for newel posts, although in higher-status houses where the staircase had become an important focus, heraldic beasts sat proudly on top of the post. Sometimes the balusters were replaced with ornamental carved panels, which cased in the stairs up to the handrail.

A further development was the open-well stair where the two flights were separated to give a more spacious effect. In some larger houses, the stairs went up around the four sides of a square stairwell.

Cut-string stairs

In the eighteenth century, the cut-string stair took over from the closed-string stair in most houses. The string was cut away to allow the tread to project slightly beyond it and capped with a nosing. In other words, the individual treads were visible from the side of the staircase.

During the Georgian period, classical influences led to changes in the style of staircases, which became more refined and less chunky than their earlier counterparts. The newel post had a less important role and the balusters became lighter and were fluted or vase-shaped. The barleysugar twist, which had first appeared in about 1690, continued to be popular for balusters for most of the century. Wrought-iron balusters were also fashionable and, as time passed, they tended to become thinner and simpler in design, culminating in the Regency period's taste for simple, slender and square iron balusters. The handrails became narrower and continued over the

Later staircases

An early-seventeenth-century staircase where decoration enhances function. The balusters are shaped from flat pieces of wood and set between the handrail or banister and the string course that supports the stairs. It is called a closed-string because it hides the treads.

Closed-strings can be found in the eighteenth century, but so could open or cut-strings. Here the riser and tread of each stop of the staircase is defined. In this 1720 example the balusters have been turned and decorated with different designs.

top of the newel and were often finished with a scroll or wreath.

Oak was appearing less by this period: mahogany was widely used for the handrail, while the rest of the stairs tended to be made of imported soft woods, like pine, which was always painted because it was considered to be a cheap and nasty wood.

New steps

During the Victorian period, closed-string staircases virtually died out and the

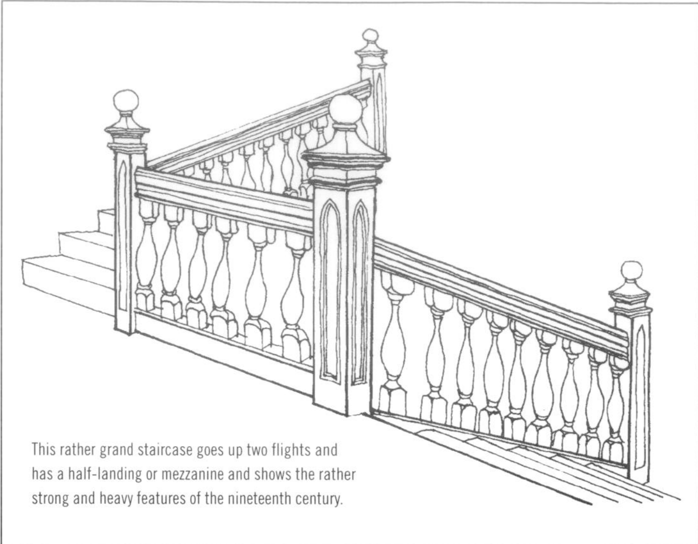

This rather grand staircase goes up two flights and has a half-landing or mezzanine and shows the rather strong and heavy features of the nineteenth century.

balusters, which were often just square sectioned wooden bars, rested directly on the stairs themselves. In the more expensive houses there were three balusters per stair, while in ordinary houses there were two. In some houses, efforts were made to decorate the staircase: a moulded nose running along the exposed sides of the treads was a popular feature and the acorn was revived as a motif for newel posts.

While the general trend was for simpler staircases, there were revivals of traditional, more elaborate staircases by the Arts and Crafts movement in the late nineteenth century and also during the Edwardian period. There was a good example of the latter in the TV series at Mulberry Cottage, Swanage, which dated from the turn of the century.

WOODWORK AND PLASTERWORK

A range of different wood and plaster ornamentation has been used in vernacular houses over the centuries and, where it has survived, it can be a useful way of dating parts of a house. However, you must beware of features which have been brought in from elsewhere.

PANELLING

Panelling is a case in point: it has often been introduced into older houses during restoration. Modern machine-made reproductions should be easy to spot, but when it comes to old panelling it is difficult to prove one way or the other whether it is part of the original construction.

Panelling was first used in high-status houses in the Middle Ages, but did not become a feature in vernacular homes until the sixteenth century. However, '*plank and muntin*' partition walls, which were sometimes chamfered or moulded, were a feature of vernacular houses from the fifteenth to the eighteenth century.

Panels were first attached to interior walls to make rooms drier and warmer, but were soon used decoratively. The earliest panelling was made of oak or other hardwoods. The panels themselves were small and the main framing members moulded.

Better quality panelling tended to have raised panels, the centre of which was in line with the face of the framing. The middle of the panels would usually be moulded with a rib and the panels set into a timber sill at the base or a frieze or moulded beam at the top. From this developed the 'linenfold' or wavy woodwork panelling where the panels were carved to look like folded cloth, a style popular in the Tudor and Stuart periods.

From the second half of the seventeenth century, the design of panelling

Panel and beam ornamentation

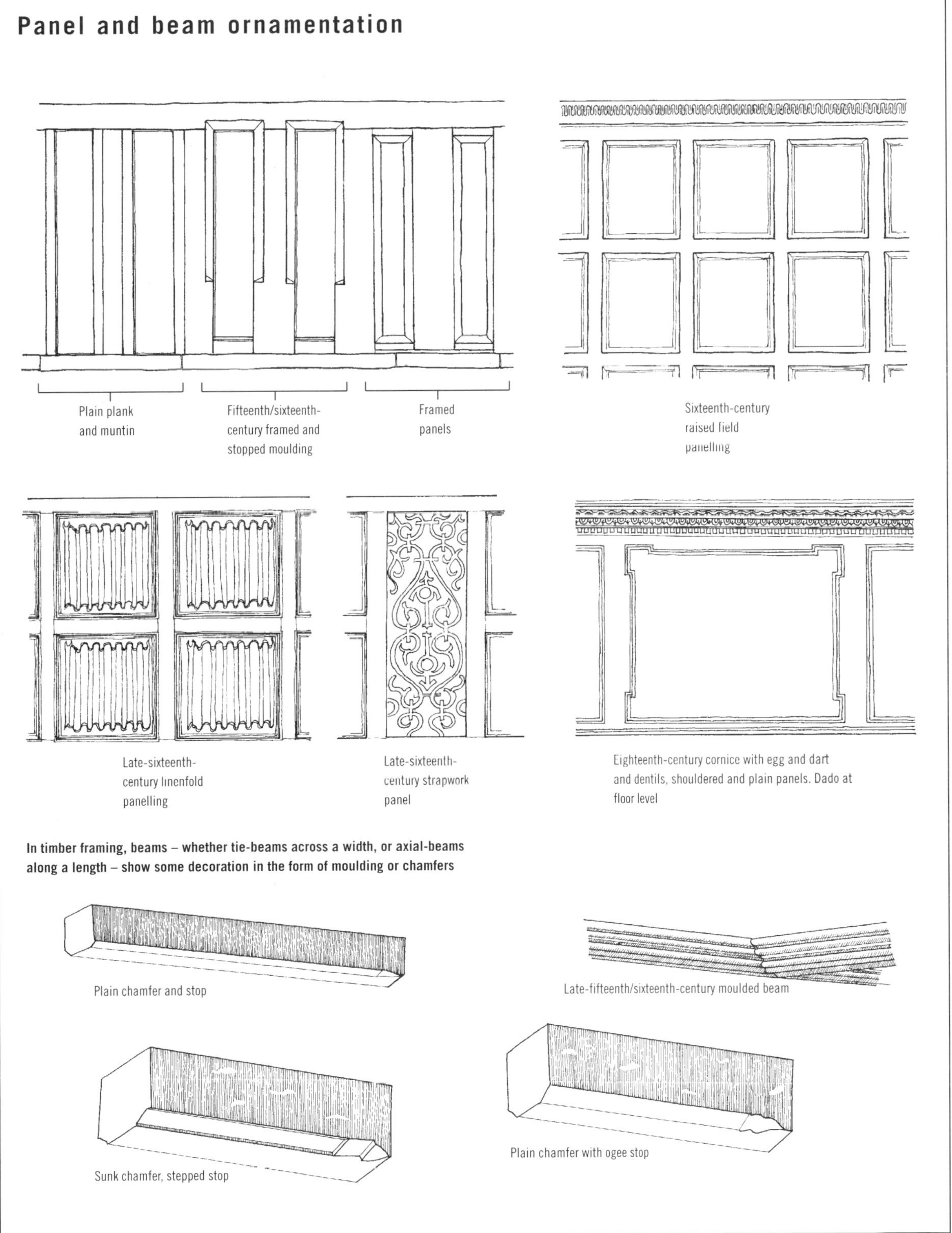

Plain plank and muntin

Fifteenth/sixteenth-century framed and stopped moulding

Framed panels

Sixteenth-century raised field panelling

Late-sixteenth-century linenfold panelling

Late-sixteenth-century strapwork panel

Eighteenth-century cornice with egg and dart and dentils, shouldered and plain panels. Dado at floor level

In timber framing, beams – whether tie-beams across a width, or axial-beams along a length – show some decoration in the form of moulding or chamfers

Plain chamfer and stop

Late-fifteenth/sixteenth-century moulded beam

Sunk chamfer, stepped stop

Plain chamfer with ogee stop

became increasingly influenced by classical styles. The panels themselves increased in size and classical mouldings were introduced. Rooms were viewed as a whole entity and the relative proportions of the skirting, dado, upper wall area and cornice were crucial. Imported softwoods began to take over from oak and for this reason panels were generally painted.

By the eighteenth century, mouldings on panelling had become more refined and delicate but, as the century progressed, panelling was overtaken by decorative plasterwork and wallpaper. Panelling did not disappear completely: into the nineteenth century it was fashionable to put in just the dado part of the panelling, while a basic form, called matchboarding, was found in cheaper housing where plain vertical boards were used as a covering for walls.

Plasterwork

Moulded plasterwork and stucco came increasingly to replace panelling in the eighteenth century. However, its history went back at least two centuries earlier than that. In important Tudor and Jacobean houses, exotic plaster friezes showing rural, hunting, mythological and other scenes were fashionable. Pargeting developed in the late sixteenth and early seventeenth century and was found on interior friezes and overmantels (see Chapter 3, p.79). Designs included birds, human figures and fables, as well as herringbone and basketwork patterns.

In medieval vernacular houses, walls were plastered and scenes featuring animals, flowers and people were painted onto the smooth surface. In most cases, these murals will have been covered by plaster, paint, limewash or wallpaper. It is a house detective's dream come true to discover medieval wall paintings: an exquisite mural showing a hunting scene was discovered in the long gallery of an Elizabethan house called Old Hall in South Burlingham, Norfolk.

Elaborate and relief plasterwork

There was a period in the middle of the seventeenth century when plasterwork was basic and functional but, by the end of the century, elaborate plasterwork in classical designs was being applied to ceilings, cornices and friezes. In the early eighteenth century, the Palladian use of plaster wall panels and framed decoration with swagged surrounds became fashionable in the houses of the well-to-do.

Early plaster was made of a mixture of lime, earth and hair and supported on laths or wattle. By the eighteenth century, new materials like stucco, papier-mâché and Roman cement were used for classical mouldings. In Georgian houses right across the social scale, relief plasterwork was highly popular: the designs included birds in flight, clouds and borders of acanthus leaves.

In polite circles during the Regency period there was a reaction against heavy ornamentation, but the burgeoning middle classes – the new money – had an unquenchable thirst for profuse decoration. Their ceilings were stuccoed and painted with landscapes and varied mythical scenes. Friezes and cornices were cast in moulds. Specific designs were borrowed from the past and there was a great revival of interest in classical decorative features.

NAMES TO CONJURE WITH

Some key figures who have helped change the way we live in houses:

1 INIGO JONES (1573–1652): He was the first great British architect and is credited with introducing classical styles to this country on his return from travelling in Italy. While his influence was on polite architecture, his work filtered downwards and, by the eighteenth century, ordinary houses began to take on a classical look.

2 FRANÇOIS MANSART (1598–1666): A French architect, he designed a double sloping roof, known as a Mansard, which permitted rooms to be built in a roof space. In the Georgian period, Mansard roofs were common in larger houses where the servants' living quarters were in the attic.

3 PRINCE RUPERT (1619–1682): He experimented with methods of controlling smoking fireplaces and invented the baffle flue, which improved the draught in chimneys in the seventeenth century. His ideas were taken up and developed by others after him. (Interestingly, he also led the Cavaliers in the battle at Ledbury in 1642 during the English Civil War.)

4 HORACE WALPOLE (1717–1797): Author, wit and letter-writer who is credited with importing the influential gothic style. After he toured Europe between 1739 and 1741, he built himself a gothic house at Strawberry Hill near Twickenham, Middlesex, with turrets, pointed arches and pinnacles, and inspired an architectural style to challenge classicism. By the beginning of Queen Victoria's reign the gothic look was widespread.

5 ELEANOR COADE (1733–1821): She gave her name to Coade stone, an artificial frost-resistant material which was used to create keystones with masks, textured archways and patterned friezes. She ran a factory in Lambeth producing the stone, a moulded aggregate akin to a concrete paste.

6 BATTY LANGLEY (1696–1751): He popularized the fine details of polite architecture in a series of pattern books. Despite being a plagiarist, his work, including *City and Country Builder's and Workman's Treasury of Designs* (1740) and *The Builder's Jewel* (1741), found favour among a new breed of speculative builders who wanted to dress up their work in fashionable classical details.

7 OWEN JONES (1809–1874): He published the most important work on ornament in the nineteenth century, *The Grammar of Ornament* (1856), which effectively laid down the rules, design, colour, etc. for the second half of the century. He also helped organize the Great Exhibition of 1851 and established the forerunner to the V&A.

8 WILLIAM MORRIS (1834–1896): He was a leading light of the Arts and Crafts movement and a designer of books, typefaces, fabrics and furniture, as well as being a prolific writer and an early socialist. He promoted a rejection of industrial mass production and a nostalgic return to the guilds and craftsmanship of the Middle Ages. Paradoxically, his beautiful work could only be afforded by the wealthy, for whom it was not intended.

9 THOMAS CRAPPER (1837–1910): He unveiled the first flush toilet in 1871, the 'valveless water waste preventor'. This was a vital breakthrough. Existing hopper-type toilets failed to keep the noxious smells of the sewer out of the room, and it was still common for people to leave out their personal 'dust', a quaint Victorian euphemism for excrement, for the dustmen to take away.

10 EBENEZER HOWARD (1850–1928): He was a social visionary and pioneer of the garden city. In his book entitled *Garden Cities of Tomorrow* he advocated the building of medium-sized towns, each with its own factories, planned layout and a surrounding green belt of countryside. As a result, his architects Barry Parker and Raymond Unwin designed the first garden city, Letchworth in Hertfordshire, in 1903. Each house had its own garden and stood in a tree-lined road.

A mania for motifs

A renewed emphasis on craftsmanship came about in the late nineteenth century, along with popular motifs in plaster of acorns, oak trees, squirrels and fairies. By this time, friezes and cornices featuring large, elaborate designs had become common in ordinary houses as new methods of mass production were developed such as flexible gelatine moulds, which appeared in 1840, and lightweight casts, which appeared at the end of the century. The houses we investigated near Preston and in Lincolnshire both had impressive friezes and other decorative plasterwork, typical of the late nineteenth and early twentieth century.

Ceiling roses were another very popular plasterwork feature in the Victorian period. They come in many different designs ranging from simple reliefs to complex and delicately ornamented motifs. The size and the style of the rose really depended on the room it was in, as well as the status of the house.

Skirting boards

Skirting boards first appeared in the eighteenth century, initially on walls that were plastered rather than panelled, and were designed to protect the walls when the floor was being cleaned.

In the smartest houses, marble skirtings were used with marble floors. In ordinary homes skirtings were wooden, though plaster became common in the nineteenth century. In Georgian and Regency homes the skirtings were moulded and beautifully carved to match the other classical features in the room. Victorian and Edwardian skirting boards tended to be much simpler, with basic, if any, moulding. Originally they would have been deep, 10–12 in (25–30 cm), but they became shallower, 2–3 in (5–7.5 cm), as the twentieth century progressed.

Dado rails

Dado rails also have their origins in the panelling of classical architecture. They were placed at the height of the middle rail in panelling, where they served the useful purpose of preventing chairs from scraping the wall. Dado rails matched the skirtings and gave rooms an important sense of symmetry. By the late nineteenth century, dado rails were dying out in most houses, surviving longest in hallways and on staircases.

COLOUR

Colour has two drawbacks for a house detective: firstly, it is highly unlikely that original colours have survived and, where they have, they will have faded. Secondly, specifying a colour for a given period, whether it be Georgian or Victorian, is an inexact science. Certain colour schemes may have been fashionable, but they were rarely universal, and the taste for them did not disappear overnight. As in other areas of interior design, revivals were inevitable. The white-and-gilt schemes associated with British and French drawing rooms of the eighteenth century made comebacks in the two succeeding centuries. We saw this at an Edwardian house we investigated in Fulwood, near Preston.

Changing tastes

It is not easy to generalize about the use of colour because for one thing you must take into account the location of your house. Lighter colours tended to be avoided in nineteenth-century urban dwellings as they became quickly sullied by soot and grime. In rural areas, light colours were more practical.

However, a brief look at how taste in colours has changed over the centuries will help you develop a picture of how your house was decorated. In the early Georgian period, lime-based 'paints', known as distemper, were applied to walls in a variety of muted colours, including drabs, stone colours, pastel blues and greens. The colour was originally a fortuitous by-product of the copper sulphate and iron sulphate that was used to prevent mildew. The precise colour varied from room to room: the drawing room could be pale blue or green, rose pink or stone colour, while the dining room would be dark green. More expensive, so-called 'fancy' colours were used for picking out details on mouldings and gilding was a fashionable technique that was also used.

From about the 1720s, white became important. (In fact, it was more of an off-white shade compared with the bright white used nowadays.) A striking 'smalt' or ultramarine blue became available in the first half of the eighteenth century, but because it was made from crushed glass it was five times as expensive as normal paints. From the middle of the century, a strong 'Prussian' blue provided a cheaper alternative and was fashionable amongst the middle classes.

Classical influences

Classical influences were dominant in the second half of the eighteenth century, when rooms were painted in rich lilacs, bright blues, green, pinks, terracotta reds, or even black. Hallways tended to be a greyish stone colour. Marbling and graining went in and out of fashion during the Georgian period. Early Georgian front doors tended to be white, but later they were painted dark colours: black, dark red, brown or green.

Dark and bold colours

The Regency period was marked by a taste for bright reds, 'a proper tint of crimson' as it was known at the time, and other bold colours, including blues and golds, and greens for libraries. Emblems, palm trees and wreaths were fashionable, as were striped fabrics and designs. In the early years of the Victorian period, walls tended to be light, except in dining rooms and libraries where darker colours were popular.

After about 1850, darker, richer colours were much more widely accepted and were perceived as enhancing the importance of a room: 'Our atmosphere clamours for sealing-wax reds, deep oranges, clear red and beautiful blues,' said Mrs Panton, a writer on interior design, in 1869. Meanwhile, white and other light colours continued to be used in bedrooms. The Victorians were able to indulge their taste in rich and vivid colours thanks to the invention of aniline dyes in the mid-nineteenth century, which allowed the production of sharp yellows, vivid blues and acid greens.

Partly as a reaction to this, the Arts and Crafts movement promoted more muted colours. 'Greenery-yallery', a muted olive-green, was popular among aesthetic designers, particularly for woodwork, while burgundy, hyacinth-blue and old

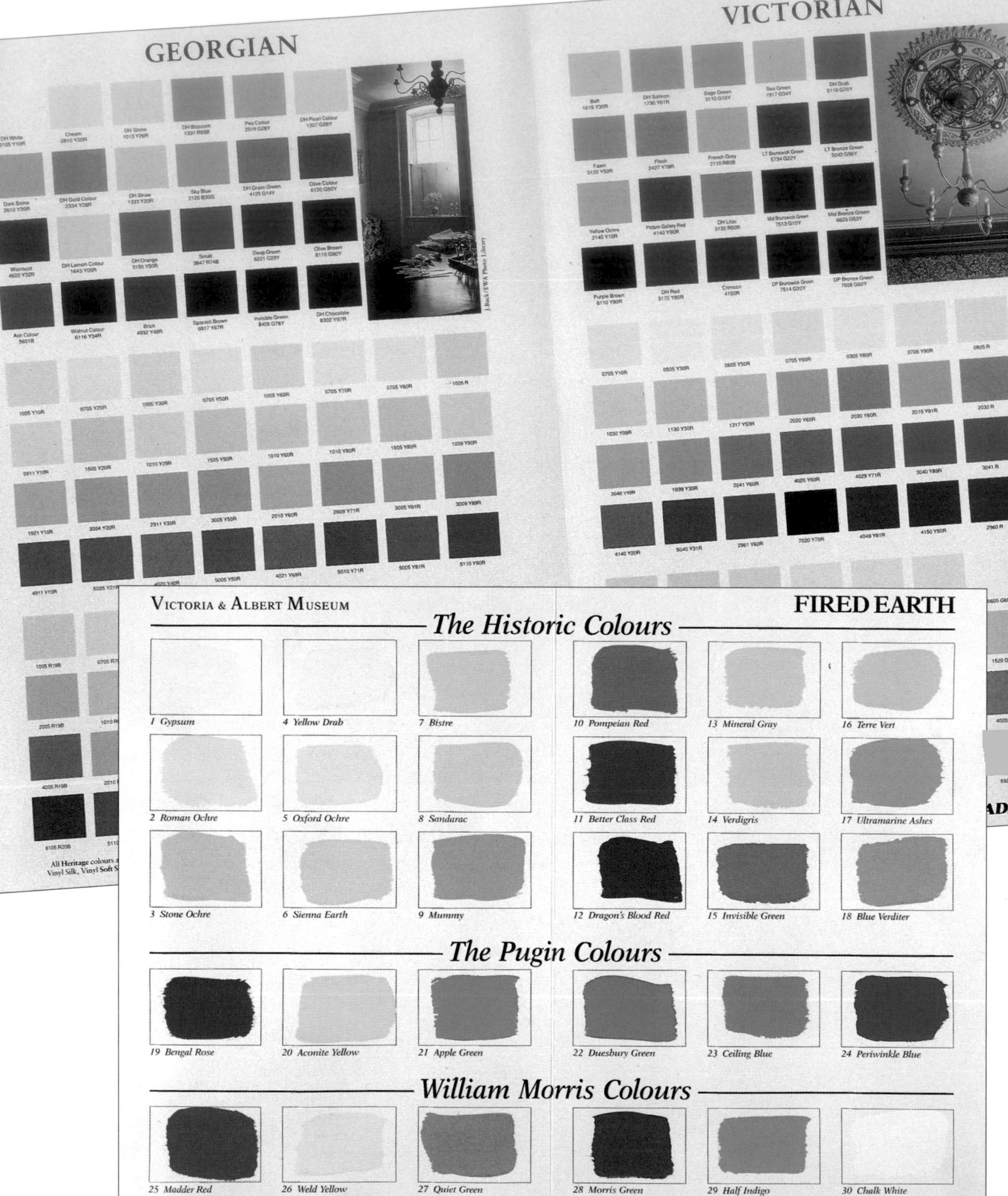
GEORGIAN
VICTORIAN
VICTORIA & ALBERT MUSEUM
FIRED EARTH
The Historic Colours
1 Gypsum
4 Yellow Drab
7 Bistre
10 Pompeian Red
13 Mineral Gray
16 Terre Vert
2 Roman Ochre
5 Oxford Ochre
8 Sandarac
11 Better Class Red
14 Verdigris
17 Ultramarine Ashes
3 Stone Ochre
6 Sienna Earth
9 Mummy
12 Dragon's Blood Red
15 Invisible Green
18 Blue Verditer
The Pugin Colours
19 Bengal Rose
20 Aconite Yellow
21 Apple Green
22 Duesbury Green
23 Ceiling Blue
24 Periwinkle Blue
William Morris Colours
25 Madder Red
26 Weld Yellow
27 Quiet Green
28 Morris Green
29 Half Indigo
30 Chalk White

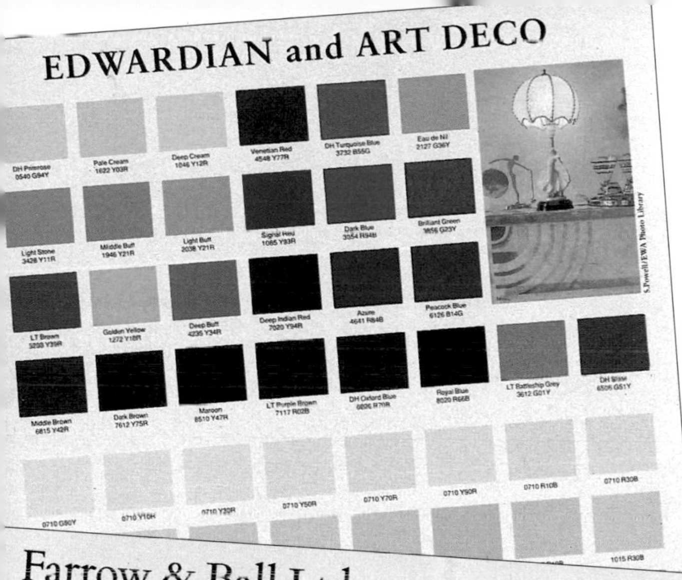

PERIOD PAINTS
Over the last 10 years there has been growing awareness of, and demand for, period paint colours. These are now available from many paint companies, including Dulux, Farrow & Ball and Fired Earth. The range is extensive and in most periods there are light and dark schemes.

Farrow & Ball Ltd — Paints Developed For The National Trust

E WHITE
1

ND
N U/C 1

HITE

ITE

CK
U/C 15

/C 10

/C 15

8 STRING U/C 1

9 LIGHT STONE U/C 15

10 FAWN U/C 15

11 STONE WHITE U/C 15

12 GREEN STONE U/C 18

13 OLIVE U/C 18

14 BERRINGTON BLUE U/C 18

15 BONE U/C 1

16 CORD U/C 15

17 LIGHT GRAY U/C 10

18 FRENCH GRAY U/C 32

19 LICHEN U/C 18

20 BUFF U/C 10

21 OINTMENT PINK U/C 10

22 LIGHT BLUE U/C 22

23 POWDER BLUE U/C 22

24 BALLROOM BLUE U/C 22

25 PIGEON U/C 22

26 DOWN PIPE U/C 26

27 PARMA GRAY U/C 22

28 DEAD SALMON U/C 10

29 SUGAR BAG LIGHT U/C 22

30 HAGUE BLUE U/C 26

31 RAILINGS U/C 26

32 COOKING APPLE GREEN U/C 32

33 PEA GREEN U/C 32

34 CALKE GREEN U/C 32

35 TRUST GREEN U/C 26

36 MAHOGANY U/C 26

AVAILABILITY OF COLOURS

OIL UNDERCOAT is available in 9 colours: Nos. 1, 10, 15, 18, 22, 26, 32, 37, 49.
DEAD FLAT OIL is available in White and all 57 colours.
OIL EGGSHELL is available in White and all 57 colours.
OIL FULL GLOSS is available in White and all 57 colours.
ESTATE EMULSION is available in White and all 57 colours.
OIL BOUND DISTEMPER is available in White and Nos. 1, 2, 3, 4, 8, 15, 16, 21, 22, 23, 27, 29, 32, 37, 44, 50, 51.
SOFT DISTEMPER is available in White and Nos. 1, 3, 4, 8, 15,
EXTERIOR MASONRY PAINT is available in Nos. 1, 3, 4, 6, 9, 15, 21, 37, 44.

We reserve the right at any time to amend any of the above colours.

37 HAY U/C 37

38 BISCUIT U/C 10

39 FOWLER PINK U/C 37

40 MOUSE'S BACK U/C 18

41 DRAB U/C 18

42 PICTURE GALLERY RED U/C 49

43 EATING ROOM RED U/C 49

44 CREAM U/C 1

45 SAND U/C 37

46 WET SAND U/C 37

47 GREEN SMOKE U/C 18

48 FOX RED U/C 49

49 PORPHYRY PINK U/C 49

50 BOOK ROOM RED U/C 49

51 SUDBURY YELLOW U/C

52 STRAW U/C 37

53 CANE U/C 37

54 DAUPHIN U/C 18

55 WAINSCOT U/C 49

56 ETRUSCAN RED U/C 49

57 OFF-BLACK U/C 26

rose were used for walls. Architects of the Gothic Revival carried out a virtually scientific study of colour, perhaps the most influential book on the subject being Owen Jones's *The Grammar of Ornament* (1856).

Paint effects

Paint effects, stencilling, colourwashing, ragging, sponging, stippling and spattering were all popular during this period. It was also common practice to use woodgrain effects to make cheap wood look like oak, mahogany, rosewood, bird's-eye maple or walnut.

House detectives should beware of being fooled by these methods because they can be surprisingly realistic. It came as something of a surprise to the owners of the houses in Preston and Swanage that their panels and doors and staircase were actually painted. One of the main reasons was that pine, which is so popular now, was considered rather downmarket in the last century, so householders went to some lengths to conceal it.

Other common decorative techniques you should look out for are staining, waxing and marbling, such as Sienna, Breche, white, black and gold, porphyry and Verde-antique.

WALLPAPER

Wallpaper goes back as far as the Middle Ages, when religious illustrations and paintings were pasted onto walls as a cheap alternative to tapestries. By the fifteenth century, paper became more widely available and printers began producing simple decorative paper panels. From the sixteenth century, there was small-scale production of designs that emulated textiles in damask or flamestitch. A century later French *dominotiers*, or factory workers who made coloured paper, had become experts at imitating fabrics on paper.

Wallpaper at this time fitted into one of two categories: repeated simple patterns created from one wood block, or

Above and right
HEIGHT OF FASHION
Recreation of flock wallpaper from the mid-nineteenth century by Coles & Son.

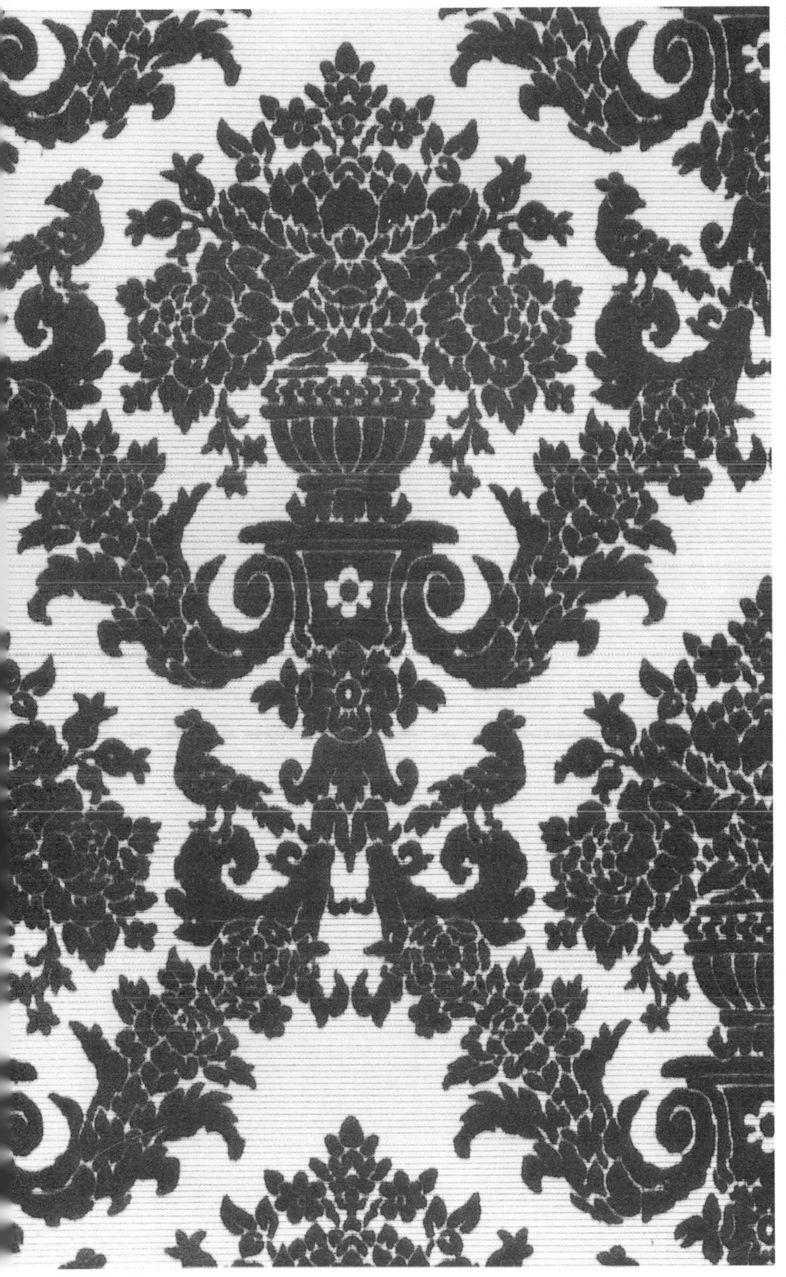

more complicated designs like shields, vases or flowers that were created from several blocks.

Flock wallpaper

In England, the most important single event was the introduction of flock wallpaper, which had its golden period between 1715 and 1745. Flock is the small shearing of wool left over in the manufacture of cloth and it was sprinkled on glued paper to achieve the desired effect. Nowadays people tend to look down their noses at flock wallpaper, but when it first appeared in the early seventeenth century it was highly regarded. No less a man than William Kent used flock wallpaper at Kensington Palace.

Imported wallpaper

By the end of the seventeenth century, sheets of paper were glued together and sold as rolls. Coloured papers became very popular in the eighteenth century and Chinese imported papers were considered to be the height of fashion all over Europe.

A growing amount of legislation reflected the rising importance of wallpaper. In 1712, a tax was levied on paper 'printed, painted or stained to serve as hangings'. France was the principal manufacturer of wallpaper, but the English industry was healthy enough for the government to repeal an act banning imports. By the early nineteenth century, wallpaper tax was so high and so lucrative to the government that in 1806 the falsification of excise duty stamps was added to the list of offences punishable by death.

British designs

As the nineteenth century wore on, British manufacturers looked to produce simple and inexpensive designs so they could reach a wider market and increase their profits. The best quality elaborately patterned scenic papers were still

a

b

c

d

imported from France and were found primarily in the reception rooms and bedrooms of the wealthy. Many of them had sophisticated *trompe l'oeil* effects: often simulations of draped and swagged fabrics such as silk damask.

The lifting of the wallpaper tax in 1836 enabled British producers to once again manufacture colourful and complicated

e

WALLPAPER STYLES
There are a large number of companies producing authentic reproductions of period wallpapers. For example:
a. 'Marivaux' by The Design Archives;
b. 'Octavia' by G. P. & J. Baker;
c. 'Sweet Pea' by Coles & Son;
d. 'Exotic Bird' by Coles & Son;
e. 'Isola Bella' by Zuber;
f. 'Fruit' by William Morris

f

patterns. Technology was improving rapidly: there was increased mechanization and papers could now be applied directly onto improved smooth plaster surfaces. Previously, papers had to be pasted onto canvas stretched over a series of battens fixed to the wall. Strangely enough, people were discouraged from putting up wallpaper in bedrooms because it was thought that bed bugs would seek sanctuary there. Distemper walls or plain panelling was considered to be much more healthy.

One of the most influential wallpaper designers was the renowned British architect, A. W. N. Pugin, who, as well as producing designs for the new Palace of Westminster, came up with several commercial designs for the decorating firm, J. G. Grace and Co. In the next chapter we look more closely at how house detectives can find clues in old wallpaper with the help of specialists on the subject.

CALLING FOR BACK-UP

If you have followed up every lead you can think of and there are still a few loose ends frustrating your investigation, do not despair. There are a number of scientific and forensic techniques that may provide the answers, or you could approach a specialist in the particular subject that has stymied you.

During the television series, we received valuable backup from dendrochronologists and dendrologists, who specialize in dating timber and trees; wallpaper conservationists; local brick experts; a pulse radar team and an expert in stained glass. The approaches we look at in this chapter range from those you can do yourself through to expensive high-tech methods that you would probably only employ if you are about to invest in a major restoration or rebuilding project on your house.

DENDROCHRONOLOGY

Dendrochronology, the science of tree-ring dating, can be very successful in helping you to find out the age of your house. For example, Neil Loader, a dendrochronologist from the Godwin Laboratory in Cambridge who we brought in on our Manningtree investigation, was able to give a precise date, 1483, for the oldest part of the house and enabled us to work out the stages by which the house was built.

A dendrochronologist works by taking samples of cores of wood from beams, wallplates, crucks, braces or other substantial timbers using a drill and a hollow bit, which works in the same way as an apple corer. The core has the diameter of a 5p piece and its length will depend on the size of the timber from which it has been extracted. The process does leave a small hole, but they will try to take their samples from less obvious places and can replace them if you wish. Samples are taken from different parts of the building, as this enables them to check whether all the timbers are the same age (and therefore from the same period).

The date at which the timber was felled is worked out by studying the sequence of wide and narrow rings on the sample. Each ring represents one year in the growth of the tree. The rings are narrow when conditions for growth were poor – for example, because of drought or blight – whereas wide rings indicate a good year when conditions allowed the tree to flourish. In theory, the combination of ring widths should correspond broadly to the prevailing weather conditions during the life of the tree. To be able to date a timber accurately, therefore, a considerable number of rings is needed: 50 or 60 is really the minimum, but 100 or more is ideal.

Having said all this, there is a proviso. Because the ring sequence from the sample is compared with the findings from other timbers tested in the same region, dendrochronology will only be useful to you if there are already sufficient records for your area. Unfortunately, if you live in an area where tree-ring data is limited or non-existent, you will be unable to benefit.

The overall picture is further complicated by other conditions affecting tree growth. For example, in areas like the southeast of England where there was great demand for timber from the Middle Ages, oak trees were grown commercially under favourable conditions over a relatively short period of about 60 years. In such cases you would expect to see a more even distribution of wider rings than on a tree that had seeded itself under natural conditions and had to struggle to grow.

Even if a dendrochronologist does have enough rings in the sample to date the timber in your house, there remains the usual drawback with relying on the evidence from timbers. Timber-framed buildings could be, and quite often were, taken down and moved to another site. Equally, individual parts could be reused elsewhere. For this reason, dendrochronologists will insist on taking a series of samples from the same building to ensure that they are not relying on a stray, unrepresentative timber.

DENDROLOGY

Dendrology is the science of dating living trees. A major advantage for house detectives is that, unlike dendrochronology, which involves experts and fees, you can do it yourself.

As explained in Chapter 1 (pp.28–29), the presence of trees in your garden or in a neighbouring field or garden can be a very useful clue to your house's age and development. Fruit trees, for example, would almost certainly have been planted by former owners, while an avenue of plane trees may represent a former driveway or approach to your house. If there is a very old tree in your garden that seems to predate your house, it could mean that a previous house once existed on the site.

Dendrology is also based on the number of rings in a tree, but unlike dendrochronology it is not necessary to take a core. This was done in the past at the risk of harming the living tree. Until recently, the only other way of calculating the age of large trees was a rather crude and inexact science that involved assuming 1 in (2.5 cm) of growth was equal to one year. However, the Forestry Commission has since devised a new and more accurate method of estimating tree age based on comparing the growth of the tree with that of others of the same species. The information is not yet complete for all trees and all local conditions so any additional data you provide will be welcomed.

All you will need is a tape measure, plus a table of readings and a calculation, which can be obtained from the Forestry Commission (see p.220). First, measure the girth of the tree: this is best done at

ROUND THE MULBERRY BUSH...
Dendrologist John White taking measurements of a mulberry tree in the garden of Mulberry Cottage, Swanage. A few quick calculations later and he was able to conclude that the tree had been planted in 1828.

chest level as long as there are no branches, swellings or abnormal lumps on the tree at that height. You then take your measurement to the tables showing tree age and ring width for the relevant species.

To be able to use the tables effectively, you will need to make some common-sense judgements about the tree's particular growing conditions. Trees grow at different rates depending on whether they are sheltered or exposed, in a sunny aspect or a shaded position. Bear in mind also how that environment might have affected its early growth: for example, a long stem with no branches may mean that the tree was once part of woodland because to survive it would have needed to grow rapidly upwards to reach the light at the canopy.

We put dendrology to good use in our investigation at Mulberry Cottage, Swanage. There was a legend that James I had ordered the planting of mulberry trees in the garden in the early seventeenth century to encourage silkworms and thus produce silk. We invited John White, a Forestry Commission dendrologist, to try and verify this. He was able to scotch the myth immediately, pointing out that the mulberry tree was the wrong variety – it produced black fruit rather than the white kind needed for hungry silkworms! On measuring the tree, he was able to date it at 1828, so with what we already knew from documents we were able to conclude that it had been planted by a woman called Hester Marsh.

RADIOCARBON DATING

Radiocarbon dating can be used to date any organic materials that have gone into the building of your house, including wood, straw, twigs, animal hair, bones or manure. It is a sophisticated method used mainly by archeologists and requires specialized laboratory equipment. As the results are accurate only to within a few decades they should be used in conjunction with other architectural or documentary evidence. There are a number of universities around the country that offer this service to the public but you will have to pay, so ask yourself whether this evidence is a crucial part of the jigsaw.

Right and below
PAPER TRAIL
Examples of Walter Crane wallpaper which came under Allyson McDermott's microscope.

Right **TO DIE FOR...**
A fragment of wallpaper bearing an excise stamp to indicate its authenticity. Such was the popularity of wallpaper that it was taxed from 1712 to 1836. It was originally brought in to finance the war of the Spanish Succession (1701–1714) but proved so lucrative that the government continued the tax long after the war and even legislated against the faking of wallpaper excise stamps as an offence punishable by death.

IDENTIFYING WALLPAPER

Even the tiniest remnant of wallpaper can be a very useful clue, but one that will require forensic backup or in-depth research on your part. As we saw in the previous chapter (pp.156–159), putting paper on walls goes back as far as the sixteenth century and even earlier; however, the production of wallpaper in Britain did not develop on any kind of scale until the nineteenth century, and you are more likely to find examples dating from that period and later.

During the television series we were able to call on the specialist skills of Allyson McDermott of Petworth House, West Sussex, who specializes in the conservation and reproduction of historic wallpaper and other decorative arts. She was able to help in our investigation at Dunsby Fen Farm by dating a tiny fragment of lining paper, while at Fayre Haven in Fulwood, Preston, she successfully restored some damaged anaglypta wallcovering on the staircase.

You may already have had the experience of stripping off what you thought to be one thickness of wallpaper, only to find layer upon layer of old wallpapers underneath. This is because in the past they simply put the new paper on top of the old lot, which can provide great evidence for house detectives.

There is a strong conservation argument for preserving old wall coverings. With the help of modern scientific techniques and trained experts, whole rooms of wallpaper can be treated safely and effectively, either *in situ* or by removing the paper and treating it in a studio. However, you are probably more likely to discover fragments of old paper, usually in places missed by a decorator such as behind a skirting board or radiator. These too can be an important record of the original interior decoration and can be used as the basis for authentic reconstructions.

Polarizing microscopy and various other analytical techniques can be used to help identify pigments, papers, dates and patterns. Bear in mind, though, that many of the colours will have changed considerably over the centuries: sunlight fades sensitive reds and blues; damp affects the bronze powders used to give an impression of gold by turning them green or brown and atmospheric pollutants turn lead white to brown and ultimately black, while acidity from pollutants may change a brilliant azurite to a dull green.

There are numerous clues to look out for when dating wallpaper. A very good one is an excise duty stamp, which was used between 1712 and 1836 when wallpaper was taxed (see Chapter 5, p.157). Others include the size and type of paper and the design, watermarks, methods and materials used in preparation and printing. For example, early wallpaper was made by joining up single sheets of rag paper, which is hand-made from recycled cloth (that is, rag paper) and then placed in a rectangular mould. A ground, or the background colour used to prepare the paper, was made by hand and the design was printed from wooden blocks. This type of wallpaper can be recognized by the depth of the colour. By the mid-nineteenth century, machinery was available to produce continuous rolls of paper, rags were being replaced by woodpulp, and the majority of designs were machine printed. Early machine-printed wallpaper can be identified by the fact that the prints are much thinner than the hand-made variety.

Ideally, you should seek specialist advice, but you can do some background research of your own. If this is a subject which really fascinates you it is worth spending the time to find out more. Several contemporary accounts of wallpaper manufacture and use have survived, the most useful being Dossie's *Handmade to the Arts* from the late eighteenth century and

Andrew Ure's *A Dictionary of Arts Manufacturers and Mines* and Charles Eastlake's *Hints on Household Taste* from the nineteenth century. You would have to contact a good library to locate these three books. These and other valuable documentary sources, including drawings, household accounts, day books, letters, pattern books and catalogues, can be found at The Victoria and Albert Museum, Temple Newsam House, Whitworth Art Gallery, The Mitchell Library in Glasgow, the Public Record Office and possibly your local County Records Office.

SURFACE-PENETRATING (PULSE) RADAR

If you want to find out whether you have a cellar under your house and do not want to take the drastic measure of digging up the floor, it may be worth considering using pulse radar, a technique used increasingly by both the police and archeologists to identify voids, buried objects or underground structures. The principle of the technology is like that of sonar, which detects submerged objects by emitting ultrasonic pulses and monitoring the way they are bounced back. The main difference is that pulse radar actually goes through solid objects.

The pulse radar antenna is moved in a straight line at a constant speed across the surface of the floor and transmits a short pulse of electromagnetic energy into the ground. This produces a multicoloured cross-sectional image of the ground beneath the floor on a computer monitor attached to the radar. The radar detects all changes in 'electrical impedance' in the materials it is passing through – in other words, it reacts differently to different materials. For example, a ceramic jar will give a different reading to the soil or material it is buried in and, on screen, this will appear as a different coloured shape. The survey is carried out systematically, traversing the floor line after line, until three-dimensional images of any objects or structures have been created. It then becomes a question of identifying the shape – if it is curved, for example, it could be part of a culvert, a drainage channel in the floor.

During the investigation into the house in Manningtree High Street, we wanted to confirm that there was a cellar, as had been indicated in the deeds. We were also curious about a local legend, which said that smugglers' tunnels linked up the cellar in this house to others in the town. A Leatherhead-based company called ERA Technology was brought in which had used surface-penetrating radar to assist in archeological digs, as well as the more gruesome task of helping the police locate bodies under the cellar of Fred and Rosemary West's house in Cromwell Road, Gloucester.

The radar came up with a number of accurate readings: it identified a double wooden floor and a stepped structure that could have been stairs or even a tunnel. The survey also showed that if there had been a cellar under that part of the house it had since been filled in. We were able to confirm this for the sake of the cameras by the rather more basic method of digging up the floor, although obviously, as a house detective, you would be seeking to avoid this by using pulse radar in the first place!

High-tech support such as this is expensive, and is only really advisable if

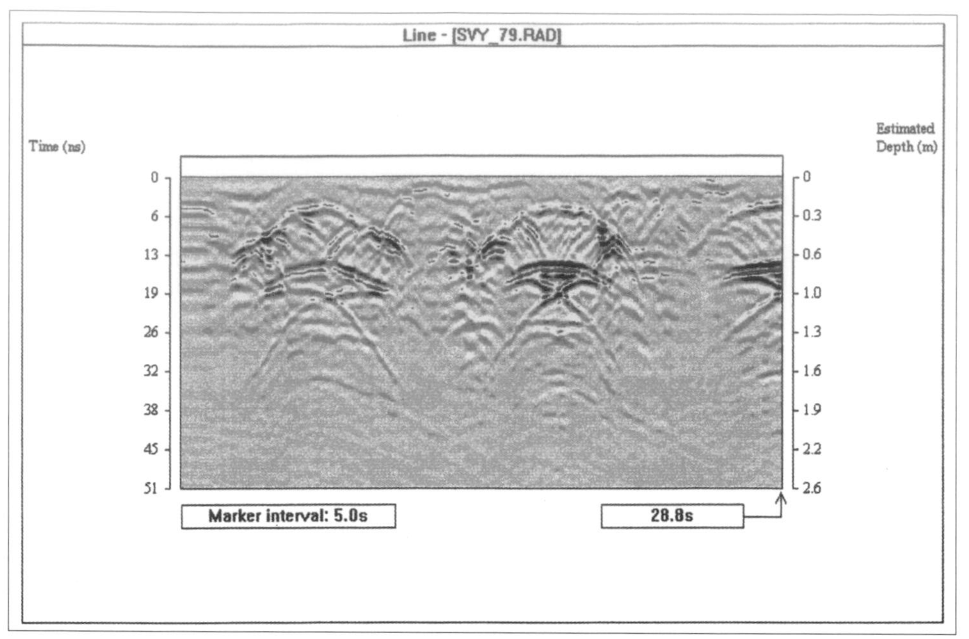

Left
CELLARIUM SECRETS
A computer printout of a pulse-radar survey carried out by ERA Technology at Fountains Abbey in North Yorkshire. The image is a cross-section of what lies below the surface in the cellarium. The horizontal section shows the distance covered at ground level while the vertical section is the depth underground. The curved shapes in red are culverts, or drainage channels.

Below **The cellarium at Fountains Abbey where pulse radar proved a useful tool to archeologists.**

you are planning major restoration work that depends on knowing if there is a cellar. Pulse radar is also very useful if you want to locate structural problems. However, conditions must also be right: the radar picture relies on the strength of the signal, which will be weaker or stronger depending on the conductivity of the soil or material below the ground.

If you are merely inquisitive about whether or not you have a cellar, you may be better advised to take the approach we did in Dunsby Fen, where we drilled a number of exploratory holes in a concrete floor and inserted a long metal probe, which revealed the existence of a void. When we withdrew the probe its tip was damp, which meant that the cellar was infilled with soil.

ENDOSCOPY

Endoscopy, which involves being able to see into areas inaccessible to the naked eye, takes the probe idea one

step further and allows you to investigate cellars without having to dig up the floor and find hidden rooms without having to knock down walls. It is the same technique used by surgeons to allow them to examine internal organs without having to cut open the patient.

The equipment needed varies from a

simple borescope – consisting of a light source and a small-diameter rigid tube with built-in optic and an eye-piece – to complicated systems with a whole range of specialized attachments. The process is simple and virtually non-destructive: for example, to look behind a modern partition wall to see if there is panelling there, all you have to do is drill a hole no more than ½ in (12 mm) in diameter and insert the tube. High-tech endoscopes can be steered to go where you want them to and you can even attach a mini stills or video camera to the end. However, all this can be rather expensive and is only suggested if it can save you money, perhaps by identifying a structural fault or discovering dry rot behind panelling.

INFRA-RED THERMOGRAPHY

Infra-red thermography is highly sophisticated and at the cutting edge of technology. It can be used by house detectives to identify what lies behind the surface and within the fabric of a house. The equipment measures and records minute variations in the infra-red radiation emitted by different structures. For example, it will allow you to see the original timber frame of a building a bit like an X-ray, without having to remove the rendering material. Thermography is very useful and can save you money if you are intending to restore or renovate an old property. It can help locate lintels or structural joints on masonry walls and identify faults like snapped headers in the brickwork.

OTHER SPECIALISTS

There is a whole range of different experts you can turn to for advice. To track them down, you may have to think laterally. For example, when we wanted to find out more about an extraordinary collection of stained glass windows at the house we investigated near Preston, we contacted the glass company Pilkington's, who, it emerged, employ an archivist, Dinah Stobbs. Not only was he able to identify the styles

Above **Block printing of wallpaper using traditional methods. The curved handle is used to apply pressure to the block to ensure a consistency of colour. Any minor gaps are then painted over by hand.**

and types of glass but she also had a pattern book dating from 1896 in which she found an example of embossed glass featuring a similar engraving of a woman (see p.193).

It would be fair to say that whatever the subject, be it bricks, stone, timber, old ovens or stair balusters, there is likely to be someone who has made the study of that feature their life's passion. Because of the huge local and regional diversity in building techniques and styles you may find it difficult to recognize and date the finest details with any accuracy. A local expert should be able to help, so it is worth phoning around societies in your area concerned with vernacular buildings, the local authority planning department, conservation societies and museums and asking them if they know of any experts in the field you are inquiring about. In many regions, including Wiltshire, Wales and the north of England, architectural information is published by local buildings' records groups which make good contacts. You will invariably find that enthusiasts will be more than happy to add your house to their list of case studies, and may even want to publish examples from it.

During our television investigations, we turned to numerous local specialists for advice. In Manningtree, for example, somebody from the county council planning department had a strong personal interest in timber-framed buildings and was able to recognize a particular type of joist. We asked for the opinion of a local brick expert, David Robinson, in the Dunsby Fen case and he was able to date bricks using his knowledge of local clay deposits and production methods.

While there is much practical detective work you can do yourself, it would be a shame to plough a long and lonely furrow without seeking the advice of specialists. How far you go down the forensic route depends on how deep you want to go into the case and how much money you want to spend. If you are planning to use the information you have discovered for restoration purposes, using the latest scientific methods could make financial sense in the long run. If not, don't get carried away: remember that while science can provide valuable backup for house detectives, it is not essential.

DETECTIVE STORIES

The best way to understand how being a house detective works is to study examples of the way the professionals do it. During the BBC series, we solved the mystery of six very different homes. Our investigations took us to six counties with contrasting architectural influences and styles: Essex, Herefordshire, Dorset, Lancashire, Lincolnshire and Merseyside. Four of the houses had their origins in the Middle Ages, but had undergone many changes since; the other two were Victorian and Edwardian. Among the houses were two former farms, an ex-vicarage, two town-centre properties and a suburban one. Each of the cases had their own challenges and surprises, with enough red herrings, myths and contradictions to test the most hardened detective.

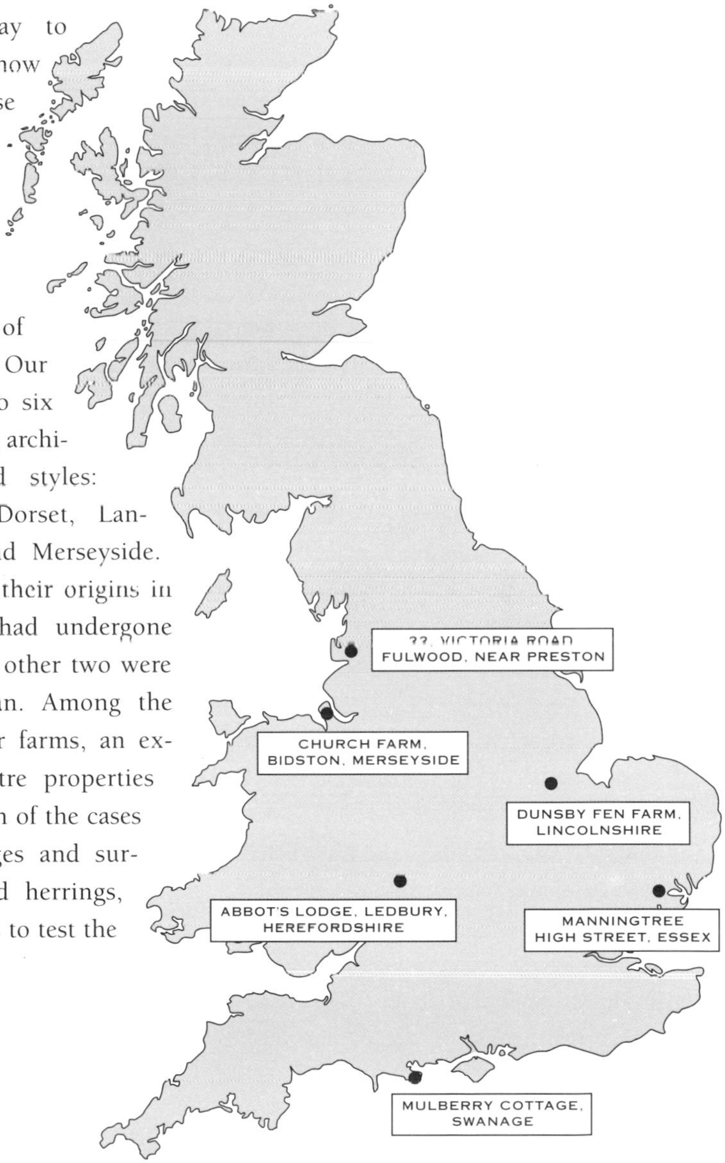

33, VICTORIA ROAD
FULWOOD, NEAR PRESTON

CHURCH FARM,
BIDSTON, MERSEYSIDE

DUNSBY FEN FARM,
LINCOLNSHIRE

ABBOT'S LODGE, LEDBURY,
HEREFORDSHIRE

MANNINGTREE
HIGH STREET, ESSEX

MULBERRY COTTAGE,
SWANAGE

CHURCH FARM, BIDSTON, MERSEYSIDE

'A RAMBLING FARMHOUSE WITH A FASCINATING HIDDEN PAST'

We were invited to look into the mystery of an old farmhouse in the village of Bidston, a few miles south of the River Mersey from Liverpool. While few people live in a 26-room house with such a colourful history, Church Farm is an excellent example to start with because it exemplifies so well what can be discovered by an unstinting approach to house detection. It also demonstrates the sort of difficulties you may come up against in your own work.

Twelve years ago, Church Farm was a virtual ruin. It was then that the O'Brien family stepped in and rescued the farm, which became home to three generations of the same family. The O'Briens wanted to know what the farm had looked like originally and to understand the mysterious maze of small rooms and staircases that made up the house. The farm was an architectural puzzle of the first order. Local architects and historians had already taken a look at the case but were left baffled. There was a local legend that monks had lived at Church Farm in the Middle Ages, but there was no clear evidence to support that. The gauntlet had been thrown down for us.

Approaching Bidston from Liverpool was like stumbling into a rural oasis amid the urban sprawl that has devoured the Wirral peninsula. On the top of the hill sits Bidston Hall, while Church Farm itself is in the heart of the village opposite the Church of St Oswald's. From the

CHURCH FARM, BIDSTON Usually the initial sight of a house can give an idea of the likely date or dates from which it has developed. However, Church Farm immediately stated, 'Early-seventeenth-century features in a stone-built house, maybe, but what are nice mullioned windows like you doing in positions like that?' It was also noted that there is a change in the way the stone courses are laid from the right and the left of the porch.

front, the house looked to be a seventeenth-century stone building, but the large number of windows, all at different levels, was confusing.

The O'Briens thought that the house was older than it appeared and that it seemed rather too grand to be an ordinary farmhouse. There was even evidence in the farmyard to suggest that this had been an important building. Among the stables and outbuildings there was a fine, high-status seventeenth-century pigsty. The sty was constructed of elaborate stonework and had clearly been built by someone wealthy.

Inside, the house was a mysterious warren of rooms, all at different levels, which certainly explained the position of the windows. There were no fewer than 13 separate staircases. The O'Briens had already uncovered one clue that suggested that the house could be older than it appeared. After peeling away *five* different fireplaces, they had come to the original inglenook hearth. Further evidence as to the age of the house was found in the cellar, so often the source of invaluable clues. In this case, there was good reason to believe that it had not always been a cellar: the stone steps leading down to it were heavily worn and there were some very good quality medieval joists and beams, as well as a filled-in door and a window surround with splayed sides and

CRUCKS OF THE MATTER
One pair of the massive crucks found in the house. When you see the amount of space such timbers occupy it is not hard to understand why the less interruptive box-framing became more popular. The two horizontal purlins show, by their texture and the way they have been cut, that they are later additions. The original purlins were cut off and you can see their ends in situation on the crucks.

a sloping sill that also dated from the Middle Ages.

It was becoming clear that the house went back well beyond the seventeenth century, so we went in search of more evidence. We found it in a box room upstairs, in the shape of a medieval cruck that would have formed an A-shaped timber frame for the house. There was a second cruck in a bedroom, with the remains of a passing brace resting on it.

From this evidence, Mac Dowdy was able to conclude that the original medieval house would have been an aisled hall. He was able to confirm this by going outside and finding where the brace had been cut off.

There was every indication that this would have been a substantial and significant house in the Middle Ages, so we decided to investigate local history. It emerged that the story about the monks came from a rather dubious source: a book of nostalgic memoirs called *Auld Lang Syne*. However, more scholarly tomes revealed that, during the Middle Ages, Bidston had been part of the Birkenhead Priory, although there was nothing to suggest that Church Farm had been home to monks.

Now it was time for David Austin's knowledge of morphology to come into play. The layout of the village was typical, with the church and its graveyard in a prime position. However, there was one major anomaly. The seventeenth-century Bidston Hall was set back on the periphery of village life on former common or pasture land. This would have been an unusual place for a medieval manor house, while Church Farm was in exactly the right sort of location.

Inside the house, Judith Miller had found further proof that a considerable amount of money had been lavished on the house in the seventeenth century. A beautiful frieze, with sea monster motifs, ran along the top of the stairs, down a corridor and into a bedroom. It was clear there had been an impressive chamber here at one time that had since been divided up. Architecturally, though, the house was proving more difficult to fathom out. Mac Dowdy was surprised to find an arched medieval doorway with chamfered sides in a utility room at one end of the house. However, it was too far from the aisled hall for it to be part of the same structure.

The only real way of finding any answers was to trawl through the archives, which were mostly held at the County Records Office in Chester. What we found was little short of extraordinary:

FRIEZE FRAME
It became obvious that the house had had extensive remodelling in the seventeenth century and that a lot of money had been spent on decorative features, including this plaster frieze displaying a flamboyant pattern of sea monsters.

HEARTH OF STONE
The village of Bidston is built on an outcrop of stone which, of course, is the material used for its houses. The inglenook fireplace is built from massive blocks of stone but it has a brick flue. It is seventeenth century but stands back to back with a very much earlier, possibly fifteenth-century, chimney found in the cellar.

it makes all the hard toil worth it when you find such excellent records.

The key to it all was Bidston Hall, which had been part of an estate granted to a Lord Kingston by Charles II. The new owner had carried out a grand survey of his lands in 1665, including beautiful colour maps and watercolours of the hall. Most significantly for our purposes, Church Farm was on the map and the tenant named as William Taylor. The survey was updated at intervals and it revealed that the farm passed to a Robert Wilson through marriage and then on to his son. The map also showed that the layout of the house had been different and that a wing attached to the original aisled hall had since disappeared.

Once names had been established, it was possible to dig a little deeper and find out about the former occupants from the local parish registers. The Wilson

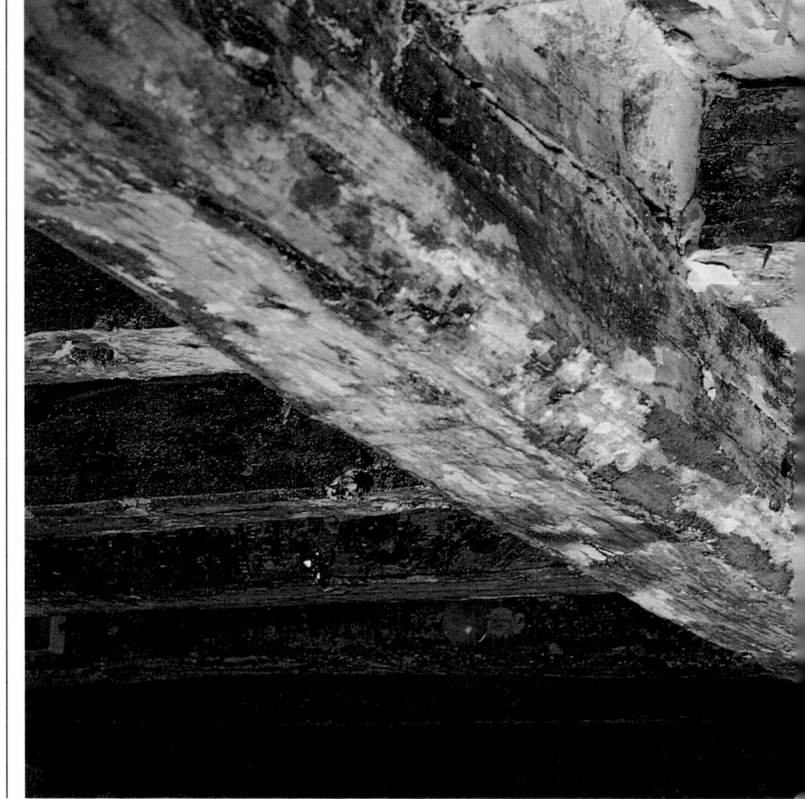

children were not baptized as normal shortly after they were born, but much later. A footnote explained that it was only after their non-conformist father, Robert Wilson, died that his children were able to be baptized.

We then turned to local court records to see if Robert Wilson's religious views had got him into trouble. Indeed they had: not only had he refused to pay his tithe or tax to the Church in 1667–68, but in 1685 he was also paid a visit by an army captain who was searching for arms. Wilson was described as a 'person dangerous to the government'. This was a time when religious dissent was tantamount to treason and non-conformists were persecuted relentlessly. There was even a legend that Wilson was involved in the Rye House Plot of 1683 to assassinate Charles II and his brother, the future James II.

After the Toleration Act of 1689, dissenters were able to meet openly, so David Austin decided to look up the Register of Dissenting Meeting Houses. This proved to be an inspired hunch, because in 1694–95 Robert Wilson was granted a licence to have his own place of worship – at Church Farm. Men like Wilson rejected what they saw to be the declining morals of the church and wanted the right to worship in their own, more devout way. (Documents we found from the period referred to bawdy vicars who frequented alehouses, used foul language and sang lewd songs.)

However, there was a twist in the plot.

Left **BARGAIN BASEMENT** **The cellar was not designed, it just happened. The timbers in its ceiling indicate that it was built in the sixteenth century when the outside ground level was raised. The space between the new floor and the old one became the cellar.**

Right **KITCHEN CLUE** **The doorway tucked closely into one corner of the kitchen was not only discovered to be chamfered, but also led into what is now a scullery, which meant that the kitchen would have been on the outside. Look towards the floor and the jamb of the doorway can be seen.**

Plan of Church Farm, Bidston

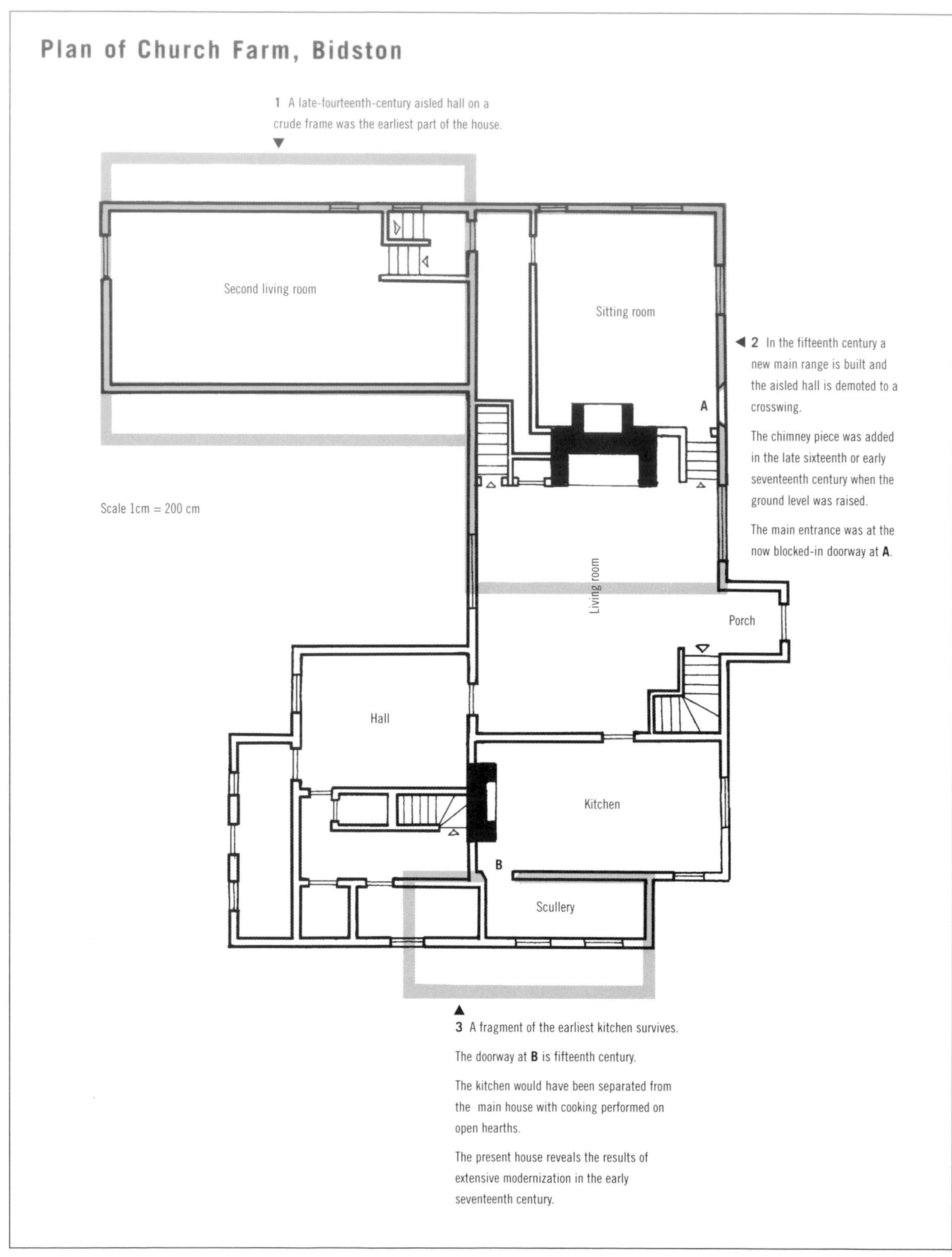

1 A late-fourteenth-century aisled hall on a crude frame was the earliest part of the house.

2 In the fifteenth century a new main range is built and the aisled hall is demoted to a crosswing.

The chimney piece was added in the late sixteenth or early seventeenth century when the ground level was raised.

The main entrance was at the now blocked-in doorway at **A**.

3 A fragment of the earliest kitchen survives.

The doorway at **B** is fifteenth century.

The kitchen would have been separated from the main house with cooking performed on open hearths.

The present house reveals the results of extensive modernization in the early seventeenth century.

Records showed that Wilson was living at Bidston Hall and farming its land along with that of Church Farm. It seemed that he had taken advantage of his Protestant connections and the fall from grace of the owners of Bidston Hall during the Civil War to acquire it on a long lease. Wills also turned out to be a very fruitful source of evidence here. It turned out that it was Wilson's wife, Ellin, who inherited Church Farm from her father, William Taylor. Taylor's will provided a telling clue as to the architectural development of the house. He left £8 for the rebuilding of the 'kitchen and house', which indicated that the kitchen had been a separate building. As part of the major modernization during Robert Wilson's time, the two medieval structures were brought together, which explained why Mac Dowdy found an old door at such a distance from the cruck frame. There was also a reference in Ellin's will which suggested that it was during her lifetime that the cellar had been created by the lowering of the ceiling (see Chapter 2, pp.52–54).

The Wilsons remained at the farm for more than a century. It was later owned by another well-known local family called Wharton. Their account books had survived, and they provided an excellent snapshot of life in the late-eighteenth and early-nineteenth centuries. The accounts showed how money was spent on ale at the Ring O Bells across the road, cock-fighting, donkey races, the April fair and quaintly named 'merry nights'.

The mystery of why the house had been carved up into a myriad of small rooms was solved by the 1881 census returns. A Thomas Lamb lived at the farm with his second wife and a grand total of 14 children. With their two Irish labourers, they needed all the rooms they could possibly muster.

Church Farm had witnessed a great deal during its 500-year history. Its position in the village and the remains of an impressive aisled hall meant that it most probably began life as Bidston's medieval manor house and was completely modernized in the seventeenth century.

Our investigation also uncovered an amazing parallel between the Wilson family and the O'Brien family. In the records we had found that in 1696, Robert Wilson's son, Obadia, bought the farm over the road from Church Farm. Exactly 300 years later, one of the O'Brien sons, David, has done precisely the same thing, so history has come full circle.

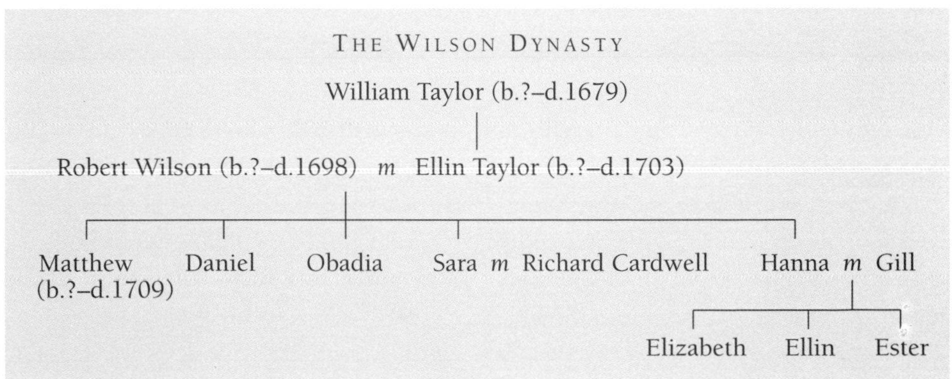

38 and 40 Manningtree High Street, Essex

'The history of English architecture in one house'

The case of two neighbouring houses in Manningtree High Street in Essex proved extremely challenging. Like Bidston, it was a complex and enthralling story. The parallels did not stop there, however. The larger of the two houses had become run-down over decades, until street entertainers David and Mandy Rose bought it in 1994. Mandy had been in love with the property since, as a young girl, she worked on Saturdays in the chemist shop at the front.

Quite by coincidence, the Roses' next-door neighbour, Ron Tanser, who owns a dry-cleaning shop, wrote to us about his house on exactly the same day as they did. Ron, David and Mandy wanted to know who had lived in their houses in the past because they had heard so many outlandish rumours about their homes.

They had been told that there were smugglers' passages running from their houses to others in the town. Manningtree is on the tidal River Stour and, in its heyday, it was a wealthy port bristling with merchants, sailors and smugglers. There were even stories that the infamous Matthew Hopkins who, in his guise as the Witchfinder General, persecuted alleged witches in Essex and Suffolk during the 1640s, had stayed in the house. Ron suspected that the two houses had been one and the same in the past, and felt that they were linked to an old chapel next door that was pulled down 30 years previously.

From the front of the two houses, at least three very distinctive architectural periods were evident: fine Georgian proportions with a portico door on the right;

Left **The garden view of the sixteenth-century chimney stack with its six angled shafts shows it rising from behind the gable. This gable appears to have been part of the entrance porch in Elizabethan times.**

Above **The Georgian-fronted house in the High Street and its near-side neighbour appear to have little in common. It was the size and position of the chimney stack that excited interest that all was not as it seemed.**

Victorian bay windows on the left and, most strikingly of all, an imposing Elizabethan brick chimney stack. David and Mandy's house was a lot larger than it looked from the front and extended a considerable distance to a back lane. It was there that we found a clue which took us even further back in history: a timber jetty overhanging the road. Inside, the timber-framed building was now being used to store junk, but it was clear it had been an important building. It was a very impressive, well-built box structure, held together with solid oak

Plan of 38 and 40 Manningtree High Street, Essex

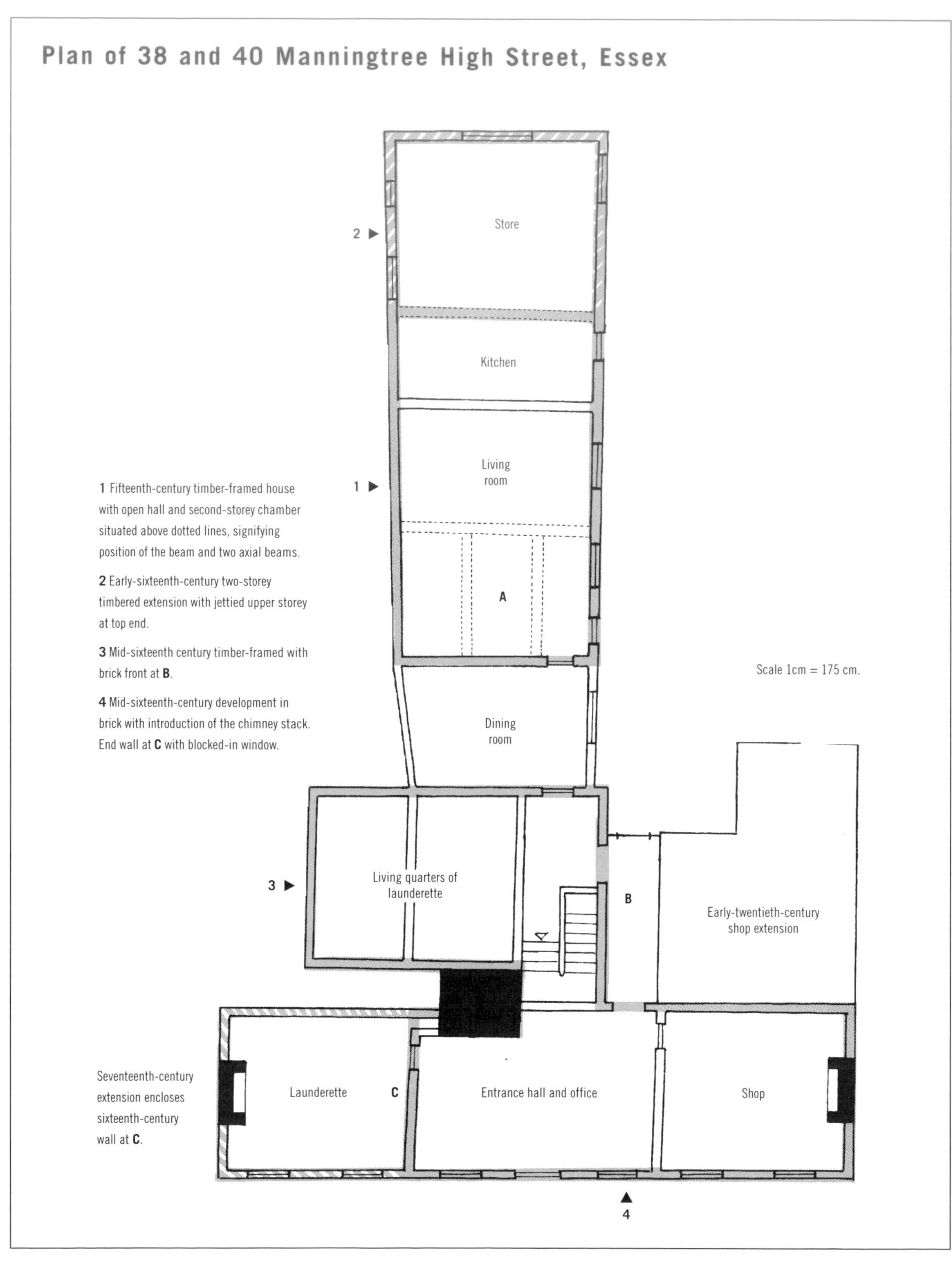

1 Fifteenth-century timber-framed house with open hall and second-storey chamber situated above dotted lines, signifying position of the beam and two axial beams.

2 Early-sixteenth-century two-storey timbered extension with jettied upper storey at top end.

3 Mid-sixteenth century timber-framed with brick front at **B**.

4 Mid-sixteenth-century development in brick with introduction of the chimney stack. End wall at **C** with blocked-in window.

Seventeenth-century extension encloses sixteenth-century wall at **C**.

wallplates and imposing tie-beams. There was also evidence of a filled-in early window with wooden mullions.

We found more early beams in the attic of the one-storey building adjoining the jettied one, so Mac Dowdy turned to dendrochronology or tree-ring dating (see Chapter 6, pp.160–161) to ascertain the age of the house. Samples were taken from different parts of the house and analyzed. The results were remarkably precise and showed that the single-storey range was built in 1483 and that it was extended in 1534 to create a two-storey building at the back of the plot. There was a further modernization around 1580 when the chimney stack was added.

A vital piece of evidence relating to this second piece of modernization was discovered in the attic. Attics often hold a house's best-kept secrets but the one above the front of the Roses' house was an exceptional example. David and Mac gained access through a hatch in the bathroom ceiling. There were steps within the attic and a roughly carved newel post, which suggested that an early staircase had come up here. Inside the attic itself there was a filled-in brick mullioned window on a wall shared with Ron's house next door. The window was facing outwards, suggesting that this house was here before Ron's was built. Next to the window there was a filled-in door, which raised the spectre of smugglers' passages.

The attic was to yield yet more telling evidence. All along the front there was a confusing array of bricks and timber. There were two brick walls: a Georgian one in front of an Elizabethan one.

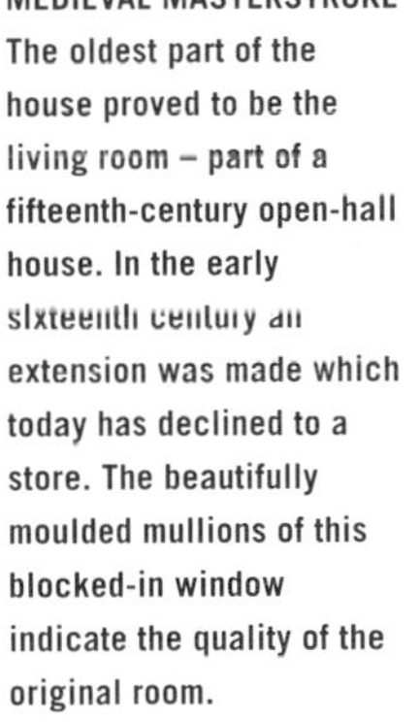

MEDIEVAL MASTERSTROKE The oldest part of the house proved to be the living room – part of a fifteenth-century open-hall house. In the early sixteenth century an extension was made which today has declined to a store. The beautifully moulded mullions of this blocked-in window indicate the quality of the original room.

ANCIENT TIMBERS
The tie-beams and rafters of what is now a store were confirmed by dendrochronology as having been built in the very early years of the sixteenth century. The modern machine-cut brace in the foreground uses the mortice and peg holes of the original.

Behind that there was a timber frame, which proved that this part of the building was late medieval too. There were also cut-off rafters in the attic, suggesting that the original roof had been replaced by a lower-pitched one.

The attic had already been a rich source of evidence, but there was more to come. As they were leaving, David and Mac stumbled upon a large hole in the floor in front of the steps. They pulled away a few loose floorboards and found a considerable cavity deliberately constructed between the ceiling below and the roof space. The hole, about 6 ft 6 in (2 m) long and 3 ft 3 in (1 m) wide and deep, had clearly been intended as a hideaway – most probably a contraband hole used by smugglers during Manningtree's days as a bustling port.

From the filled-in window it seemed likely that Ron's house had been built later than the Roses'. Was there any evidence, then, to support Ron's theory that the two houses were ever one? Mac Dowdy set out to answer the question by looking for clues in Ron's flat above the shop. In an attic bedroom he found an axial beam that abutted up against the Roses' house. From the joists, which had a greater horizontal

SECRETS OF THE ATTIC
The roof of the street range gave up so many clues. The horizontal timber is a purlin from the sixteenth-century house and its rafters have been cut off. These rafters rise from a wallplate from a timber-framed building that had been cased in brick – we can see the upper part of the wall. For some extraordinary reason a new brick wall is built just outside it in the eighteenth century and a new roof covers the old.

dimension than the vertical, Mac worked out that this was a seventeenth-century building that had been added on to the one next door. His theory was later corroborated by documents showing that the two houses had had the same owners until the turn of this century.

From the outset, David had been struck by the size of the burgage plot or property on which the house was built. It stretched from the high street right to the back lane, which in itself was not unusual but it was unexpectedly wide. By studying local maps, he deduced that the plot was twice the size of others in the high street, suggesting that it was two plots that had been amalgamated. This was evidence pointing to the fact that a former owner of the house had come into money and was able to buy up the neighbouring plot to expand his holding.

The imposing chimney stack also suggested that somebody wealthy had owned the house, though it was something of a mystery at first: it had six shafts in beautiful, multicoloured moulded brick, but was located at one end of the building. There was no way that it could have served six separate fireplaces. It emerged that the chimney was primarily a status symbol designed to show off the wealth of its owner. In reality, there were just two hearths.

By this stage, a profile of the sixteenth-century owner of the house was coming together. He was wealthy and almost certainly involved in Manningtree's prosperous trade. To put a name to him, and to any other former owners, we had to investigate the archives in Colchester and Chelmsford. The census returns of 1841 (see Chapter 2, pp.50–52) were useful and gave the names of the occupants of the house. Unfortunately, it seemed that the original deeds had been destroyed and lost for ever until we had a remarkable stroke of luck. A local historian, Clarice Jacques, had copied them out by hand 40 years earlier. Her handwritten copies revealed that the house had been a tavern in the eighteenth century at the height of the town's popularity as a trading centre. The local tavern was exactly the sort of place that smuggling would go on, so this went some way to explaining the contraband hole in the attic. The deeds also referred to cellars and vaults,

which came as news to David and Mandy.

The trail of documentary evidence began to go a little cold before 1700, but we found the evidence we needed in manorial records. A rental of 1628 referred to two properties either side of the chapel. This gave us two suspects: Richard Edwards or Robert Taylor. Richard Edwards was the most likely candidate, because he held two burgage plots. Edwards, it turned out, was a yeoman, which meant effectively that he was a prominent middle-class member of Manningtree society. He was also an overseer of the poor, which would have given him local power and prestige.

One of the most fascinating insights into Richard Edwards the man came from a petition of 1611 calling for the building of a new chapel in Manningtree because the existing one had fallen into disrepair. Richard Edwards was one of the main signatories and, from the sanctimonious tone of the petition, we were able to build up a clearer picture of the sort of man he was. The petition, which did indeed lead to the building of the new chapel next to Edwards' house in 1616, referred to declining morals in the town and bitterly condemned stage players, who it accused of abusing the old chapel. Richard Edwards was quite clearly a puritan and the sort of person who would have supported the Witchfinder General during the feverish days of the English Civil War in the 1640s. In the absence of any solid evidence, it would be fair to say that the legend about the Witchfinder General had some credence.

Above **The former chemist's shop on the premises, which had been run by the Winter family and later the Co-Op. Prior to being a chemist's, it was a bank.**

Right **The three steps lead up into the main range roof space. They move in a spiral from a roughly carved newel post which must have been at the top of a staircase.**

David and Mandy still wanted to know if there was a cellar. With the help of pulse radar, we were able to ascertain that there had been a cellar at some point but that it was likely to have been filled in. A quick look under the floorboards proved that this was the case.

There remained one more mystery to solve. Mandy had been told by a builder that he had covered up some medieval murals in a room upstairs. We decided to take a peek by cutting a small, neat hole in the hardboard wall. There was no ancient wall painting, but good-quality Georgian panelling instead. The rest of the partition wall was ripped down in a flurry of excitement: this was a wonderful surprise. While we knew this part of the house had been modernized in the eighteenth century, we had no idea that any interior features had survived. (Just to add a note of caution, though, before you get carried away: in the case of listed buildings or houses in Conservation Areas it is important to consult the relevant authorities before removing partition walls and other features.)

High Street, Manningtree is a classic example of a house built 500 years ago that has been modernized numerous times. This made it very complicated to understand. What made it ultimately so rewarding was that it reflected accurately Manningtree's social and economic history. From being home to a Puritan who hated stage players, it went on to become a tavern, a bank, a chemists and then home to modern-day street entertainers. The Witchfinder General and smugglers may well have passed through its doors, which goes to prove that there may be something in the old myths after all.

DUNSBY FEN FARM, LINCOLNSHIRE

'THE QUEST FOR A RELUCTANT HEIRESS'S POSSESSIONS SEALED IN THE CELLAR'

Our next case took us to the wild and remote fenlands of Lincolnshire. Dunsby Fen Farm is an isolated farmhouse, cut off from the rest of the world by a flat, featureless landscape that stretches as far as the eye can see. Dunsby Fen Farm had a secret history and the owners, the Mentzel family, wanted to get to the bottom of it.

They were intrigued as to why such an apparently grand house was built in the middle of nowhere. They had also heard an extraordinary tale of a reluctant heiress who was said to have put all of her furniture in the cellar and sealed it over. The Mentzels did not even know if there was a cellar, but suspected that its entrance may have been in what is now an understairs cupboard.

We were immediately struck by the layout of the buildings. Access from the road was from the back of the farm through an old disused farmyard. The brickwork in the feeding troughs suggested that this was a classic model farm

DUNSBY FEN FARM
The main entrance to the house, a really grand-looking porch, appeared to be on the wrong side of the house as it is used today. It was obvious that there must have been a more suitable driveway when the house was built in the nineteenth century. However, the service end of the house would not enhance the entrance in any way. The furthest three very narrow openings gave ventilation to the games room, now the larder.

AT HOME WITH THE CASSWELLS
This photograph shows members of the Casswell family in the front garden around the early twentieth century. It confirmed the conjecture: here is the driveway to the entrance, and the service range was hidden by the hedge.

of the eighteenth or nineteenth century. The front of the house, with its grand entrance, looked out onto a lawn and beyond over the fenlands.

This seemed paradoxical: the front was at the back, and there was no approach road on that side, not even a path leading up to the front door. It was almost as if the house was facing the wrong way. The house had a typical upstairs-downstairs layout but, architecturally, it was not quite as you might expect: one side of the façade was symmetrical, while the other half, which appeared to be the servants wing, was not.

While the old farm dairy was typically nineteenth century with handmade bricks, the interior of the house raised further questions. The entrance hall was covered with beautiful encaustic tiles and its centrepiece was an impressive late-nineteenth-century staircase with a good-quality frieze. Whoever had the house built quite clearly had taste and was style conscious as a considerable amount of money had been spent on decorating it.

To put a date to the decorations forensic back-up was needed, so we called in wallpaper expert Allyson McDermott. She thought the embossed paper design, which had been painted many times, was from the 1880s. What she needed to confirm the date were original fragments of wallpaper. Using tweezers, she was able to find tiny pieces of old paper behind skirting boards and under the edge of the fire surround – places decorators often miss when they are stripping wallpaper. Allyson took her samples away for chemical analysis. Unfortunately, most of them did not reveal anything, except one tiny fragment of lining paper taken from the dining room. She compared this with a known example and the fibres were the same, enabling her to date the paper accurately at 1890.

The main mystery remained, however: why was the house facing the back?

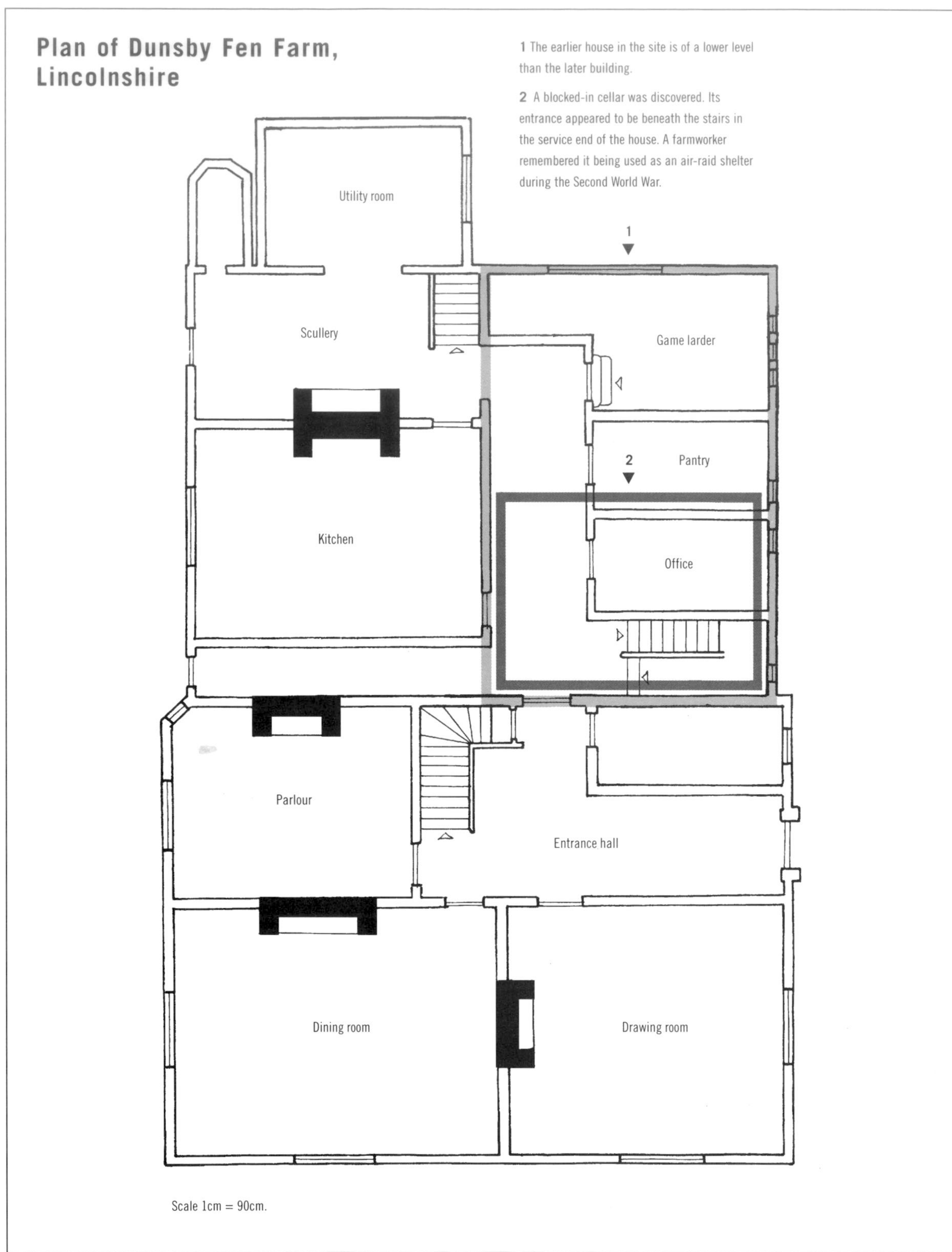

Plan of Dunsby Fen Farm, Lincolnshire
1 The earlier house in the site is of a lower level than the later building.
2 A blocked-in cellar was discovered. Its entrance appeared to be beneath the stairs in the service end of the house. A farmworker remembered it being used as an air-raid shelter during the Second World War.
1
Utility room
Scullery
Game larder
Pantry
2
Kitchen
Office
Parlour
Entrance hall
Dining room
Drawing room
Scale 1cm = 90cm.

Armed with Ordnance Survey maps, David set out to find the answer. At the edge of the front lawn, he discovered an old wooden gatepost that would have signified the front of the house. Well-established plane trees extending towards the dyke in the distance were also clues as to an earlier development in the now-deserted area in front of the house. Beyond the trees there was an old bridge, called Casswell's Bridge, crossing the dyke. It is now disused and dangerous, but at one time it would have been an important crossing point. As he approached the bridge, David found old rubble and the remnants of building debris in the grass. There was a lump of limestone – a local building material – and an old brick. A brick expert, David Robinson, was able to confirm that the brick was handmade and older than the ones used to build the house or the farm buildings. There was, therefore, clear evidence that there had been an earlier settlement in front of the current farm.

David also established from the topography of the farm that a cellar was not out of the question, because the house was built on ground raised above the level of the drainage dyke. Meanwhile, Mac decided to investigate more closely and uncovered several clues in the understairs cupboard which suggested that the cellar entrance may have been there. The floor of the cupboard had been concreted over fairly recently and the underside of the service stairs had been rendered, suggesting that this had once been an area that was meant to be exposed. Pulling back the carpet in front of the cupboard he found that the stone steps were worn, indicating that this had been a busy thoroughfare in the past. Although Charterhouse had indicated on their house-style plan that this was the place for an earth closet (or toilet) it seemed more likely that these were steps leading to a cellar.

Dunsby Fen Farm was blessed with some excellent archive material because for most of its history it had been owned by one of the great estates, the Charterhouse charity, which kept extensive records. Charterhouse's connection with Dunsby Fen went right back to 1612, but the first building on our site did not come until 1771. A handwritten document said that it was constructed from local bricks made on the farm with silt from the fens. The documents showed that in 1772 the tenant farmer at Dunsby Fen was called William Carter. In 1842, a yeoman farmer, Thomas Casswell, took over, and within six years the money was available for him to develop the farm buildings in the style of a model farm. The dairy and the arched brickwork in the feeding troughs dated from this period. It was Thomas who built the bridge and gave it his family name. The bridge made the journey to the local market town of Spalding much more direct for the Casswells.

According to the accounts, the current farm was built in the 1870s by Charterhouse for Thomas's son, Frederick Casswell. There was a detailed plan in the records drawn up by a London architect for the building of the new house. The final building did not correspond exactly to the plan, but the variations probably reflected ad hoc adjustments made locally. Accounts ledgers showed that no expense had been spared on the new house, with

FLIGHT OF FANCY
The house was clearly divided into two social areas, the family end and the service side. It had two staircases, here the principal one with its elegant joinery rises from quite a spacious stairhall.

quite considerable sums being spent on wall papering and painting.

The Casswells must have been influential tenants. Frederick's wife, Emily, came from a wealthy Stamford family and had high standards to keep up. She even employed a London governess for the children. Judith was able to build up a profile of Emily as somebody who was up to speed on the latest fashions. She was the sort of person who would have devoured the latest fashions in classical revival wallcoverings and would have decorated her home in rich colours and

empire fabrics with fancy tassels and other trimmings.

From the Charterhouse records, it was clear that the area around the farm was once a vibrant community made up of a large family, staff and farmworkers. There had been an old school house on the other side of the bridge, an alehouse and farm-workers' cottages. All of these buildings have now gone. But what about the original farmhouse? Mac had found some heavily worn tiles under the main stairs in the current farmhouse that appeared to be earlier than the rest of the building. We were able to conclude, therefore, that the new house was built on the site of the old farm.

Mac was still determined to track down the cellar. A former farmworker, Fred Parkinson, who had been at Dunsby Fen in the 1950s, remembered being told that the cellar had been converted to an air-raid shelter and remembered filling it in after the war. Mac turned to dowsing to see if that could help solve the mystery and found what appeared to be the entrance to the cellar in a cupboard beneath the service stairs. He failed to locate a cavity in the scullery, but was able to find one in the understairs cupboard. He proceeded to drill a series of holes in the concrete floor to see if there was a void below. Mac then inserted a long metal probe into one of the holes: it went smoothly down through some soft infill and down still further into a void. When he pulled the probe out the end was damp, suggesting that the cellar was infilled with soil.

All of this left the Mentzels with an agonizing decision: should they dig up the whole floor to see if the reluctant heiress had buried her possessions in the cellar? The possible identity of the heiress also remained a mystery. The farm stayed in the Casswell family for five generations. Russell Casswell bought it from the Charterhouse estate in 1919, but remained there for only two years before moving to Spalding because his wife, Annie, felt it was too remote. They had two children, Gordon and Laura, but they were not interested in taking over the farm. Gordon preferred the thrill of fast cars, while Laura emigrated. Perhaps Laura was the reluctant heiress of local legend, or even her mother? The secret may lie hidden in the cellar forever...

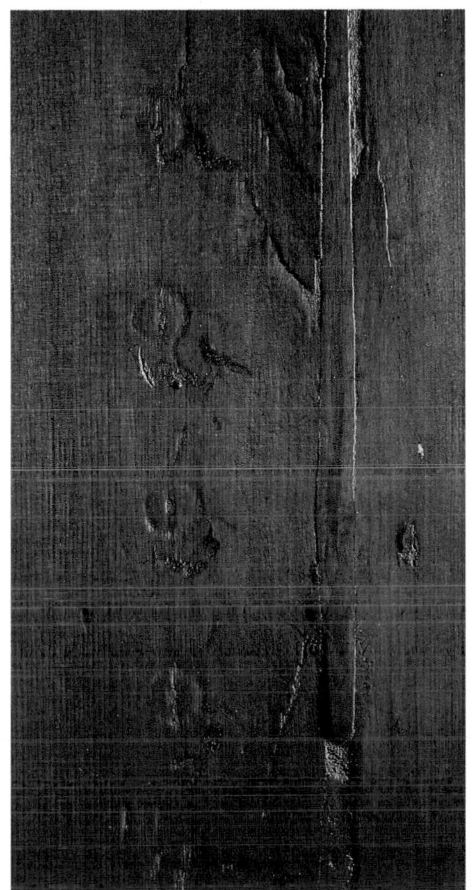

WHAT'S BEHIND THE GREEN DOOR? The door between the family and service end was insulated on one side from potentially offensive noises. This detail shows the holes made by the brass tacks that held the green baize in place.

22, VICTORIA ROAD, FULWOOD, NEAR PRESTON

'EDWARDIAN SPLENDOUR FOR A SELF-MADE MAN'

Fayre Haven is in a suburb of Preston, Lancashire, and was the youngest house in the series and the only twentieth-century one. But its history was as rich as the others because it mirrored so clearly the social and architectural mores of the Edwardian period. It was also rewarding because it reflected the life and career of one exceptional man. With its ostentatious turret the house gives the impression of being a fairy-tale castle and is a source of endless fascination to local people. Whether you view such houses as the height of Edwardian elegance or a tawdry piece of pretension, Fayre Haven was to prove a delightful investigation.

Anne Conchie and Phil Hulme fell in love with the house as soon as they set eyes on it, so they put a note through the letterbox saying they were interested in buying it. They moved in just three weeks later. The interior turned out to be even more over-the-top than the exterior, with its exotic anaglypta wallcoverings and elaborate stained-glass windows. For many years the house had been split up into separate flats and bedsits and it was a far cry from its heyday at the beginning of the century.

The couple wanted to restore it to how it would have been then, but needed some guidance as to what was original and what was fake. They were also intrigued to find out who had built the house and how they had lived. It was obvious that a considerable amount of money had been spent blending such a bizarre mix of styles to create the architectural equivalent of a wedding cake. It was fashionable during the later years of Queen Victoria's reign through to the Edwardian period for the wealthy middle classes to build with a flourish of exuberance, even eccentricity. Fayre Haven, with its fine garden and folly of a turret, was all about showing off the owner's wealth.

Inside, the house was a real treasure trove with much of the original Edwardian decoration on the walls and ceilings remaining intact. There were also Jacobean and classically inspired styles: a fine example of new money trying to ape the country's great stately homes. It was all rather hit-or-miss though: some of the details, including pillars in the living room, were rather tacky. Anne had thought about pulling them out, assuming wrongly that they were a later addition. Beneath the carpet, the floor had been painted to give the impression of high-class and expensive parquet flooring. There was such a vast range of different decorative details that Judith thought that its original owner had been connected with the decorating business. To follow up this gut feeling she decided to track down some catalogue books from the period.

Under the floorboards, Phil had discovered a bell pull system for servants. This was excellent evidence that the owners had been wealthy. The servants would have lived in the attic rooms, which were spartan in contrast to the rest of the house. From the outside, the turret was the most striking feature, so we took a closer look.

Our first impressions were correct: the

turret was merely a folly. Access to it was not easy and little attention had been paid to finishing off the interior: the rafters were all uneven. This was a room not designed to be seen from the inside. The turret was another striking example of frivolous showing off, probably by a middle-class person who had come into money. The history of Fulwood supported the new-money theory. During the first half of the nineteenth century, Preston emerged as an important centre for the cotton industry. As millworkers moved into the town, the middle classes headed out and created their own utopian suburbs, like the Fulwood estate, which was founded in 1851.

With a profile of the original owner emerging, the investigation turned to the key question of naming him. The big advantage of younger houses is that there is a wealth of documentary evidence available, including old rate books and census returns until 1891. We tracked down the name of the owner, J. R. Hodgson, in local street directories from the early 1900s and went on to find out from Barrets trade directory for 1901 that he was 'a plumber, painter and paper-hanging merchant with a substantial shop in Church Street'. It seemed that John Hodgson was using his home as a showcase for his wares.

His was a real rags-to-riches story. The census returns for 1871 showed that a young J.R. had been living with his unmarried mother in a poor part of Preston, and that he was illegitimate. Within 30 years he was living in the relative splendour of Fayre Haven: a house he had planned and built himself. By an amazing stroke of good fortune, his own rather amateurish plans from 1898 were kept in the records office. A commercial directory from the same year described J.R. Hodgson as 'a well-respected businessman and an authority on sanitary engineering'. It also listed all the different materials he sold in his builders' merchants.

J.R. Hodgson had got quite carried away doing up his own house and had used a bewildering display of stained glass. He was also a glazier and went to extraordinary lengths to add colour to his windows in a dazzling array of different patterns. Decorative windows were all the rage during the late Victorian and Edwardian period and there were many variations on a theme. To assess J.R.'s collection, we needed specialist support. Dinah Stobbs, an archivist from Pilkington Glass, immediately recognized the glass as being of the high-street variety because it had colour right the way through it unlike truly *stained* glass found in churches and cathedrals. Dinah acknowledged that all self-respecting villas of this period would have had a coloured transom, but felt that J.R. Hodgson had gone just a little too far. It was as if he was determined to use every single shade of glass listed in his commercial directory. Dinah recognized a heady mix of different types: figured glass called Murinese, painted glass and red flash. She was most excited by one panel which was made using a technique called mechanical embossing. It featured a fine image of a woman and Dinah was able to locate the design in the Pilkington pattern book from 1896.

J.R. also drew extensively from his pattern books to decorate his home with fake plasterwork or anaglypta. All over the house there were elaborate designs

moulded with a mixture of wood pulp and cotton. Some of the anaglypta by the stairs had been damaged over the years. This was another case for Allyson McDermott, the wallpaper expert who had already identified the decoration of Dunsby Fen Farm. Allyson worked out what materials had been used and demonstrated to Phil how to create a mould and repair the damage. She also found out that the anagylpta had originally been painted dark brown to make it look like wood panelling. Phil was not tempted to return it to its original colour, which he felt was much too dark for modern tastes.

Further investigations into the archives at the Harris Museum in Preston yielded much more about J.R.'s career. It emerged that he was an aspiring local politician: in 1900, he was elected as a councillor and 16 years later, he became an alderman. Then, in 1924, came his greatest triumph – he was elected Mayor of Preston.

***Above* FANTASTIC FAÇADE** **Fayre Haven presents an intriguing face to Victoria Road. A feast of decorative features meets the eye: there is mock Tudor mixing with Jacobean strapwork motifs and a mixture of window bay shapes and a turreted tower looking like a fugitive from Denmark. At least the styles all come from the early twentieth century!**

Above **NOT ALL IT SEEMS** The garden view offers further surprises: the two-storey front has become a three-storey back and the line of the front gable has turned into a range parallel with the road. The blank white wall between the square-bay windows turns out to have been an enclosed balcony.

Above right **DIGNITARY'S DELIGHTS** John R. Hodgson in his mayoral robes from his time as mayor of Preston in 1924. He used Fayre Haven as a living catalogue for the materials sold by his builders' merchants firm.

Right **BUSINESS AFFAIRS** The panelled room which J. R. used as his office. The timber frame is strips of wood pinned to the plaster wall. This room is the one with the larger bay on the facing page.

During his term of office, J.R.'s house became a focus for polite society in Preston. We even uncovered a wonderful press cutting about a garden party, which read: 'A charming function took place on Thursday at "Fairhaven", Fulwood, the residence of his Worship the Mayor. A garden party had been arranged and some charming dresses were worn in light summer shades...great amusement was caused by the men's hat trimming competition which was won by a clergyman...' Reports like this bring so much colour to the history of a house. You need a strong lead before you can hope to find anything in a newspaper, but it's certainly something that is well worth bearing in mind.

Architecturally there was something about Fayre Haven that troubled Mac. Everything about the house was flamboyant, except a balcony area at the back that was strangely white and bare. It looked so out of place. The iron balustrade was clearly more modern than the rest of the house and was a later addition. Mac found evidence of wooden posts which had been cut off and noticed some louvres, or horizontally hung windows, higher up the wall that were intended for ventilation. These clues suggested a former balcony conservatory, which was a popular feature at the time the house was built. Mac asked an illustrator, Anny Evason, to draw an impression of what the house would have looked like with its first-floor conservatory.

David, meanwhile, had placed an advertisement in a local newspaper seeking information that could lead us to any of J.R.'s surviving relatives. The quest was a big success and well worth the effort. Three of J.R.'s surviving grandchildren were tracked down to different parts of the country. They all agreed to return to Fayre Haven to tell Anne and Phil their childhood memories and to show them their old family photos. One of them, J.R. Hodgson the Third, had not been back in 70 years. Among the old photos they brought was one showing the balcony conservatory how it used to look, which compared favourably with the painting Mac had commissioned. Moments like this are very special and moving and allow house detectives to get in touch with the emotional history of their homes.

This, however, was not the end of the story. According to the electoral registers, J.R. Hodgson left Fayre Haven in 1926 and let it out. This marked the end of Fayre Haven's period of grandeur, but J.R. was going up in the world. On his retirement, be bought a real Jacobean mansion, Oxendale Hall in Osbaldeston. J.R. Hodgson lived till the ripe old age of 81, when he died a contented man, his journey from the back streets of Preston to a stately home complete.

MIXED BUNCH
A recurring decorative feature at Fayre Haven is panels of these embossed motifs in anaglypta. The frieze above the panels follows a form of Jacobean patterning while the main decoration in the panels brings together a mixture of Elizabethan and the classical with a flair for the baroque, the figures being part-Eastern, part-Mediterranean with the men having faces of Edwardian gentlemen. In their day they were a popular buy.

MULBERRY COTTAGE, SWANAGE

'THE MYSTERY OF THE TEETOTAL POLTERGEIST'

Mulberry Cottage in the picturesque seaside town of Swanage in Dorset provided a stern examination of our detective skills. It proved, if proof was needed, that you cannot take anything at face value when investigating the history of a house. This is a detective story with many twists and turns and it exemplifies the need to keep digging below the surface and to keep questioning your assumptions about your home.

The property is situated in the oldest part of Swanage on the High Street. It forms part of a Grade II listed building, which was called Springfield House before it was split up into cottages. Sara Robinson and Rob Grindon wanted to bring the history of their home to life and to know more about who had lived there in the past. They also had a rather unusual request: they wanted to know the identity of a ghost who they believed haunted the house. From house detectives to ghostbusters all in one day...

From the front, the house looked to be straightforward. On one side it was clearly eighteenth century with a symmetrical elevation and chimney stacks where you would expect them to be. The right-hand side appeared to be a nineteenth-century extension.

Stepping through the front door, we were immediately struck by a staircase that seemed too grand and out of proportion with the rest of the house. It was trying to pass itself off as eighteenth century, but was clearly much later. The newel post was a mixture of Jacobean and Georgian details and Judith immediately dated it as Edwardian, somewhere between 1900 and 1905. The staircase was built of fine Canadian pine which had been painted to make it look like a darker, more exotic wood. A window at first-floor level suggested that a first-floor room had been sacrificed to create the big open hallway. This was definite evidence of gentrification at the turn of the century.

While David set to work on local maps, Mac busied himself with sketching plans of the house. When they conferred, their theories were wildly different: David thought the back of the house was older than the front, while Mac believed the

SPOOKY FIND
It was important to know whether a window or door was hidden behind the plasterwork. Sara and Rob were for knocking all the plaster off, but the detectives thought an examination near the skirting board would prove the point. It did – there was a door... the one used by the ghost!

Above left
UPFRONT CLUES
The street front, though sporting nineteenth-century features – some of them quite early enough to be eighteenth century – can be seen to be long and rangy. The proportion of the front range (as shown in the photo) suggests seventeenth-century beginnings.

Right **SET IN STONE**
Part of a vertical join appears in the stonework just to the right of the upper part of the doorcasing. This is the side wall of a house further up the street from Mulberry Cottage and it was one of the factors that proved that the road was once set back further than today and that the back range of the cottage was older than the front.

Below left **REAR VIEW**
The ashlaring of the front has disappeared at the back, or rather it has never been here. Apart from the windows introduced into it, parts of the stonework were identified as seventeenth century. However, it was the interior discoveries that really told the story.

front to be older than the back. Sara had her own theory that the kitchen had been altered at some stage. She told a story of how a visitor sleeping in the front room once had been terrified to see a ghostly figure walking through the wall from the kitchen. Sara had taken a hammer to the wall and uncovered what looked like a wooden lintel, which suggested that there could have been a door or window there. Mac took a closer look and by chipping away the plaster further found evidence of bricks that had been used to fill in the doorway.

Despite this rather spooky discovery, there was nothing to suggest at this stage that the house was earlier than eighteenth century. Sara and Rob had mentioned that the dining room was damp and smelt musty, and wondered if the original name of the house, Springfield House, meant that there was a stream nearby. Mac got out his dowsing rods and was able to recognize signs of a stream beneath the dining-room floor and plotted its course right up through the garden at the back. The dining room, which was part of the Victorian extension, had been built over a water source.

David, meanwhile, was getting closer to proving his theory that the back of the house was the oldest part. From a 25-inch Ordnance Survey map he deduced that the front of the house had been built out onto part of the original High Street. From the layout of the roads it was evident that Mulberry Cottage had encroached forwards into what would have been a wider marketplace in the past. He also felt that the back of the house had at one time been a one-storey building similar to the outhouse next to it, and that a second storey had been added later. When a roof has been raised you expect to find a change in the coursing of the stone, which is just what David went on to discover at the back of the house: a string course of narrower stone that would have marked the line of the eaves of an older, lower roof.

David's theory was coming together very nicely indeed. He went on to find a hidden clue in a most unexpected place: the kitchen larder. The interior walls of the cupboard were cut at an angle pointing outwards. The only logical explanation for the splaying of the walls was that this had at one time been a window in an external wall. The only problem with this was that the splay continued right to the floor. However, Mac was able to answer

Plan of Muberry Cottage, Swanage

1 The bricks in the upper part of the chimney stack were dated to the early sixteenth century and, as the fireplace had been an introduction, the house itself must be earlier, conservatively late fifteenth century. The documentary evidence supported this.

A Earlier window found in cupboard.

B Earlier door discovered in the wall.

2 Some surviving roof timbers put this building at the same date as the house. The evidence that the building was longer was discovered at **C** when the remnants of the extended walls were discovered.

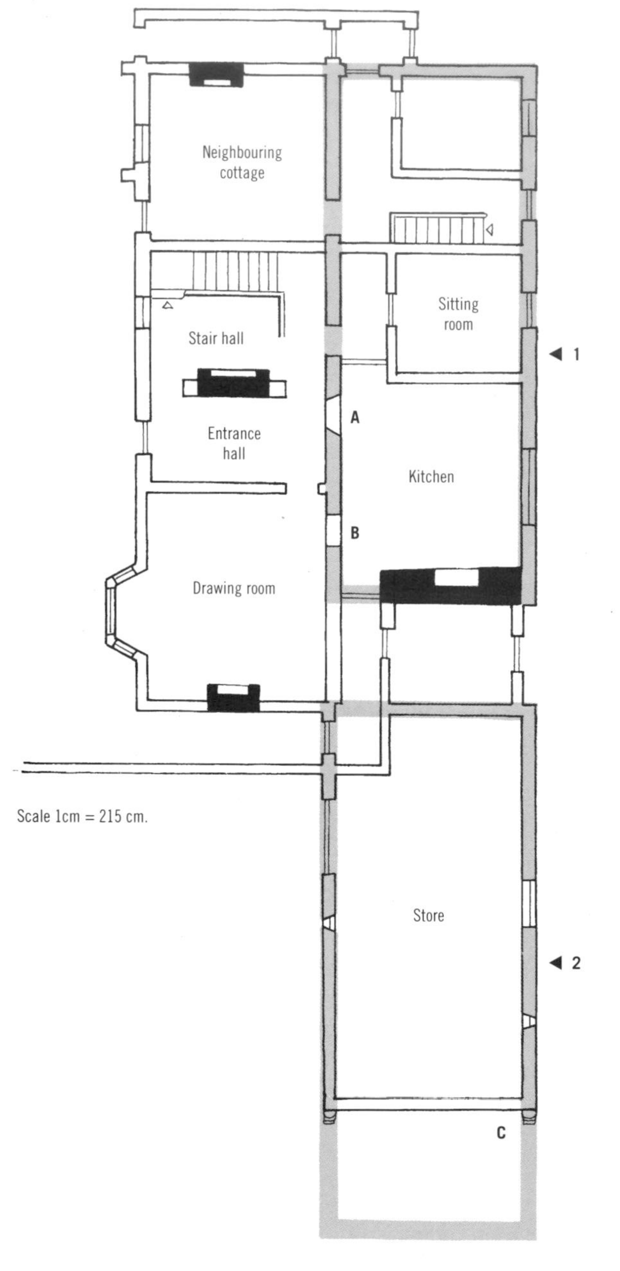

this query: the splay was also designed to accommodate a window seat.

The interior of another cupboard further along the same wall displayed the same characteristics, so there was evidence of two filled-in windows, the filled-in ghost door and the current doorway. This was almost certainly an external wall at one time and the original front of the house, but we still wanted more corroborative evidence. David and Mac found it further along the High Street. Other buildings on the same side showed signs, including differences in stonework, of being extended outwards into the street. In other words, the modern High Street was narrower than it had been.

David's theory had been proved, but this was not the end of it. Our original estimate of the age of the oldest part of the house turned out to be wrong by several centuries. It was in the roof space at the back, the classic place for hidden clues, that Mac was surprised to find early brickwork. The bricks were long and narrow, and from the variable mortar course it was clear they were irregular shapes. Mac recognized them as typically sixteenth century. This work must have been done when the second storey was added, which meant that the earliest one-storey building on the site was older still.

Mulberry Cottage had undergone many changes. To find out who orchestrated them, it was necessary to delve into the archives. The owner, Sara, had a theory that the ghost was Hester Marsh, who lived in the house in the first half of the nineteenth century. Sara had found her name in a local history book and discovered a plaque commemorating Hester and her husband Peter in the local church.

The story of Peter and Hester Marsh was brought to life by a rate book. Peter, it turned out, had been a successful and wealthy young businessman and the house at that time was listed as a 'malt-house, brewhouse and dwelling'. He was to die at the relatively young age of 45. Sara claimed that the ghost disapproved of alcohol and that a friend had witnessed a bottle of wine falling from a wine rack and tipping its contents over her. Could it be that Peter Marsh drank himself to an early grave? We decided against holding a séance to find out...

Hester lived until 1845, so it must have been she who had had the mulberry tree planted in 1828, a date that was worked out for us by a dendrologist, John White (see Chapter 6, p.162). Around this time, her nephew, William Cole, was living with her, and this apparently prompted her to add to the house in 1830 by building over the spring. Her husband Peter had already extended the house forwards and out into the High Street 40 years earlier.

After Hester Marsh, the house was owned by a James Kent and, on his death, it passed to his two daughters, who lived there until 1920. It was they who put in the grand staircase and fine Edwardian decoration at the turn of the century. Springfield House was split up by the next owner in 1933. However, it was the earlier history of the house that was most revealing. The discovery that the house was on an estate owned by a local gentleman called Barland led us to his estate records and a deed in the name of Thomas Newborough, which referred to the original building on the site. This was dated as 25 July 1494. Mulberry Cottage had started life as a late medieval long-house more than 500 years ago.

There was *still* another twist in the tale, however. David had been puzzling over the morphology throughout the investigation. Mulberry Cottage had been inserted at the top of a long narrow strip of land that extended all the way down to the sea. These long strips repeated themselves all the way up the High Street, each with separate boundaries. David finally concluded that the basic shape of the landscape was more than 4000 years old and that Mulberry Cottage's boundaries could go back as far as the Bronze Age.

More than any other example, Mulberry Cottage demonstrated how deeply inquisitive you need to be. For much of the investigation, we could not agree among ourselves about its development. The lesson to be learned from it is not to leave any stone unturned, any cupboard unopened or any attic unexplored.

OUT OF THE CLOSET
An important discovery was made in this kitchen cupboard. It was a window facing outwards and today the entrance hall is the other side. It proved that the rear range of the house was the oldest part. The angled splay on the right gives us the thickness of the wall.

ABBOT'S LODGE, LEDBURY, HEREFORDSHIRE

'GIVING BACK A HOUSE ITS TRUE HISTORY'

'The seventeenth-century timber-framed "Abbot's Lodge" may at one time have been the Tithe Barn. The present building was modified and added to in Victorian times.' Case closed. Or was it?

ON A RISE
The garden elevation of Abbot's Lodge is curious. It appears to be a timber-framed building one storey high and to have two giant angled bay windows. Then it is noted that the gable end is the conventional two storeys. The house is not so much built on a slope as it has had the level of the garden rise. The large brick building on the left is a service range dating to the eighteenth century.

The mystery of Abbot's Lodge took us to one of the most beautiful parts of Britain, on the edge of the Malvern hills. Ledbury itself is an ancient market town, renowned for its collection of well-preserved timber-framed buildings, including the famous seventeenth-century Market House perched on stilts. There is an almost tangible sense of history and the local council has produced a useful booklet for visitors called *Ledbury Walk-about*. On page three, the house we were investigating gets a mention:

The owners of Abbot's Lodge, David and Ann Tombs, were not convinced that the accepted version of their home's history was correct. They already knew that the house had traditionally been the residence of the local vicar from the early 1800s until 1959 when it was sold by the Church. After living there for 20 years and seeing their family grow up, David and Ann felt instinctively that Abbot's Lodge had been a home for even longer than that and was not merely a tithe barn. David was also sceptical about the house being seventeenth century because he had found timbers in the loft that seemed much older.

Abbot's Lodge is at the far end of the narrow and picturesque Church Lane, which is lined with timber-framed buildings dating from the seventeenth century and earlier. The house looks out onto the church of St Michael's and All Angels and is next to Church House, which was reputed to be the original vicarage. We entered Abbot's Lodge through a side entrance that led into a large courtyard and were immediately struck by how far back the house was from the boundary wall with the churchyard. From the front, the house appeared to be a seventeenth-century structure that had been modernized in the nineteenth century to add bay windows, a new roof and a parapet.

Inside, the proportions of the rooms also suggested that the house had been developed over the centuries and undergone changes in its status. However, the interior features gave little away. It was the attic, as is often the case, that yielded the house's most surprising secret: that it was originally two separate buildings that had been amalgamated.

The evidence was provided by a change in level and differences in the timber construction. Even more revealing was that the timbers on one side went right back into the depths of the Middle Ages. The clue to this was an early king post coming down from the apex of the

ON THE LEVEL?
The stairhall makes sense when you know that the garden has been built up – you now realize that the house is apparently two rooms thick and that most of the garden side rises to a ceiling at roof level and that the remainder of the house has two storeys. The stairs going down reach the proper ground-floor level

roof to a solid collar, which Mac dated as thirteenth century. The timbers in the other half of the house were fifteenth century and the two buildings abutted very tightly together. From the outside, the joins were completely invisible.

This is why it is so important to search out the hidden clues. While we knew a date for the timbers, there was nothing to say that they had not been moved from elsewhere and reassembled on this site. Therefore more evidence was needed. Mac was able to disprove the tithe barn theory at this stage, though, as in the Middle Ages, two single-storey halls would not have been placed side by side like this to form a tithe barn.

Morphology, or the shape, pattern and form of the landscape, proved to be a crucial source of evidence here. Using a first edition 6-inch Ordnance Survey map, David Austin was able to draw some pertinent conclusions about the location of Abbot's Lodge.

The first key fact was that while the modern axis of Ledbury runs north-south, it used to go in an east-west direction. On the map, there were two early roads running either side of a small valley and two important areas of Church land, the Minster and the Sanctuary, lay between the roads. There was also a holy stream, running under the church, Abbot's Lodge and down to St Katherine's Hospital and the almshouses in the High Street. The borough, or town itself, came along later, in the twelfth century, and David felt that there was a strong possibility that Abbot's Lodge and not Church House was the true vicarage, but hard evidence was still required.

It was in the archives that Abbot's Lodge's true identity was found. In the knowledge that the house's history was linked to that of the church, David and Ann had already enlisted the support of the local vicar, the Reverend Dr Colin Beevers. It is a major bonus if your house was ever owned by the Church: in this case, the records went back as far as the thirteenth century, although the Minster itself was probably founded in the early ninth century.

The Hereford Bishoprick Estates Red Book was a rich mine of information about the house: it was a survey of the borough of Ledbury commissioned by the Bishops of Hereford in 1288. By walking up one side of the street with a copy of a rental document, David was able to ascertain that Abbot's Lodge had been two dwellings side by side. 'Roger the Vicar' held half a burgage, which was the basic unit of tenure in a medieval town, while 'Richard the Deacon' had another quarter. The other quarter was the modern-day courtyard. A terrier or survey of Church property from 1607 showed that by this time the vicar held one full burgage, so it looked likely that the two houses were amalgamated soon after the Reformation.

The archives proved that Church House, supposedly the original vicarage, had never been owned by the Church and had only been a vicarage for a few years at the end of the sixteenth century. The documents also explained why people in Ledbury had been so confused about the vicarage. In the late 1500s, a Reverend Davis, who was from a wealthy family, bought Church House and modernized it for his own use, effectively turning it into the vicarage for a short period.

Plan of Abbot's Lodge, Ledbury

1 and **2** Outline plan of the two fifteenth-century timber-framed houses.

A Position of thirteenth-century king post

B The beams from each house are set side by side. This was the evidence proving the existence of two buildings

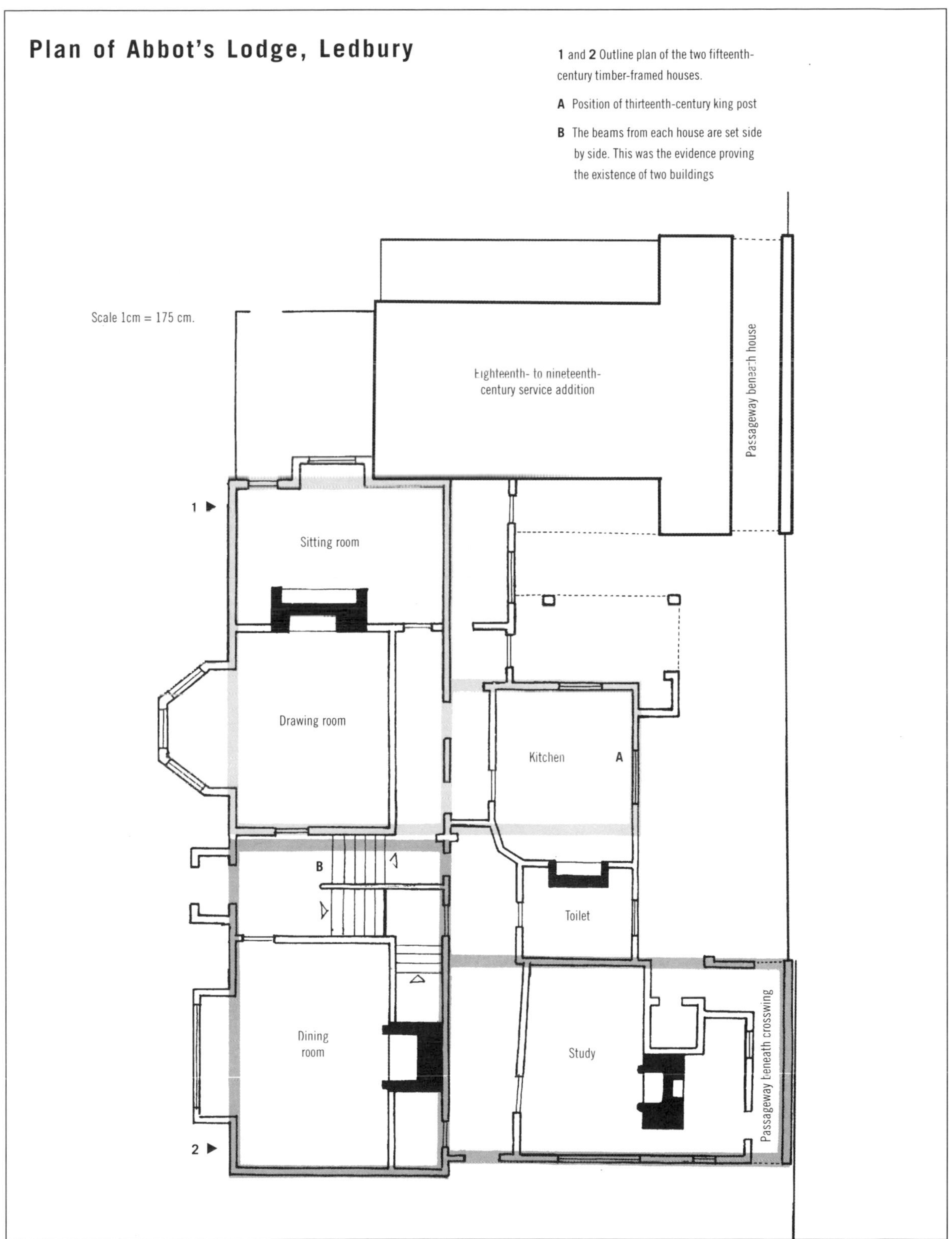

The Church records told us a great deal about the lives of the vicars who had resided at Abbot's Lodge. One of them, John de Beverley, had fallen victim to the Black Death after ministering bravely to the needs of his dying parishioners. In the late seventeenth century there was a less virtuous vicar called Benjamin Pritchard, who also held the more powerful position of church portionist. He was a snob and did not think the vicarage was good enough for him. Pritchard really wanted to live in nearby Upper Hall, which was owned by the Church but leased out to the Skippe family. Pritchard did not hide his intentions, so much so that the Skippes' gardener, Moses Greenway, was instructed to say a very loud amen every week at church services during the Reverend Pritchard's reading of the Tenth Commandment, 'Thou shalt not covet thy neighbour's house'.

However, the Reverend Pritchard was not the only vicar to become embroiled in local controversy. During a service by the Reverend John Jackson in the nineteenth century, a young servant girl walked up the aisle carrying a baby she claimed to be his. He spent the next two years trying to disprove the allegation.

The documents not only provided lots of colour about the lives of vicars, they also helped explain the fabric of the house. In the early nineteenth century, the vicar, James Watts, applied for a grant, a Queen Anne's Bounty, to do some work on the vicarage. He received the considerable sum of £600, which he invested in a new roof, a fine staircase, a new door and the bay windows at the front. He would probably have splashed out on some expensive fabrics, drapes

and furnishings for the interior to show off his fashionably classical tastes. It is also possible that it was he who built the service block extension on the side of the house and a garden wall in matching red brick. From his will it was clear that

Left **LIFE RAFTERS**
The roof and its timbers told the story of Abbot's Lodge. A plan was made of the timber construction and there emerged two houses almost touching each other, both having open halls – now the rooms with bay windows and crosswings.

Right **FULL BEAM AHEAD**
The two horizontal beams were at the ends of the two timber-framed houses. They were not quite the same size, but near enough to be enclosed as one house in the early nineteenth century.

James Watts was a wealthy man: there was also a hint of fraud on his part. When he applied for the bounty, he claimed that he did not own any stocks or shares, but in his will he left some.

From the history books and primary sources we were able to trace the remarkable history of Abbot's Lodge. During the English Civil War, the Battle of Ledbury raged in the churchyard and around the house. The Roundheads, led by Edward Massey, advanced up from the town, only to be beaten back by the flamboyant Prince Rupert's Cavaliers. You can still see bullet holes in the church door, although any physical evidence of the combat has long since disappeared from Abbot's Lodge.

Abbot's Lodge is a wonderful example of house detection in two main ways. First, every approach – architectural, morphological and documentary – yielded vital evidence. Secondly, we were able to give the house back its true history. For years, people had been getting its identity and its age completely wrong. It is strange really, because the truth was not that far away.

The moral of this tale is that house detectives should never accept second-hand accounts about their homes without first scraping below the surface and questioning perceived opinions, and then checking for corroborative evidence. Ann Tombs is planning to write an alternative guide to Abbot's Lodge.

HIDDEN CLUES

During your investigation, you may have encountered hidden clues that do not match with the overall picture you have been piecing together of your house. In some cases, these fragmentary pieces of evidence will add up to another, older house, concealed and enveloped by the existing one.

From the six case studies in the previous chapter it is clear that there is much more to a house than meets the eye. There was a Georgian façade hiding a sixteenth-century timber-framed building, a medieval long-house buried within an eighteenth-century structure and a seventeenth-century farmhouse constructed around the basis of a much earlier manor house. Each of these discoveries was a surprise, and a wonderful one at that.

But how do you identify these hidden clues, by definition few in number and sometimes disparate in character? The answer is to continue your detective work on two fronts. If there is architectural evidence to suggest an earlier building, start thinking in terms of the type of documentary records that may survive from that period. You might already have discovered that the site of your house was part of a manorial estate or was owned by a religious order but discarded the information because you did not think your house went that far back. A freshly uncovered piece of evidence, for example remnants of a timber-framed building, may mean that you need to return to the archives. Equally, a new lead found in the documents may prompt you to take a second look at the fabric of the house.

The further back in history you go, the more circumstantial and patchy the evidence will become, which means you will have to use your imagination and think in a more lateral way. If, from your study of maps, you have found that the site of your house lies at the heart of a medieval town or borough, then there is a strong possibility that a building, even if it was not your house, existed on the same plot during the Middle Ages. You might have heard about earlier settlements, Roman or Anglo-Saxon, from local archeologists; if so, ask yourself whether this may have affected the location of your house. Modern-day landscapes sometimes reflect settlements going back thousands of years. For example, near the Hertfordshire village of Eastwick, the site of a Roman villa appears to have caused the old main road to make a sudden

WINDOW ON THE WORLD
A brick gable end in the roof of the Manningtree house. Here is a blocked-in sixteenth-century window with a surviving fragment of a finely moulded brick mullion. The door was cut through in the seventeenth century when it joined with a new extension, now part of the launderette. It was blocked in when the premises were divided in the nineteenth century.

diversion and this in turn influenced the layout of the village.

To interpret hidden clues requires an unstinting analytical approach combined with unswerving attention to detail. A good example is the contraband hole we found in the attic of the house in Manningtree. Our first impression was that it could have been a priest's hiding hole, a feature common to sixteenth-century Catholic households during a period of religious persecution. The hole was definitely big enough for a priest to curl up in but, on closer inspection, we found evidence of eighteenth-century lath-and-plaster work, which meant that the space was too late to be a priest hole. We knew that Manningtree had been a thriving port during that period and that smuggling was common, and were able to conclude that the hole was built to stash contraband and would have been accessed by pulling away the top part of the stairs. This was corroborated when we later discovered that back then the house had been a tavern and was most probably a centre for nefarious activities.

Once you embark on this level of detective work there are no rules, only the most general guidelines – in some cases, you may just have to take a view. In the Dunsby Fen Farm investigation, we agreed that the current house had been built on the site of an earlier one. However, David and Mac begged to differ on whether or not some ancient-looking, heavily worn tiles under a staircase had belonged to an earlier house. Ultimately, you have to judge for yourself in cases like this.

Hidden clues can be architectural, stylistic or buried in a document or a map. You are most likely to find them as you poke around in attics or cellars, beneath floorboards or suspended ceilings or in cupboards. Certain anomalies – butt joins between parts of the building, changes in roof line and blocked-in windows – should all raise questions in your mind, so stay alert to conflicting evidence.

Equally, it could suddenly dawn on you that something you have always taken for granted is an important clue. For example, if the proportion of the house is untypically long and rectangular, it could just mean that it started life as a late-medieval long-house. This would of course need further evidence to back it up, which would most likely be found in the timbers in the attic. You should try to develop a feeling of space in your house and an intuitive sense for which parts of the building sit comfortably together and which do not.

When you are thinking about hidden clues you should consider the topography of your area in relation to the way vernacular buildings have developed. The eastern and southern edges of Dartmoor in Devon are a good case in point: it is not immediately obvious just how old some of the farms there really are. As long ago as the late twelfth century there was considerable growth in farming activity and new farms began appearing. Growing prosperity in the fifteenth and sixteenth centuries meant that many of these were rebuilt in the popular long-house style. In the intervening years these houses have undergone further modernization: they may have been Georgianized in the eighteenth century and had the animal byre incorporated into the living space.

The hidden clues you need to look for are external doors directly opposite each other, which would suggest a long-house's cross-passage; differences in the brick or stonework reflecting the addition of a second floor, or changes in level within the house resulting from the conversion of the byre.

Maps can also help propel your investigation into the distant past: look for archeological sites, ancient streams, evidence of old lanes and complex patterns of small fields around farms and don't forget the soft architecture. It is also worth examining the stone walls around your house: if they are dry-stone they are going to be earlier than if they are bonded together by lime mortar.

There are many different ways in which clues hidden over the centuries reveal themselves. Perhaps the best way to look at the house unseen is through a series of examples we have drawn from our own personal casework files.

UPPER LAMPHEY PARK, LAMPHEY, PEMBROKESHIRE

While doing fieldwork in Pembrokeshire, we looked at a farmhouse in Lamphey, which was built on parkland once owned and hunted by the bishops of St David's. The farmhouse was clearly a Pembrokeshire long-house in origin, possibly sixteenth or seventeenth century. There was nothing surprising about that. However, the farmer wanted to show us something in his barn. Initially, it appeared to be a late-seventeenth or eighteenth-century hay barn with a curious faceted south gable around which had been wrapped, at a later date, an external stone-built staircase to a loft.

At the north end of the barn we made an extraordinary discovery: the remains of a fourteenth-century tower house. Three of the exterior walls were hidden by later construction, but the inner walls were clearly visible and the *pièce de résistance* was a stone spiral staircase in a corner turret. This suggested that the tower had once had three storeys, since it continued above the doorway to the first floor.

On the ground floor there was also a medieval fireplace in the south wall and in the opposite wall there was a blocked entrance to a building that had since been lost. Directly above this on the next floor there was another blocked door and a rather more elaborate fireplace with a stone hood sitting on two moulded corbels (masonry blocks projecting from a wall, usually to support a beam). On another wall was the entrance to the stair turret and yet another door that was blocked.

David Austin was able to conclude that this was a good-quality medieval building that may well have been used as a hunting lodge by the bishops. It was feasible that it would have been a free-standing tower, but evidence of an earlier building alongside it suggested that it may have been a semi-fortified camera (a vaulted or arched room) attached to a hall.

There was also corroborative evidence. In the background of a 1740 Buck print of Lamphey Palace the tower can clearly be seen surrounded by buildings. Revelations of this kind are, admittedly, rare, but it does show how important it is not to assume that the current focus of a house is necessarily the oldest part and that it is worth spending time examining outhouses and barns.

NANT-Y-BAI WATER MILL, WALES

First impressions suggested that Ystradffin Farm was an eighteenth-century house with a nineteenth-century mill, Nant-Y-Bai, that would have run on a flow of water coming down from a small pond above. From the documents, we knew that the farm had been a grange belonging to the Strata Florida Cistercian Abbey, which hinted that there was something older here.

Four separate pieces of architectural evidence proved this. First, the dam holding back the pond was a massive structure built of dressed stone, possibly by the masons who built the medieval abbey. Second, there were the remnants of a purpose-built stone channel running down from a sluice in a different position and at a higher level than the one used for the nineteenth-century mill. Third, on close inspection, the lower foundations of the mill were found to be built of medieval stonework. Finally, we found evidence of an axle hole on a side wall that would have at one time supported an earlier wheel than the nineteenth-century water wheel, which is now on the end wall. Put together, these hidden clues added up to a substantial medieval water mill that had been completely modernized in the nineteenth century.

STOWE HALL, STOWE, GLOUCESTERSHIRE

Superficially, Stowe Hall appears to be a double-pile Georgian house rendered in false ashlaring. However, closer inspection revealed that numerous features did not ring true, indicating that the house was considerably older than the eighteenth century.

In a room now used as a study there was an early inglenook fireplace, so the room was almost certainly a kitchen in the past. Next to the fireplace, stone steps went down into the front of a cellar, which was clearly older than the rear. The most striking thing about this side of the building was that the walls were extremely thick – about 4 ft (1.2 m) – in comparison with those in the rest of the house.

In one corner of the modern-day dining room (next to the study) the wall seemed to have been scooped out and a door put in. In a bedroom upstairs there was an equally curious semi-circular recess, now housing a window. These shapes were consistent with the remains of a stone spiral staircase. In medieval buildings it was typical for a spiral staircase to be built alongside a fireplace. It was in the attic that the overall picture finally became clear. There were the remnants of a fireplace, which was the proof we needed that this had at one time been a lived-in third floor.

From this, it could be concluded that Stowe Hall's original incarnation had been as a medieval three-storey tower house that had been developed on at least three separate occasions, culminating in its Georgian gentrification.

The tower house theory fitted perfectly with the historical context of the area, which was the scene of cross-border skirmishes between the English and Welsh during the Middle Ages and earlier. Because of the violence, people chose to live in tall narrow houses which afforded them better protection: the more exposed ground floor was generally used for storage while the family lived on the more secure upper floors. Once the Western Marches became more stable, these houses were no longer practical and were expanded.

(Similarly, if you live in the northern marches of Cumbria and Northumberland, it is worth considering if your house ever had a defensive function. Look for evidence that your home started life as a bastle house. Bastles were fortified first-floor blockhouses with thick stone walls, outside stairs and no windows. The Border regions were for centuries volatile and ungovernable, so houses were designed with security as the main priority.

The moral of this tale is that it pays to be aware of the specific traits of houses in and around your region.)

LAMB'S LANE, COTTENHAM, CAMBRIDGE

This is actually Mac Dowdy's home and an inspiration to all house detectives. It is a story about peeling back layer after layer to find one surprise after another. Ostensibly, the house is a small double-fronted brick-built building with angled bay windows on the ground floor. It looks much like any other nineteenth-century village house with its double-span blue slate roof. From the exterior, two periods of building in the last century are evident, as well as a flat-roofed single-storey extension dating from this century. The interior also indicates three possible periods of modernization in the nineteenth or early twentieth century.

However, there was one key anomaly: in the south room of the street range the quarry-tiled or brick floor appeared to be seventeenth century judging by the texture and cut of each brick. The bricks are laid directly onto the earth. Further evidence of an older house was found when a hessian-based wallcovering, on which many layers of wallpaper had been pasted, was peeled away to reveal low-cost eighteenth-century pine panelling.

There were yet more hidden clues to come: a door was uncovered when some hardboard panels were removed from a curiously angled corner of the same room. The door had led out to a lobby at the foot of a very steep staircase. When the staircase was removed to be replaced by a less steep one, fragments of old wallpaper suggested that the stairs had been put in to replace an earlier ladder in the nineteenth century. This helped to confirm that the pine panelling, which predated the stairs, would fit in to the eighteenth century.

When the old wallcovering on the outer side of this south room was removed, very poor-quality timber framing was uncovered. It appeared to date from the eighteenth century. The timber was not very substantial and had been left in place when a builder encased the building in brick, making it sound.

Mac discovered that he had a cob ceiling when tragedy struck during a heavy gale and water seeped into it from the bay bringing almost half of it down. If the sight of the collapsed ceiling wasn't enough, the stench of the sixteenth-century cob ceiling, made of cow dung and straw, was devastating – an unpleasant way of discovering the history of one's house.

While the south room appeared to be older, it was still assumed that the north room was built in about the 1860s, with bay windows added about 30 years later.

The north wall of the room had a fireplace with recessed bays on either side. When work had to be done on the fire place it emerged that it had been built in two phases – in house detectives' jargon, it was a two-build wall. The outside of the wall did show a projection rather like a boundary wall that the house had been built against. In fact, the boundary wall had been incorporated into the building of the house wall. It was found to be part of a sixteenth-century wall.

In a final twist, it was discovered that the south room had been the tack-room to the stables of the Lordship Manor, home in the seventeenth century to Katharine Pepys, who was a cousin of the renowned diarist Samuel Pepys!

PENIARTH UCHAF, LLANEGRYN, TYWYN, GWYNEDD, WALES

Situated in the beautiful Snowdonia National Park, Peniarth Uchaf is an elegant house with a verandah on two sides and an alpine-looking roof. You would probably guess that it is a minor gentry home built in the last century.

However, the core of an original, earlier house reveals itself as soon as you go upstairs and into a long corridor typical of an early-eighteenth-century Welsh farmhouse. It turned out that the house had been reroofed and modernized to include an extra wing and the verandah by an owner in the last century on his return from serving with the Indian Army.

'THE GROVE', BRINKLEY, NEAR NEWMARKET

Judging from the façade alone, you would be forgiven for thinking that 'The Grove' is an early-nineteenth-century house with its creamy-grey brickwork and low-pitched, hipped roof in blue slate. It has sash windows and an elegant doorcasing with echoes of the eighteenth century in its broken triangular pediment and the nicely proportioned ray pattern of glazing bars in the fanlight.

A walk around the outside of the house gave us a feel of the plan: a front main range with two crosswings at right angles to it. From the brickwork, the crosswings seemed to have been added to the front range at different times: the earliest appeared to be the north one while the second one extended from the middle of the front range.

The interior had lofty ceilings typical of the period, but the kitchen had a large inglenook fireplace that looked to be early seventeenth century, possibly even older. The first door on the left, moving down the central corridor, led into a small cupboard called the boot room. In one corner of this tiny room was a jowel post: a vertical post that spreads out at its top to take wallplates. This was clear evidence of an older building and, after a lot of measuring and closer inspection, it emerged that the north crosswing was not square with the rest of the building.

It was time to take a look in part of the central roof that had been closed off and it rapidly emerged that the rafters were seventeenth century. Floorboards in one of the front rooms were lifted to reveal a timber sole or wallplate on which the façade wall was positioned. This was further telling evidence, and we were able to conclude that a seventeenth-century house had been on the same site and had been drastically altered.

INTERIOR REVELATIONS

For the majority of house detectives, the house unseen will not be about finding the remains of a medieval building but, even so, it does not mean you have to be deprived of the joys of discovery. There was a fine example during our investigation in Manningtree when a flimsy partition was ripped away to reveal some good-quality Georgian panelling. We already knew that this part of the

CHEERING VIEW
A house in a lovely setting in North Wales. This is Peniarth Uchaf. The oldest part of the house, based on the proportions of the elevations, is the range slightly obscured by the nearer building. The size and position of the chimney stacks hint that the house may be eighteenth century or even a little earlier. The house appears much restored and the verandahs are cunningly positioned so that, no doubt, the resident could follow the sun down indulging in a 'quiet lemonade'!

house had been totally modernized during the eighteenth century but we had no idea that any features from the period had survived.

Original features can also be concealed underneath false ceilings. It is normally easy to recognize a dropped ceiling because the proportions of the room will look all wrong: the distances between the skirting board, the dado and the ceiling will be asymmetrical. Hidden ceilings can also be detected by measuring the thickness of floors or can be seen by pulling up floorboards in the room above.

We visited a Regency house in Barnsbury, north London, where a fine cornice was discovered hidden, almost criminally, behind a dropped ceiling. The drawing room had a plain ceiling and was out of keeping with other rooms, which all had high ceilings. The owners pulled up the floorboards upstairs, saw evidence of the cornice and decided to remove the offending ceiling. All but a small section of the cornice was undamaged, but coat after coat of distemper and oil paint had clogged up the fine details. It was a painstaking process to scrape off all the old paint with a carving tool, but it was worth it when the delicate palm leaf and floral design was restored to its true beauty.

The best surprises are not always concealed: there may be a feature you look at every day without realizing what it is or how it is meant to look. When Judith Miller moved into her new home there was a good-quality Edwardian fireplace in the master bedroom. The fireplace was by then out of proportion with the room, which had been divided to create a bathroom. Meanwhile, a less than tasteful 1970s York stone fireplace had been inserted in the dining room. It made perfect sense to remove this out-of-character addition and replace it with the fine fireplace from upstairs. What was more exciting, though, was that the true beauty of the Edwardian cast-iron insert had been concealed by black paint. When the paint was removed, the surround was restored to its full stylish glory, the sweeping Art Nouveau lines and delicate pomegranate motif once again exposed in shining metal. Restoring features like this is time-consuming and you will need to consult experts or specialist books, but the effect can be stunning.

CONCLUSION

At some point, you may reluctantly have to face up to the fact that you have exhausted every possibility and you still want to know more. The advantage of this sort of detective work is that you do not need conclusive proof to present in a court. You can develop your own narrative of the history of your home which, while it may not be 100 per cent accurate, is based on your empowered imagination, constrained by a sense of the possible. The most important thing is to have fun being a house detective and to record the fruits of your work for posterity.

Glossary of Architectural Terms

Adze: an early axe-like tool used for dressing wood. It has an arched blade at right angles to the handle.

Aisled hall: an open hall divided into three aisles by lines of wooden or stone posts.

Anaglypta: an embossed and textured type of wallpaper introduced in 1887.

Anthemion: a flower-like ornament used in art and design.

Apron: a panel below a window.

Arcading: a series of arches on columns or piers which can be freestanding or attached to a wall.

Architrave: moulded frame around a window or door, or the lowest part of the entablature in Classical architecture.

Art Nouveau: style based on natural lines with tendrils and sinuous curves *c.*1890–1940.

Arts and Crafts: late-nineteenth-century decorative style based on traditional skills of craftspeople.

Ashlar: stone cut into smooth rectangular blocks.

Axial beam: the main, central roof or ceiling beam which follows the axis of the house; the beam from which all other ceiling supports extend.

Baluster: a vertical piece of timber or stone supporting a handrail on a staircase.

Bargeboard: plain or decorative wooden board fixed to the verge of a roof.

Baroque: rather extravagant and flamboyant architectural style.

Batten: thin strips of timber.

Bay: a single structural unit: the space between two roof trusses or between the truss and end wall.

Bay or bow window: a window which projects beyond the wall, in square, angled or circular plan.

Bolection: double curved moulding covering a joint. Popular in the seventeenth century.

Bond: the pattern of laying brick walls.

Boss: an ornamental knob at the intersection of a ceiling or vault.

Brace: a diagonal reinforcement.

Bressumer: a beam spanning an opening, e.g. a timber supporting a chimney breast over a fireplace.

Bull's eye window: a small circular or oval window.

Burgage plots: pieces of land in the town granted by the lord of the manor.

But and Ben: a two-roomed Scottish highland house.

Byre: the end of a long-house used for housing animals.

Came: strip of metal, usually lead, used to separate panes of glass in windows.

Capital: the top or crowning feature of a column.

Casement window: a window with vertical hinges which opens inwards or outwards.

Ceiling rose: plaster decoration in the centre of a ceiling.

Chamfer: a splayed effect created by removing the sharp edge of timber or stone.

Cob: building material consisting of mud and straw.

Collar: a horizontal beam linking rafters.

Common rafters: pairs of rafters forming a pitched roof.

Console: a carved or moulded support for a doorhood or canopy.

Coping: dressed stone or brick capping along the top of a wall.

Corbel: a masonry block projecting from a wall to support a beam.

Corinthian: the most ornate of the Classical columns.

Cornice: a moulding at the junction of a wall and the ceiling in a room, or a moulding on an external wall at the eaves line.

Cove: usually a quarter circle concave moulding.

Crenellation: a parapet with battlements.

Cross-passage: a passage crossing house from front to back.

Crown post: a vertical post rising from a tie-beam in a roof.

Crowstep: a gable built like a flight of steps.

Crucks: large curved timbers used to support a roof from the ground.

Dado: panelling or rail on the lower part of an internal wall, usually extending to about a metre above the floor.

Dais: a raised platform found typically at the upper end of a hall.

Dentillation: small toothlike block used in cornices.

Dogleg: a type of stair with a 180 degree turn and no central well.

Doric: simplest of the Classical order columns.

Dormers: windows built into the slope of a roof.

Dowel: a headless wood or metal peg used to hold timbers in place.

Dragon beam: a diagonal beam in hipped roofs and jetties.

Eaves: overhang of the roof slope.

Encaustic tiles: colourful ceramic tiles with matt finish. Popular for Victorian and Edwardian hallways and paths.

Entablature: a decorative band above a column made up of architrave, frieze and cornice.

Fanlight: a window above a doorway.

Faux finish: a surface finish of paint or lacquer intended to imitate another material, wood or marble.

Fielded panel: a panel with centre raised in profile.

Fireback: cast iron plate at the back of a fireplace.

Firedogs: a pair of raised iron bars in which to burn logs in fireplaces.

Frieze: a band, sometimes ornamented, along the top of a wall just below the cornice. In Classical architecture it is the centre of an entablature.

Gable: a triangular end wall.

Gothick: eighteenth century revival of Gothic or medieval styles of architecture which was a branch of the English Rococo. A 'k' is added to help differentiate.

Gothic revival: a revival of a more authentic Gothic style which began in the late eighteenth century and flourished in the nineteenth century. (It derived from a greater interest in the medieval and ecclesiastical.)

Hall: in early houses, the hall was the main living area, but it later came to be used for the entrance area.

Harling: external wall coating of lime and gravel.

Headers: bricks laid headwise.

Hipped roof: a roof without a gable, i.e. sloping on all sides of the building.

Hood mould (or rainhood): a moulding above a door or window designed to protect the opening from water running down the wall.

Inglenook: a recess with a seat next to a fireplace.

Ionic columns: fluted columns with scrolled capitals.
Jamb: the side post of a door or window opening.
Jetty: an overhanging wall in timber-framed buildings.
Joist: a timber carrying the floor or ceiling.
Keystone: a central tapering stone in an arch.
King post: a vertical timber rising from a tie-beam or collar to support the ridge piece.
Label: protruding stone or brick course above Tudor doors.
Laithe house: a type of long-house found in northern areas which has no internal access to the byre.
Lap joint: a type of joint in which one timber fits into a cutaway on another.
Lath: a thin strip of sawn or split wood used to support plaster.
Limewash: a mix of slaked lime and water used to paint walls.
Linenfold: a carved pattern which looks like folded cloth.
Lintel: a horizontal beam or stone across an opening, window, door or fireplace.
Long-house: an early type of single-pile house, with a byre for animals at one end.
Louvre: a slatted opening.
Mansard roof: a roof with two pitches, with the lower part steeper than the upper section.
Manse: a clergyman's house.
Mathematical tiling: special tiles resembling brick.
Modillions: small blocks or scrolls supporting the cornice.
Mortice and tenon: a carpentry joint, the protruding tenon slots into the mortice hole.
Mullions: wooden or stone uprights dividing a window into sections, known as lights.
Newel post: a vertical post at the end or corner of a handrail or staircase, or the central post of a spiral staircase.
Nogging: brick infill of a timber frame.
Ogee: a double-curved arch.
Oriel: a projecting bay window.
Outshut: an extension at the back of a house.
Overmantel: an ornamental structure above a mantelpiece.
Oversailing brickwork: overhanging or projecting courses.
Ovolo: convex moulding, which is a quarter circle in section.
Padstone: a stone footing for the post in a timber frame.
Painted glass : A cheaper method of achieving the effect of stained glass. The colours are metallic oxides which are painted onto the glass and hardened in a kiln (similar to ceramics) where the colour fuses into the glass.
Palladian: Neo-Classical style of Italian architect, Andrea Palladio (1508-1580).
Pantile: an S-shaped roof tile.
Parapet: a low wall extending above a roof, at the eaves or at a gable.
Pargeting: ornamental plasterwork used on external walls.
Parquet: flooring made of wood blocks in a geometrical pattern.
Pebbledash: a rendering of mortar with pebbles.
Pediment: a shallow triangular or arched head to a door or window opening.
***Piano nobile*:** principal floor for reception rooms where guests were entertained (eighteenth century).
Pier: a solid vertical masonry support.
Pilaster: a half-column decorative column projecting from a wall, often next to a door opening.
Pile: a building. Single pile: one room deep. Double pile: two rooms deep.
Pitch: the angle of the roof.
Pitch floors: flooring made from small pieces of stone laid like cobblestones and arranged in patterns.
Plank and muntin: an early form of timber partition made up of vertical muntins linked by thinner planks.
Plat band: a protruding line of brickwork covering a beam or support.
Pointing: mortar finishing of brick or stonework.
Principal rafters: the main rafters in a roof truss.
Purlin: the main horizontal timber in a roof, it supports the common rafters.
Queen posts: vertical roof posts which come in pairs and rise from a tie-beam and support the principal rafters.
Quoins (pronounced coins): dressed stones used on corners of buildings.
Rafter: sloping timber which directly supports the roof.
Rail: a horizontal member in a door frame or panelling.
Rainhood: *see* Hood mould.
Rebate: a rectangular recess in wood or stone.
Reeding: parallel ridge on moulding.
Rendering: weatherproof coating for exterior wall.
Repoussé: ornamental metalwork.
Reveal: the side of an opening in a wall for a window or door.
Roughcast: a type of rendering made of cement mixed with gravel.
Rubble: roughly-cut stone in a wall.
Sash window: a vertical window which slides up and down.
Screens passage: the passage at the lower end of a hall, which is separated from the hall by a screen.
Shingles: thin pieces of wood used for roofing.
Skirting: the moulding at the base of an internal wall.
Smoke hood: timber-framed hood above a hearth.
Solar: a private room often used for sleeping in medieval houses.
Stanchions: the more substantial uprights in railings.
Stile: vertical framing part of a door.
Strapwork: decoration of interlaced bands, similar to cut leather.
Stretchers: bricks laid lengthwise.
String: the outer part of a staircase, into which the treads and risers are framed.
Strut: roof timber connecting rafter to collar or king post.
Stucco: smooth plaster or cement coating for exterior wall.
Stud: a non-structural vertical timber.
Terriers: inventories of estate land marking the end of the open-field system.
Tessellated floor: covering made up of small cubes of marble, stone or glass embedded in cement.
Tie-beam: a beam joining the feet of principal rafters in a roof truss.
Transom: a horizontal bar dividing a window opening.
Truss: a framed structure supporting a roof.
Tudor arch: a flattened arch coming to a point.
Undercroft: room below a medieval first-floor hall.
Vault: an underground chamber.
Vermiculated: wormlike patterns or markings.
Volutes: curved scroll on a pillar or column.
Voussoir: wedge-shaped stone in an arch.
Wainscot: wood panelling on an internal wall.
Wallplate: longitudinal timber running along a wall.
Wattle and daub: wall infill of woven willow or hazel withies covered with mixture of mud, clay, chalk and dung.
Wealden house: a late medieval and Tudor type of open-hall house.
Weatherboarding: horizontal planks used to clad an exterior wall.
Wychert: earth and clay walling material.

Bibliography

The Arts and Crafts Movement by Steven Adams (Grange Books)

At Home: An Illustrated Historyof Houses and Homes by Anthony Ridley (Heinemann)

Authentic Decor, The Domestic Interior 1620–1920 by Peter Thornton (Weidenfeld & Nicolson)

The Buildings of England by Nikolaus Pevsner (Penguin Books) (46 volumes)

Clay and Cob Buildings by John McCann (Shire Publications Ltd)

A Dictionary of Arts' Manufacturers and Mines by Andrew Ure (Longman)

Discovering Your Old House by David Iredale and John Barrett (Shire Publications Ltd)

The Edwardian House by Helen Long (Manchester University Press)

Edwardian House Style by Hilary Hockman (David & Charles)

Elements of Style: Encyclopaedia of Domestic Architectural Details by Stephen Calloway (Mitchell Beazley)

The English Farmhouse and Cottage by M.W. Barley (Routledge & Keegan Paul)

The English Home by Doreen Yarwood (B.T. Batsford Ltd)

The English House Through Seven Centuries by Olive Cook (Penguin Books)

English Interiors by Doreen Yarwood (Lutterworth Press)

The English Medieval House by Margaret Wood (Phoenix)

English Vernacular Houses by Eric Mercer (HMSO Books)

Genealogy for Beginners by Arthur Willis and Molly Tatchell (Phillimore & Co. Ltd)

The Georgian House by Steven Parissien (Aurum Press Ltd)

The Glamour of Ornament by Owen Jones (first edition 1856)

Going to Pot? The Great British Chimney by John Chatham (Baron)

Handmade to the Arts by Robert Dossie (last edition printed in 1796)

Hints on Household Taste by Charles Eastlake (Dover)

The Historic Home Owners Companion by Matthew Saunders (B.T. Batsford Ltd)

House and Home by Anthony Quiney (BBC Books)

Houses & History by Maurice Barley (Faber & Faber)

Houses of the Welsh Countryside by Peter Smith (2nd edition) (HMSO Books)

How Old is Your House? by Pamela Cunnington (Alphabooks)

How to Read Old Documents by E.E. Thoyts (Phillimore & Co. Ltd)

Illustrated Handbook of Vernacular Architecture by R.W. Brunskill (2nd edition) (Faber & Faber)

Inventories of the Royal Commission on Historical Monuments (HMSO Books)

The Making of the English Landscape by William Hoskins, commentary by Christopher Taylor (Hodder & Stoughton)

The Papered Wall: History, Patterns and Techniques of Wallpaper by Lesley Hoskins (Thames and Hudson)

Period Details by Judith and Martin Miller (Mitchell Beazley)

The Period House, Style, Detail and Decoration 1774 to 1914 by Richard Russell Lawrence and Teresa Chris (Weidenfeld & Nicolson)

Period Houses – a Guide to Authentic Architectural Features by Anthony Quiney (George Philip Ltd)

Period Style by Judith and Martin Miller (Mitchell Beazley)

A Social History of Housing by John Burnett (David & Charles)

The Tax on Wallpaper by H. Dagnall (H. Dagnall)

Tiles in Architecture by Hans van Lemmen (Laurence King Publishing)

Timber Building in Britain by R.W. Brunskill (Victor Gollancz Ltd)

Timber-framed Buildings in Wales by Gerralt D. Nash (National Museum of Wales)

Tracing Your Ancestors in the Public Record Office by J. Cox and T. Padfield (HMSO Books)

Traditional Buildings of Britain by R.W. Brunskill (Victor Gollancz Ltd)

The Traditional Buildings of England by Anthony Quiney (Thames and Hudson)

Traditional Farm Buildings of Britain by R.W. Brunskill (Victor Gollancz Ltd)

Traditional Style by Stephen Calloway and Stephen Jones (Pyramid Books)

Uppark Restored by Christopher Rowell and John Martin Robinson (The National Trust)

The Victoria County History: An Encyclopaedia of English Local History (Dawson Publishing, Folkestone. Originally published by Oxford University Press)

Victorian and Edwardian Furniture and Interiors by Jeremy Cooper (Thames and Hudson)

Victorian Ceramic Tiles by Julian Barnard (Studio Vista/Christie's)

Victorian Style by Judith and Martin Miller (Mitchell Beazley)

Village Buildings in Britain by Matthew Rice (Little, Brown)

Wallpapers by Charles Oman and Jean Hamilton (Sotheby Publications with the V&A Museum)

Welsh Long-houses by Eurwyn Wiliam (University of Wales Press)

Your House – the Outside View by John Prizeman (Hutchinson & Co. Publishers Ltd)

Useful Addresses

Allyson McDermott
Conservation of the Fine & Decorative Arts
The Battery House
Petworth House
Petworth
West Sussex GU28 0DP
01798 343700

Ancient Monuments Society
St Ann's Vestry Hall
2 Church Entry
London EC4V 5HB
0171 236 3934

The Borthwick Institute of Historical Research
(part of the University of York)
St Anthony's Hall
Peasholme Green
York YO1 2PW
01904 642315

British Archaeological Association
1 Priory Gardens
London W4 1TT
0181 994 1019

British Library
British Museum
Great Russell Street
London WC1B 3DG
0171 636 1544

British Newspaper Library
Colindale Avenue
London NW9 5HE
0171 412 7353

The Brooking Collection
University of Greenwich
Oakfield Lane
Dartford
Kent DA1 2SZ
0181 331 9897

Cadw
(Welsh Historic Monuments)
Brunel House
2 Fitzalan Road
Cardiff CF2 1UY
01222 500200

Church of England Record Centre (includes the Church Commission's Records Office)
15 Galleywall Road
South Bermondsey
London SE16 3PB
0171 231 1251 (the Record Centre prefers written enquiries)

Church of Jesus Christ of Latter Day Saints Hyde Park Family History Centre (for the Mormons International Genealogical Index)
64–68 Exhibition Road
Kensington
London SW7 2PA
0171 589 8561

Civic Trust
17 Carlton House Terrace
London SW1Y 5AW
0171 930 0914

Council for the Protection of Rural England
Warwick House
25 Buckingham Palace Road
London SW1W 0PP
0171 976 6433

Dr Williams's Library
– for information on Nonconformist congregations.
14 Gordon Square
London WC1H 0AG
0171 387 3727

English Heritage
23 Savile Row
London W1X 1AB
0171 973 3000

ERA Technology
(Pulse radar)
Cleeve Road
Leatherhead
Surrey KT22 7SA
01372 367000

The Forestry Commission
(includes The Forestry Authority)
Communications Officer
Alice Holt Lodge
Wrecclesham
Farnham
Surrey GU10 4LH
01420 22255

General Register Office and Office for National Statistics
Myddelton Place
Myddelton Street
London EC1
0151 471 4200
General Register Office (Scotland)
New Register House
Edinburgh EH1 3YT
0131 334 0380

General Register Office (Northern Ireland)
Oxford House
49-55 Chichester Street
Belfast BT1 4HH
01232 252000

General Registry (Isle of Man)
New Courts of Justice
Deemsters' Bucks Road
Douglas
Isle of Man IM1 3AR
01624 685242

General Register (Guernsey)
The Greffe
Royal Court House
Guernse, GY1 2PB
01481 725277

General Register (Jersey)
Judicial Greffe
Burrard House
Don Street
St. Helier
Jersey JE2 4TQ
01534 502300

Georgian Group
6 Fitzroy Square
London W1P 6DX
0171 387 1720

Glasgow Museum
See **The Mitchell Library**

The Godwin Laboratory
(for dendrochronology)
Free School Lane
Cambridge CB2 3RS
01223 334870

Guildhall Library
Aldermanbury
London EC2P 2EJ
0171 606 3030

Historic Homes of Britain
21 Pembroke Square
London W8 6PB
0171 937 2402

Historic Houses Association
2 Chester Street
London SW1X 7BB
0171 259 5688

Historic Scotland
Longmore House
Salisbury Place
Edinburgh EH7 1SH
0131 668 8600

Hunting Aerofilms
Gate Studios
Station Road
Borehamwood
Hertfordshire WD6 1EJ
0181 207 0666

Imperial War Museum Archives
Lambeth Road
London SE1 6HZ
0171 416 5000

Institute of Agricultural History & Museum of English Rural Life
University of Reading
P.O. Box 229
Whiteknights
Reading
Berkshire RG6 6AG
01734 875123

Irish Georgian Society
74 Merrion Square
Dublin 2
Ireland
00353 16767053

John Rylands University Library of Manchester
Deansgate
Manchester M3 3EH
0161 834 5343

Lambeth Palace Library
London SE1 7JU
0171 928 6222
(prefers written enquiries)

The Mitchell Library
The Glasgow Room
North Street
Glasgow G3 7DN
0141 287 2000

National Library of Aerial Photography
NMR Customer Services
National Monuments
Records Centre
Kemble Drive
Swindon
Wiltshire SN2 2GZ
01793 414100

National Library of Scotland
George IV Bridge
Edinburgh EH1 1EW
0131 226 4531

National Library of Wales
Aberystwyth
Ceredigion SY23 3BU
01970 623816

National Monuments Record (*see* Royal Commission on Historical Monuments)

The National Museum of Wales
Cathay's Park
Cardiff CF1 3NP
01222 397951

National Register of Archives
Quality House
Quality Court
Chancery Lane
London WC2A 1HP
0171 242 1198

The National Trust
36 Queen Anne's Gate
London SW1 9AS
0171 222 9251

The National Trust for Scotland
5 Charlotte Square
Edinburgh EH2 4DU
0131 226 5922

Pilkington Glass Museum
Prescot Road
St Helens WA10 3TT
01744 28882

Principal Registry of the Family Division
Somerset House
The Strand
London WC2R 1LP
0171 936 6960

Public Record Office
Chancery Lane
London WC2A 1LR
0181 876 3444

Public Record Office
Ruskin Avenue
Kew
Surrey TW9 4DU
0181 876 3444

Public Record Office of Northern Ireland
66 Balmoral Avenue
Belfast BT9 6NY
01232 251318

Railway and Canal Historical Society
17 Clumber Crescent North
The Park
Nottingham NG7 1EY
0115 941 4844

Royal Commission for Ancient and Historical Monuments in Scotland
16 Bernard Terrace
Edinburgh EH8 9NX
0131 662 1456

Royal Commision of the Ancient and Historic Monuments of Wales
The Crown Building
Plas Crug
Aberystwyth
Ceredigion SY23 1NJ
01970 621227

Royal Commission on Historical Monuments
(Headquarters)
National Monuments Record Centre
Kemble Drive
Swindon
Wiltshire SN2 2GZ
01793 414600
(London office)
Public Services
55 Blandford Street
London W1H 3AF
0171 208 8200

Royal Incorporation of Architects in Scotland
15 Rutland Square
Edinburgh EH1 2BE
0131 229 7205

The Royal Institute of British Architects (RIBA)
66 Portland Place
London W1N 4AD
0171 580 5533

Scottish Civic Trust
24 George Square
Glasgow G2 1EF
0141 221 1466

Scottish Record Office
HM General Register Office
2 Princes Street
Edinburgh EH1 3YY
0131 535 1314

Society for the Protection of Ancient Buildings
37 Spital Square
London E1 6DY
0171 377 1644

Society of Friends Library
Friends House
173--177 Euston Road
London NW1 2BJ
0171 387 3601

Society of Genealogists Library
14 Charterhouse Buildings
Goswell Road
London EC1M 7BA
0171 251 8799

Temple Newsam House
Temple Newsam
Leeds
LS15 0AE
01132 647321

Twentieth Century Society
70 Calcross Street
London
EC1M 6BP
0171 250 3857

Vernacular Architecture Group
16 Falna Crescent
Coton Green
Tamworth
Staffordshire B79 8JS

Victorian Society
1 Priory Gardens
Bedford Park
London W4 1TT
0181 994 1019

Wallpaper History Society
The Victoria & Albert Museum
South Kensington SW7 2RL
0171 938 8500

Weald and Downland Open Air Museum
Singleton
Near Chichester
West Sussex
PO18 0EU
01243 811348

Museum of Welsh Life
St Fagan's
Cardiff
01222 569441

The Whitworth Art Gallery
University of Manchester
Oxford Road
Manchester M15 6ER
0161 275 7450

INDEX

Illustrations in **bold**